More Praise for
The BELIEF INST...

"[Bering's] writing is witty, crammed with pop-culture references, and he employs examples and analogies that make his arguments seem like common sense rather than the hard-earned scientific insights they really are. This fascinating book presents gentle, nuanced but convincing arguments for atheism." —Michael Brooks, *New Scientist*

"Bering presents a refreshingly scientific take on the adaptive benefit of religious beliefs." —Bob Grant, *The Scientist*

"Bering ranges comfortably among evolutionary biology, psychology and philosophical concerns, and finds the good science in belief."
—*Kirkus Reviews*

"The author approaches these dicey subjects with a dazzlingly insightful reading of the empirical literature on human cognition and development, a sly sense of humor, and an obvious compassion for those who do not share his beliefs. He also has a lot of fun. Richard Dawkins . . . and others have surveyed some of this terrain before, but few have done it as convincingly and enjoyably."
—R. R. Cornelius, *Choice*

"Far from asking us to toss aside our beliefs, *The Belief Instinct* simply opens our eyes to the genesis of belief and a higher power in our wonderfully complex minds." —Josh Shiode,
Berkeley Science Review

"There's a place in our minds where God goes. This spellbinding book explains how: We humans find the idea of God inviting because we evolved to perceive minds all around us. Bering's own clever research on children's perceptions of the supernatural is the centerpiece in his rich portrayal of the newly unfolding science of belief in God." —Daniel M. Wegner, Harvard University, author of *The Illusion of Conscious Will*

"Since God didn't exist, our human ancestors found it necessary to invent him. In this scintillating book, Jesse Bering explains, with characteristic wit and wisdom, how, in the course of human evolution, God returned the compliment—by helping individuals, despite themselves, lead better lives." —Nicholas Humphrey, professor emeritus, London School of Economics, and author of *Soul Dust*

"Jesse Bering is a brilliant young psychologist, a gifted storyteller, a careful reader of Jean-Paul Sartre, and a very funny man. And his first book, *The Belief Instinct*, is a triumph—a moving, provocative, and entertaining exploration of the human search for meaning."
—Paul Bloom, professor of psychology, Yale University, and author of *How Pleasure Works*

The
BELIEF
INSTINCT

THE PSYCHOLOGY OF
SOULS, DESTINY, AND THE
MEANING OF LIFE

Jesse Bering

W. W. NORTON & COMPANY New York · London

For information about permission to reproduce selections from this book,
write to Permissions, W. W. Norton & Company, Inc., 500 Fifth Avenue,
New York, NY 10110

For information about special discounts for bulk purchases, please contact
W. W. Norton Special Sales at specialsales@wwnorton.com or 800-233-4830

Manufacturing by Courier Westford
Book design by Dana Sloan
Production manager: Anna Oler

Library of Congress Cataloging-in-Publication Data

Bering, Jesse.
[God instinct]
The belief instinct : the psychology of souls, destiny, and the meaning of life /
Jesse Bering.—1st American ed. 2011.
p. cm.
Originally published in Great Britain under the title: The God instinct.
Includes bibliographical references and index.
ISBN 978-0-393-07299-0 (hardcover)
1. Spirituality—Psychological aspects. 2. Psychology and religion.
3. Psychology—Religious aspects. I. Title.
BF51.B47 2011
200.1'9—dc22

2010047252

ISBN 978-0-393-34126-3 pbk.

W. W. Norton & Company, Inc.
500 Fifth Avenue, New York, N.Y. 10110
www.wwnorton.com

W. W. Norton & Company ltd.
Castle House, 75/76 Wells Street, London W1T 3QT
1 2 3 4 5 6 7 8 9 0

For my father, William

CONTENTS

THE CHILD: I'm frightened.

THE WOMAN: And so you should be, darling. Terribly frightened. That's how one grows up into a decent, god-fearing man.

—*Jean-Paul Sartre*, The Flies *(1937)*

ACKNOWLEDGMENTS

LET'S FACE IT—BOOKS about science and religion can be awfully dull. And there isn't exactly a shortage in the marketplace in this particular genre. So for these reasons I'm especially grateful to a patient group of people in the publishing world who listened to me long enough to realize that, perhaps, I might have something a little bit different to say on that tired old horse of a subject, the existence of God. Were it not for these people's support, the book that you're holding in your hand right now would probably be busily growing cobwebs in a rare bookseller's boutique, sandwiched among a dozen obscure, self-published books on metaphysics or reincarnation or some such impenetrable emanations of the authors' strange, hallucinatory matter.

These supportive people include my agent, Peter Tallack of The Science Factory, who patiently held my hand from the very first day and helped me navigate a publishing universe that was quite foreign to me; and Angela von der Lippe and Nick Brealey, my editors at W. W. Norton and Nicholas Brealey Publishing, respectively, whose critical and talented eyes forced me to rethink, reedit, and rewrite this book a few times over. As such things go, I'm reasonably certain that, in a few years' time, should I survive that long, I'll look back with embarrassment on many things that I've written in this volume. But hopefully this blushing regret will be owing to the personal anecdotes rather than to the central arguments, and Angela and Nick certainly cannot be held accountable for those unfortunate bits of my own ridiculous life. In addition, publishing assistants Laura Romain and Erica Stern, of W. W. Norton, were exceedingly helpful at both ends of the production process. Last but not least, I would like to thank my copy editor, Stephanie Hiebert, who performed miracles worthy of the Almighty in cleaning up this text.

My students, as well as many other people in my day-to-day life, graciously endured many fleeting bouts of crankiness and my occasional absence of both body and mind while I was working on this manuscript. I only hope they forgive me these things someday. My partner, Juan Quiles, is still miraculously with me, in spite of everything. I'm also very grateful for the many friends, family members, and colleagues who generously gave their time to read early chapter versions (in some cases, the entire unedited manuscript) and whose clear comments and ideas helped give shape to the finished product. Among others, these include David Bjorklund, Paul Bloom, Joseph Bulbulia, Nicholas Epley, Margaret Evans, Gordon Gallup, Marc Hauser, Nicholas Humphrey, Dominic Johnson, Deborah Kelemen, E. Thomas Lawson, Graham Macdonald, Joel Mort, Shadd Muruna, Karen Schrock, Todd Shackelford, David Sloan-Wilson, Richard Sosis, Paulo Sousa, Henry Wellman, and Harvey Whitehouse. My former and present PhD students at the Institute of Cognition and Culture at Queen's University Belfast, particularly Natalie Emmons, David Harnden-Warwick, Bethany Heywood, Gordon Ingram, Hillary Lenfesty, Jared Piazza, Lauren Swiney, Claire White, and Neil Young, have contributed substantially to my thinking, through their clever insights and innovative research ideas.

Finally, because the theoretical story simply took me where it led, no more and no less, I wish to give a special thanks to all those talented scholars whom I have inadvertently offended by failing to cite their work in this book. There are probably many and sundry otherwise gentle intellectuals and scientists who will want my head for this.

The BELIEF INSTINCT

INTRODUCTION

GOD CAME FROM an egg. At least, that's how He came to me. Don't get me wrong, it was a very fancy egg. More specifically, it was an ersatz Fabergé egg decorated with colorful scenes from the Orient.

Now about two dozen years before the episode I'm about to describe, somewhere in continental Europe, this particular egg was shunted through the vent of an irritable hen, pierced with a needle and drained of its yolk, and held in the palm of a nimble artist who, for hours upon hours, painstakingly hand-painted it with elaborate images of a stereotypical Asian society. The artist, who specialized in such kitsch materials, then sold the egg along with similar wares to a local vendor, who placed it carefully in the front window of a side-street souvenir shop. Here it eventually caught the eye of a young German girl, who coveted it, purchased it, and after some time admiring it in her apartment against the backdrop of the Black Forest, wrapped it in layers of tissue paper, placed it in her purse, said a prayer for its safe transport, and took it on a transatlantic journey to a middle-class American neighborhood where she was to live with her new military husband. There, in the family room of her modest new home, on a bookshelf crammed with romance novels

1

and knickknacks from her earlier life, she found a cozy little nook for the egg and propped it up on a miniature display stand. A year or so later she bore a son, Peter, who later befriended the boy across the street, who suffered me as a tagalong little brother, the boy who, one aimless summer afternoon, would enter the German woman's family room, see the egg, become transfixed by this curiosity, and crush it accidentally in his seven-year-old hand.

The incident unobserved, I hastily put the fractured artifact back in its place, turned it at an angle so that its wound would be least noticeable, and, to this day, acted as though nothing had ever happened. Well, almost. A week later, I overheard Peter telling my brother that the crime had been discovered. His mother had a few theories about how her beloved egg had been irreparably damaged, he said—one being a very accurate and embarrassing deduction involving, of all people, *me*. When confronted with this scenario—through first insinuation and then full-blown accusations—and wary of the stern German matriarch's wrath, I denied my guilt summarily. Then, to get them off my back, I did the unthinkable. *I swore to God that I hadn't done it.*

———◆———

Let's put this in perspective. Somewhere on a quiet cul-de-sac, a second-grader secretly cracks a flashy egg owned by a woman who's a little too infatuated with it to begin with, tells nobody for fear of being punished, and finally invokes God as a false witness to his egged innocence. It's not exactly the crime of the century. But from my point of view, at that moment in time, the act was commensurate with the very worst of offenses against another human being. That I would dare to bring God into it only to protect myself was so unconscionable that the matter was never spoken of again.[1] Meanwhile, for weeks afterward, I had trouble sleeping and I lost my appetite; when I got a nasty splinter a few days later, I thought it was God's wrath.

I nearly offered up an unbidden confession to my parents. I was like a loathsome dog whimpering at God's feet. Do with me as you will, I thought to myself; I've done wrong.

Such an overwhelming fear of a vindictive, disappointed God certainly wasn't something that my parents had ever taught me. Of course, many parents do teach their children such things. If you've ever seen *Jesus Camp* (2006), a rather disturbing documentary about evangelically reared children in the American heartland, or if you've read Sam Harris's *The End of Faith* (2004), you'll know what I mean. But my family didn't even own a copy of the Bible, and I doubt if I had ever even heard the word "sin" uttered before. The only serious religious talk I ever heard was when my mother—who as a girl was once held down by exuberant Catholic children sifting through her hair for the rudimentary devil horns their parents told them all Jews have—tried to vaccinate me against all things evangelical by explaining how silly Christians' beliefs were. But even she was just a "secular Jew," and my father, at best, a shoulder-shrugging Lutheran.

Years later, when I was a teenager, my mother would be diagnosed with cancer, and then, too, I had the immediate sense that I had fallen out of favor with God. It felt as if my mother's plight were somehow related to the shenanigans I'd been up to (nothing worse than most teenagers, I'm sure, but also certainly nothing to commit indelibly to print). The feeling that I had a *bad essence* welled up inside me; God was singling me out for special punishment.

The thing is, I would never have admitted to having these thoughts at the time. In fact, I didn't even believe in God. I realized there was a logical biological explanation for the fact that my mother was dying. And if you had even alluded to the possibility that my mom's ailing health was caused by some secret moral offense on my part or hers, you would have forced my intellectual gag reflex. I would probably have dismissed you as one of those people she had warned me about.

3

In fact, I shook off the "God must really hate me" mentality as soon as it registered in my rational consciousness. But there's also no mistaking that it was there in my mind and, for a few bizarre moments, it was clear as a whistle.

It was around that time that God struck me as being curiously similar to the Mafia, offering us "protection" and promising not to hurt us (or kill us) as long as we pay up in moral currency. But unlike a hammer to the shin or a baseball bat to the back of the head, God's brand of punishment, at least here on earth, is distinctively symbolic, coming in the form of a limitless array of cruel vagaries thoughtfully designed for us, such as a splinter in our hands, our stocks tumbling into the financial abyss, a tumor in our brains, our ex-wives on the prowl for another man, an earthquake under our feet, and so on. For believers, the possibilities are endless.

Now, years later, one of the key motivators still driving the academic curiosity that fuels my career as an atheistic psychological scientist who studies religion is my own seemingly instinctual fear of being punished by God, and thinking about God more generally. I wanted to know where in the world these ideas were coming from. Could it really be possible that they were *innate*? Is there perhaps something like a "belief instinct"?

———

In the chapters that follow, we will be exploring this question of the innateness of God beliefs, in addition to many related beliefs, such as souls, the afterlife, destiny, and meaning. You're probably already well versed in the man in the street's explanations for why people gravitate toward God in times of trouble. Almost all such stories are need-based accounts concerning human emotional well-being. For example, if I were to pose the question "Why do most people believe in God?" to my best friend from high school, or my Aunt Betty Sue in

Georgia, or the pet store owner in my small village here in Northern Ireland, their responses would undoubtedly go something like this: "Well, that's easy. It's because people need . . . [fill in the blank here: *to feel like there's something bigger out there; to have a sense of purpose in their lives; to take comfort in religion; to reduce uncertainty; something to believe in*]."

I don't think these types of answers are entirely intellectually bankrupt actually, but I do think they just beg the question. They're perfectly circular, leaving us scratching our heads over why we need to feel like there's something bigger out there or to have a sense of purpose and so on to begin with. Do other animals have these same existential needs? And, if not, why don't they?[2] When looked at objectively, our behaviors in this domain are quite strange, at least from a cross-species, evolutionary perspective. As the Spanish author Miguel de Unamuno wrote,

> *The gorilla, the chimpanzee, the orangutan, and their kind, must look upon man as a feeble and infirm animal, whose strange custom it is to store up his dead.* Wherefore?[3]

Back when I was in graduate school, I spent several years conducting psychological research with chimpanzees. Our small group of seven study animals was housed in a very large, very sterile, and very boring biomedical facility, where hundreds of other great apes—our closest living relatives—were being warehoused for invasive testing purposes under pharmaceutical contracts. I saw too many scenes of these animals in distress, unsettling images that I try not to revisit these days. But it occurred to me that if humans were in comparably hopeless conditions as these chimpanzees, certainly the question of God—particularly, what God could possibly be thinking by allowing such cruel travesties—would be on a lot of people's minds.

So what exactly is it that can account for that instantaneous bolus of "why" questioning secreted by our human brains in response to pain and misfortune, a question that implies a breach of some unspoken moral contract between ourselves, as individuals, and God? We might convince ourselves that it is misleading to ask such questions, that God "isn't like that" or even that there is no God, but this is only in answer to the knee-jerk question arising in the first place.

To help us understand why our minds gravitate toward God in the wake of misfortune (as well as fortune), we will be drawing primarily from recent findings in the *cognitive sciences*. Investigators in the cognitive science of religion argue that religious thinking, like any other type of thinking, is something done by a brain that is occasionally prone to making mistakes. Superstitious thinking, such as seeing causal relations where none in fact exist, is portrayed as the product of an imperfectly evolved brain. Perhaps it's understandable, then, that all but a handful of scholars in this area regard religion as an accidental byproduct of our mental evolution. Specifically, religious thought is usually portrayed by scholars as having no particular adaptive biological function in itself, but instead it's viewed as a leftover of other psychological adaptations (sort of like male nipples being a useless leftover of the default human body plan). God is a happenstance muddle of other evolved mental parts. This is the position taken by the evolutionary biologist Richard Dawkins, for example, in *The God Delusion* (2006):

> *I am one of an increasing number of biologists who see religion as a byproduct of something else. Perhaps the feature we are interested in (religion in this case) doesn't have a direct survival value of its own, but is a byproduct of something else that does . . . [Religious] behavior may be a misfiring, an unfortunate byproduct of an underlying psychological propensity which in other circumstances is, or once was, useful.*[4]

Evolutionary by-product theorists, however, may have been a bit hasty in dismissing the possibility that religion—and especially, the idea of a watchful, knowing, reactive God—uniquely helped our ancestors survive and reproduce. If so, then just as with any other evolved adaptation, we would expect concepts about supernatural agents such as God to have solved, or at least to have meaningfully addressed, a particular adaptive problem in the evolutionary past. And, indeed, after first examining the mechanics of belief, we'll eventually explore in this book the possibility that God (and others like Him) evolved in human minds as an "adaptive illusion," one that directly helped our ancestors solve the unique problem of *human gossip*.

With the evolution of language, the importance of behavioral inhibition became paramount for our ancestors because absent third parties could now find out about their behaviors days, even weeks, after an event. If they failed to bridle their selfish passions in the face of temptation, and if there was even a single human witness to their antisocial actions, our ancestors' reputations—and hence their reproductive interests—were foolishly gambled away. The private perception of being intelligently designed, monitored, and known about by a God who actively punished and rewarded our intentions and behaviors would have helped stomp out the frequency and intensity of our ancestors' immoral hiccups and would have been strongly favored by natural selection. God and other supernatural agents like Him needn't actually exist to have caused such desired gene-salvaging effects, but—just as they do today—the mental biases we'll be examining certainly gave our ancestors reason to think that they did.

———•———

One of the important, often unspoken, implications of the new cognitive science of religion is the possibility that we've been going about studying the God question completely wrong for a very long time. Perhaps the question of God's existence is one that is more for psychologists than for philosophers, physicists, or even theologians. Put the scripture aside. Just as the scientist who studies the basic cognitive mechanisms of language acquisition isn't especially concerned with the particular narrative plot in children's bedtime stories, the cognitive scientist of religion isn't much concerned about the details of the fantastic fables buried in religious texts. Instead, in picking apart the psychological bones of belief, we're going to focus on some existential basics. Perceiving the supernatural isn't magic, but something patently organic: a function of the brain.

I should warn you: I've always had trouble biting my tongue, and we're going to address head-on some of life's biggest questions. Is there really a God who cares about you? Is there really a special reason that you are here? Will your soul live on after you die? Or, alternatively, are God, souls, and destiny simply a set of seductive cognitive illusions, one that can be accounted for by the unusual evolution of the human brain? It seems Nature may have had a few tricks up her sleeve to ensure that we would fall hook, line, and sinker for these spectacular ruses.

Ultimately, of course, you must decide for yourself whether the subjective psychological effects created by your evolved cognitive biases reflect an objective reality, perhaps as evidence that God designed your mind to be so receptive to Him. Or, just maybe, you will come to acknowledge that, like the rest of us, you are a hopeless pawn in one of natural selection's most successful hoaxes ever—and smile at the sheer ingenuity involved in pulling it off, at the very thought of such mindless cleverness. One can still enjoy the illusion of God, after all, without believing Him to be real.

Either way, our first order of business is to determine what kind of mind it takes to think about God's mind in the first place, and one crucial factor—indeed, perhaps the only essential one—is the ability to think about other minds at all.

So, onward we go.

I | THE HISTORY OF AN ILLUSION

Gorgias had a way with words. He was also a bit of a charlatan. While draped, as the story goes, in flowing purple robes, the charismatic former student of the philosopher Empedocles stood before listless hordes of gangly slaves, bored plebes, and the bloated politicians of ancient Greece and gave them all a show. During public debates on the most serious matters of the day—from the rape of Helen, to the economy, to the nature of existence itself—he was rumored to have disarmed his grim-faced opponents with a sudden burst of good-natured laughter. When the other side returned his laughter amicably, he would obliterate the attempts at humor by a return to seriousness, questioning why they were making light of such an important and sobering subject.

On stage, Gorgias achieved astonishing feats of verbal acrobatics and delivered poetic rejoinders said to dumbfound even the most eloquent of his learned adversaries. Although Gorgias's booming voice had long since vanished from the site of the Olympic Games, where he had once orated before tens of thousands of restless, sweaty forms, one admirer, the Greek lexicographer Suidas, gushed that Gorgias "was the first to give to the rhetorical genre the art of deliberate culture and employed tropes and metaphors and figurative language and hypallage and catachresis and hyperbaton and doublings of words and repetitions and apostrophes and clauses of equal length."[1] In the *Phaedrus* (circa 370 BC), Socrates refers to Gorgias as being, "skilled in tricking out a speech." Even the notoriously hard-to-please Plato couldn't help but marvel at Gorgias's verbal skills. "I often heard Gorgias say that the art of rhetoric differs from all other arts," wrote Plato. "Under its influence all things are willingly but not forcibly made slaves."[2]

To "Gorgianize" became synonymous with bamboozling listeners with seductive wordage. Gorgias charged exorbitant fees for his public performances and was so sought after as a teacher that he was made fantastically rich by the amount he earned from his many pupils. (Just in case anyone doubted his superfluous wealth, he commissioned a dazzling, solid-gold statue of himself and had it erected prominently in the temple at Delphi.) Such was Gorgias's prowess in persuasion that in the theater at Athens he often boldly provoked the crowd, challenging them to pose to him a question that would leave him speechless. "Suggest a topic," he would say, paring idly away at his fingernails. But to the very day he died, his tongue refused to tie. At the age of at least 105, Gorgias lay down on his bed and began drifting off to sleep. When a friend asked him if he was okay, Gorgias is said to have responded with characteristic wit, "Sleep already begins to hand me over to his brother Death."[3]

Yet for all his eloquence, there was something that pestered Gorgias throughout his life. In spite of his inimitable ability to domesticate language so that even the most elusive of concepts would play like docile animals at his every command, he was frustrated by the fact that even a wordsmith such as he couldn't effectively communicate his innermost experiences to another listener in a way that perfectly reflected his private reality. Dressed up in language and filtered through another person's brain, one's subjective experiences are inevitably transfigured into a wholly different thing, so much so that Gorgias felt it fair to say that the speaker's mind can never truly be known. Thoughts said aloud are mutant by nature. No matter how expertly one plumbs the depths of subjective understanding, Gorgias realized to his horror, or how artistically rendered and devastatingly precise language may be, truth still falls on ears that hear something altogether different from what exists in reality.

Gorgias would have found a commiserating fellow scholar in a modern-day (and unusually poetical) psychologist from the London School of Economics named Nicholas Humphrey. "How hard it is to come to terms with this result," Humphrey laments in "The Society of Selves." "To have to face the fact of being oneself—one self, this self and none other, this secret packet of phenomena, this singular bubble of consciousness. Press up against each other as we may, and the bubbles remain essentially inviolate. Share the same body even, be joined like Siamese twins, and there still remain two quite separate consciousnesses."[4] To Humphrey, this fundamental and unbridgeable "otherness of others" induces a unique kind of loneliness in human beings—one that, paradoxically, is exacerbated by the physical presence of other people.[5] This type of psychological loneliness is perhaps felt most acutely when we are as close to another person's body as is humanly possible. As the poet William Butler Yeats wrote rather dramatically, "The tragedy of sexual intercourse is the perpetual virginity of the soul."[6]

This sentiment that other minds are insufferably just out of reach isn't all reason for despair, though. One can, in fact, arguably derive a rather pleasing sense of narcissistic control from such an understanding. Each of us, utterly alone, carries the whole world in our heads, and other people exist only insofar as we have minds capable of harboring them. The upside of being alone in the universe, of having sovereign psychological reign, is expressed rather nicely in the poem "Mad Girl's Love Song" (1953), in which the somewhat lugubrious Sylvia Plath tells us, "I shut my eyes and all the world drops dead; I lift my lids and all is born again."

Actually, Gorgias's reasoning about the inherent solitude of the individual (and the population-level "societies of selves," as Humphrey refers to human cultures) has been the plaything of a diverse group of thinkers and writers. Author Thomas De Quincey, in *Confessions of an English Opium-Eater* (1821), notes that, "all men come into this world alone and leave it alone." This is true in a very literal sense. But, if you really think about it, we also take others with us when we die. Because the only knowledge that we have of another person is contained in our heads as a mental representation of that individual, in a sense our own death will steal their lives away too. If the entire universe is all in our heads, so to speak, Plath is justified in her musing that, "all the world drops dead."

Gorgias went even further than simply noting the illusion of a true intersubjectivity. He concluded that, because other minds cannot be known in reality but only perceived, perhaps they don't exist at all. After all, one can't actually see, feel, or weigh another person's mind; rather, all we can really observe is bodies moving about, mouths talking, and faces contorting. For this reason, Gorgias is still regarded by many scholars as the world's first *solipsist*—someone who denies, on philosophical grounds, the very existence of other minds.[7]

———————

Although believing yourself to be the only subjective entity in all the world may sound patently ludicrous, if not mildly psychopathic, in fact such thinking is just as logical today as it was in the fourth century BC, when Gorgias, struck by the impotence of mere words in conveying his reality, declared himself to have the only mind that ever was. Long after the seventeenth-century philosopher René Descartes, questioning even the existence of his own mind, muttered his existentially consoling *Cogito, ergo sum* ("I think, therefore I am"), the task of proving beyond a shadow of a doubt that other minds exist remains fundamentally impossible. A scientist can no sooner capture and study a mental state than trap a kilogram in a bottle or caress an ounce in the palm of her hand.

Even with all the technological sophistication of today's brain-imaging equipment, or with the recent discovery of mirror neurons (neurons that fire both when an animal acts and when the animal observes the same action performed by another), other minds still exist only in theory. How would you prove to someone else, incontrovertibly, that you have a mind? Consider that if confronted with Shakespeare's celebrated plea from *The Merchant of Venice* (1598)—"If you prick us, do we not bleed? If you tickle us, do we not laugh? If you poison us, do we not die?"—the solipsist might answer, "Yeah. *And?*"

Even in modern Hollywood, the concept of true intersubjectivity is rather hard to get one's head around. In one of my all-time favorite films, *Being John Malkovich* (1999), a lowly puppeteer played by John Cusack is forced to take on a remedial office job on the "7½ floor" of a low-ceilinged building in New York City, only to discover a wormhole hidden behind a filing cabinet that leads straight into actor John Malkovich's subjective universe. As members of the viewing audience, we're told that Cusack's character (and later, other paying customers given access to this strange wonderland of Malkovich's head before being vomited out of the wormhole and onto the side of the New Jersey Turnpike) can see and feel what Malkovich is experiencing. But what is supposed to be a merging of consciousnesses can only be portrayed on-screen as Cusack's character looking through Malkovich's eyes as a voyeur into the actor's world. Cusack is a sort of homunculus listening to the muffled voice of its host like a fetus in utero hearing its mother. Later in the movie, when his skills are put to use in manipulating Malkovich's behavior, Cusack is a puppeteer. But Malkovich's consciousness is never truly punctured. Rather, the film is about two separate minds in one head; "being" John Malkovich amounts to being inside John Malkovich's body.

What a multimillion-dollar studio budget cannot do, however, was nearly achieved on a shoestring budget in a psychological laboratory. Harvard University psychologist Daniel Wegner demonstrated that, under certain unusual conditions, people may actually mistake someone else's mental experiences as their own. In one classic study, participants were asked to dress in long-sleeved medical scrubs and stand before a mirror with their arms behind them. Another person of the same sex, roughly the same size, wearing identical clothes, stood behind a curtain and inserted his or her arms along the participants' sides, so that when the participants glanced in the mirror, it looked as though this other person's arms were their own. If participants saw the foreign hand snapping its fingers and were made to feel in control of this behavior, a rather curious thing happened: when a rubber band on this other person's wrist was snapped against the stranger's skin, the participants themselves responded with a spike in their own skin conductance in the same wrist area, which was resting, of course, comfortably out of sight behind them.[8]

The notable exception of some quirky laboratory experiments notwithstanding, we are indeed contained entirely in our own skulls. The only reasonable defense against solipsism is reason itself. Psychologists Steven Platek and Gordon Gallup from the State University of New York at Albany are cautiously optimistic that we're on fairly safe ground in assuming that other people are just as conscious as we ourselves are. "Because humans share similar receptor mechanisms and brains that are organized roughly the same way," they point out, "there is bound to be considerable overlap between their experiences."[9]

We all have our doubts from time to time—I've stared, square in the eyes, my share of somnambulistic students who I would swear were cleverly rigged automatons. But generally speaking, most of us seldom doubt that other people are indeed fellow conscious creatures. In fact, we're forced to exert far greater effort trying to comprehend solipsism than we are its more intuitive antithesis, which is that the world is continually breathing with conscious activity, infused by those ethereal minds that exist only in theory. That is to say, for most of us, others are more than just ambulant objects fitted out with brains and programmed with behavioral algorithms leading them to act *as if* they were conscious.

Even individuals with a somewhat misanthropic bent cannot help but, occasionally at least, see other people as deeply psychological entities—compatriot souls being driven by similar likes and desires. A good example comes from Portuguese writer Fernando Pessoa's semiautobiographical *The Book of Disquiet* (1916). Speaking to us through the voice of his alter ego, Bernardo Soares, an accountant aware of his own mediocrity as a midlevel employee but nonetheless someone who secretly relishes his intellectual superiority, Pessoa recalls a particular incident in which his own solipsistic worldview was caused to wobble:

> *Yesterday, when they told me that the assistant in the tobacconist's had committed suicide, I couldn't believe it. Poor lad, so he existed too! We had all forgotten that, all of us. We who knew him only about as well as those who didn't know him at all. We'll forget him more easily tomorrow. But what is certain is that he had a soul, enough to kill himself. Passions? Worries? Of course. But for me, and for the rest of humanity, all that remains is the memory of a foolish smile above a grubby woolen jacket that didn't fit properly at the shoulders. That is all that remains to me*

*of someone who felt deeply enough to kill himself, because, after
all there's no other reason to kill oneself.*[10]

———◆———

One researcher who has given considerable thought to these sorts of
questions is Yale University psychologist Paul Bloom. In his book
Descartes' Baby (2004), Bloom posits that human beings are "commonsense dualists." His central thesis is that, unlike any other species,
we're unusually prone to seeing others as being "more than bodies"—
rather, we see bodies as being inhabited by souls. Yet depending on
the particular social parameters and the conditions we're dealing with,
we can become more or less likely to see others as objects rather than
as fellow human beings. On some occasions, such as the suicide case
described by Pessoa, other people's souls stare out at us so vividly that
our thinking is tilted heavily toward seeing them as richly experien-
tial agents like ourselves. On other occasions, however, such as when
relations with our neighbors grow sour or during periods of intense
sociopolitical turmoil and violence, we're vulnerable to diminishing
other people's humanity, objectifying other human beings as mere
"disgusting" or stock bodies. The Nazi regime's systematic dehumanization of Jews, Bloom points out, is a case in point:

> *The clearest modern example of how this works comes from Nazi
> propaganda, which described the Jews as dirty, filthy, disease-
> ridden; they were portrayed as rats, garbage, and bacillus, agents
> of infection . . . Having trapped the Jews in conditions in which
> hygiene was difficult or impossible—as in the concentration camps
> and, to a lesser extent, the ghettos—[the Nazis] would speak with
> satisfaction of their filthiness . . .*
>
> *Disgust is not the only way to diminish people. One can also*

try to rob them of individuality—describing them as "cargo,"
designating them by number, and so on.[11]

In fact, Nick Haslam, a psychologist at the University of Melbourne, has found that we don't have to be in the midst of genocide to catch a very scary glimpse of dehumanization at work—or at least, a slightly less toxic version of dehumanization he calls "infrahumanization." In a 2009 article for the popular social psychology online magazine *In-Mind*, Haslam and coauthors Peter Koval and Joonha Park write, "It should be a sobering thought that mild forms of humanness denial are pervasive in our everyday perception of groups."[12] They base this conclusion on laboratory findings indicating that people implicitly perceive those of other groups (for example, Indonesians or Britons from the Australians' point of view) as having emotions starker and less subtle than their own. While we're happy enough to acknowledge that strangers from other groups have blunted, animal-like emotions such as happiness, fear, and anger, we're much more reluctant to endow them with the more sumptuous, complicated affects, such as nostalgia, embarrassment, and admiration.

But the truth is, unless we're professional mental health care providers or are unusually empathic, seldom do we really strive to understand someone else's private reality—not in any meaningful way anyway. Instead, somewhere between solipsism and psychoanalysis is an everyday form of "mind reading," one in which we tend to see others as doing things intentionally and for a reason but we stop short of trying to crawl into their skin to get a perfect phenomenological picture of their inner universe.

For instance, not so very long ago I found myself at a small academic conference at Cambridge University seated behind the noted philosopher Daniel Dennett. What was strange about this was that I couldn't help but stare at the back of Dennett's head—at the perfectly oblong shape of his skull, the sun-speckled skin stretched taut around it, the neatly trimmed ring of white hair . . . What irony, I thought, that I would be staring at the particular cranium containing the very mind that first posed the formal question of why understanding other minds is so central to evolved human psychology, only to realize that, though it literally lay at my fingertips, even this mind was no more than an airy hypothetical.[13]

Among cognitive scientists, Dennett is perhaps best known for his argument that humans are unique among other organisms because evolution has crafted our brains in such a way that we cannot help but assume an "intentional stance" when reasoning about others:

> *The intentional stance is the strategy of interpreting the behavior of an entity (person, animal, artifact, whatever) by treating it as if it were a rational agent who governed its "choice" of "action" by a consideration of its "beliefs" and "desires" . . . the basic strategy of the intentional stance is to treat the entity in question as an agent, in order to predict—and thereby explain, in one sense—its actions or moves.*[14]

If Dennett were to have, say, turned suddenly around in his chair at that Cambridge conference and winked twice at me, well then I wouldn't have simply seen the torso of a six-foot-three-inch human body capped by an oblong head that held a pair of eyes, one of which was peering peculiarly at me from under the fluttering sheath of a thin piece of skin. Rather, I would have instinctively asked myself what on earth these winks were supposed to be in reference to. In other words, I would have wondered what was going through Dennett's mind that would cause him to act in such a manner. Perhaps the speaker we were both listening to just said something that reminded him of me? Maybe he just realized I was sitting behind him and he was simply saying hello? Perhaps it had something to do with our secret rendezvous from one very magical night before? When someone winks at you— or does anything else unexpected, for that matter—your brain isn't content with just processing the superficial layer of behavior being exhibited by this other person, but without any conscious effort it launches a search of the other person's mental reasons for acting this way. In other words, we ask, "What is the behavior we're witnessing *about*?" Back at the conference I might think to myself, "Oh, I get it. Dan probably believes that I'm antagonistic to the speaker's posi- tion, and he wants to show a sort of good-natured teasing with me by winking at me in playfulness."

Consider how your everyday social experiences would look with- out this capacity to instantaneously translate other people's behav- iors into ideas, emotions, and thoughts. Developmental psychologists Alison Gopnik and Andrew Meltzoff provide a nightmarish example in their book the *The Scientist in the Crib* (2000). Imagine, the authors tell us, taking the perspective of a guest sitting at a restaurant table and simply observing a banal dinner party conservation among the members of a young family, one of whom, a child, erupts into tears after a bout of teasing by an older sibling:

> We seem to see husbands and wives and little brothers. But what we really see are bags of skin stuffed into pieces of cloth and draped over chairs. There are small restless black spots that move at the top of the bags of skin, and a hole underneath that irregularly makes noise. The bags move in unpredictable ways, and some- times one of them will touch us. The holes change shape, and occasionally salty liquid pours from the two spots.[15]

———◆———

Dennett's landmark set of essays on the subject of perceiving other minds in *The Intentional Stance* (1987) was published on the heels of an important change in attitude and mind toward other animals. Through the mainstreaming of scientific findings, more people than ever before were being made aware just how much we had in common with other animals. Much of this awareness could be traced directly back to the early 1960s, when the well-known paleontologist Louis Leakey encouraged the first of a trio of young women to begin studying our closest living relatives—the great apes—in their natural environments. Jane Goodall, a British graduate student who had previously accompanied Leakey as an assistant during his archaeological digs for prehuman fossils at Olduvai Gorge in eastern Africa, soon set up camp in Tanzania, where for the next few decades she took copious field notes revealing the secret, everyday lives of wild chimpanzees. It was Goodall, of course, who obliterated the old definition of our species as being "Man the Toolmaker" when she observed the chimps at Gombe fashioning twigs and inserting them into termite mounds, fishing for insects. When Leakey learned of this behavior, he replied excitedly in a telegram to Goodall, "Now we must redefine tool, redefine Man, or accept chimpanzees as humans!"[16]

A few years later, another of Leakey's young protégés, a Canadian student named Biruté Galdikas, set up her own camp at the edge of the Java Sea in Borneo and began the world's first observational studies of wild orangutans. By contrast to Goodall, Galdikas didn't initially spy any such clear incidences of tool use. But, like her colleague's observations of chimp behavior, Galdikas's observations of orangutan social behavior were often mirror images of our own proclivities; and what the mirror reflected wasn't always so pretty. Among a few other things in her many years spent watching these elusive red apes, Galdikas discovered that human males aren't the only animals on earth that, occasionally, brutally rape females while they are struggling to get away. According to Galdikas's autobiography, in fact, one adolescent orangutan even had his way with an unsuspecting human field-worker from her camp.

Finally, the third of "Leakey's Angels," as they came to be known, was American Dian Fossey, portrayed in the Academy Award–nominated performance by Sigourney Weaver in the film *Gorillas in the Mist* (1988). Before she was martyred in her campaign to save mountain gorillas from extinction, Fossey captivated members of the public with her heartfelt descriptions of these giant, very humanlike creatures living deep in the Virunga Mountains of Rwanda.

Meanwhile, as these primatological field endeavors were gaining ever-wider press, making starlets of Leakey's Angels and stirring up heated, popular debates about Darwinian evolution and the nature of human nature, a somewhat lesser-known researcher working along-side the Rwanda team had his own peculiarly staggering thought:

In the grandeur of the mountains, half-accepted into the gorilla family, watching and watched by a dozen black eyes, far from any other person, left with my own thoughts, I began musing about an issue that has fascinated me ever since: What's it like, for a gorilla, to be a gorilla? What does a gorilla know about what it's like to be me? How do we read minds? . . .

It dawned on me that this could be the answer to much that is special about human evolution. We humans—and to a lesser extent maybe gorillas and chimps too—have evolved to be "natural psychologists." The most promising but also the most dangerous elements in our environment are other members of our own species. Success for our human ancestors must have depended on being able to get inside the minds of those they lived with, second-guess them, anticipate where they were going, help them if they needed it, challenge them, or manipulate them. To do this they had to develop brains that would deliver a story about what it's like to be another person from the inside.

The researcher in question was a young Nicholas Humphrey, the psychologist we met earlier bemoaning the impenetrableness of other minds. But here he was, many years earlier as the twenty-eight-year-old assistant director of research at the Cambridge Department of Animal Behavior, swatting away insects, crouching in montane forest, the air laden with the musky odor of gorilla sweat, first realizing that we might well be the only species on the planet (perhaps even the universe) able to ponder the question of other minds to begin with.[17]

Over the ensuing years, it was largely Humphrey who reminded scholars that, although the religiously inspired *scala naturae* (or the "great chain of being," which placed beasts in orders of magnitude below humans and humans below only the angels) had been thoroughly—and justly—knocked off its base by Darwinian logic, this didn't imply that there weren't in fact meaningful, evolved psychological differences between humans and other animals. Actually, there might well be one very big difference: the human capacity to think about minds.

Soon, two American psychologists, David Premack and Guy Woodruff, would become the first experimental researchers to explore the question under controlled laboratory conditions. Their 1978 article "Does the Chimpanzee Have a 'Theory of Mind'?" kick-started a sort of revolution in the social cognitive sciences. (They answered "yes" to their own question, but this answer was based on such a flawed study that it's hardly worth describing here.) This rather jargony term, "theory of mind," was defined by the authors as follows:

A system of inferences of this kind may properly be viewed as a theory because such [mental] states are not directly observable, and the system can be used to make predictions about the behavior of others.[18]

Again, we can't see minds, feel them, or weigh them in any literal sense; rather, we can only infer their existence through observing other actors' behaviors. So Premack and Woodruff's "theory of mind" was simply a more formalized version of Humphrey's initial inklings out in that lonely African rain forest, and for our purposes it can be considered synonymous with Humphrey's "natural psychologist" construct, as well as Dennett's more philosophical "intentional stance."

It's perhaps easiest to grasp the concept of a theory of mind when considering how we struggle to make sense of someone else's bizarre or unexpected behavior. If you've ever seen an unfortunate woman at the grocery store wearing a midriff-revealing top and packed into a pair of lavender tights like meat in a sausage wrapper, or a follicularly challenged man with a hairpiece two shades off and three centimeters adrift, and asked yourself what on earth those people were thinking when they looked in the mirror before leaving the house, this is a good sign that your theory of mind (not to mention your fashion sense!) is in working order. When others violate our expectations for normalcy, or stump us with surprising behaviors, our tendency to mind-read goes into overdrive.

The evolutionary significance of this mind-reading system hinges on one gigantic question: Is this psychological capacity—this theory of mind, this seeing souls glimmering beneath the skin, spirits twinkling behind orbiting eyes, thoughts in the flurry of movement—is this the "one big thing" that could help us finally understand what it means to be human? Forget tool use, never mind culture—and, for that matter, monogamy, love, play, politics, warfare, and all those other categories of behavior once deemed exclusively human. Leakey's

Angels and other anthropologists were scratching these candidates off the list of possibly unique human traits one by one. One prominent researcher, the Dutch primatologist Frans de Waal, summed up his highly respected work on chimpanzee social behavior as showing that great apes were "inching closer to humanity."[19] Even our unique claim to language was up in the air. A few ragtag animals were allegedly learning human sign language in closely guarded studies in which they were raised, essentially, as children. One of the key researchers involved in this line of work, Sue Savage-Rumbaugh from Georgia State University, years later declared that she had met the mind of another species (in this case owned by one of her bonobo chimpanzee subjects) and discovered that it was just as human as her own: "I found out that it was the same as ours. I found out that 'it' was me!"[20]

A handful of more reluctant scholars, however, worried that in trying to show just how human other animals are, we might end up overlooking something equally important. Isn't it possible, they countered, that despite this striking overlap in behavioral similarity with other primates, human minds still work in this very different, mind-reading way? After all, when compared to the brains of the other African apes, cognitive neuroscientists have found that the area of the brain believed to be responsible for reasoning about other minds is significantly larger in human beings and occupies more of our cerebral mantle. This area, right behind your forehead, is called the prefrontal cortex, and images from functional MRI (fMRI) studies suggest that it houses special neural systems dedicated to theory of mind.

So although the previous century had seen Darwin's theory of evolution forcing people to come to grips with their own unprivileged, amoebic origins, and more recent studies showed just how much we have in common with other animals, a few academics were beginning to think that, perhaps, there's still one thing—theory of mind—that makes our species truly unique.

———◆———

Ironically, such scholars found themselves in a definite minority. The tide had turned. People who now subscribed to the view that humans are "special" carried a suspicious whiff of bias and were looked at askance by the larger scientific community. Many saw them as being either secretly religious and endorsing an outmoded view of the natural world or, even worse, simply not "getting it" when it came to the standard processes of evolution by natural selection, which implied a basic continuity in function and form between members of shared ancestral lineages. After all, hadn't Darwin himself written that "the difference between the mind of the lowest man and that of the highest animal is . . . one of degree and not of kind"?[21]

In a 2004 article in the journal *Animal Law*, Roger Fouts, a psychologist from Central Washington University who had been involved with some of the pioneering sign language work with chimpanzees back in the 1960s, argued for new legislation that would dissolve the "delusory" species barrier between humans and great apes—a legal action that would, in effect, grant personhood status to simians. Fouts writes that in accepting the foregoing Darwinian logic, we can finally

accept the reality that our species is not outside of nature and that we are not gods. We might lose the illusory heights of being demiurges, but this new perspective would offer us something greater, the full realization of our place in this great orchestra we call Nature.[22]

Fouts inveighs against those disbelieving, coldhearted scientists who have "indulged in such pandering [of human uniqueness] to human arrogance," especially those of the past century who "did not have the excuse of being ignorant of Darwin." Such a point of view, he reasons, "is derived from our long established theological, political, and metaphysical beliefs about humans." Fouts confesses that he, too, was once sadly just like these sanctimonious and delusional academics. But after decades of devotedly raising, studying, and interacting with a chimp named Washoe—who was captured as an infant in Africa, her mother killed by poachers—he's had to come face-to-face with the harsh emotional realities of Darwinian continuity:

> *I had to recognize that I was part of a research project, in the ignorance of the times, which was party to a baby being taken from her mother and the killing of her mother. It was a project that condemned a young girl [referring to Washoe] to a life where she could never fully reach the potential for which she was born. It was a project that took a young girl from her culture and family where she could have learned and given so much. It was a project that condemned her to life in prison, though she never committed a crime . . . I have to accept the Darwinian fact that Washoe is a person by any reasonable definition, and that the community of chimpanzees from which she was stolen are a people.*[23]

Fouts's story is very touching. But is there any scientific substance to what he's saying? Perhaps the real issue, some might balk, isn't about vanity and human arrogance, or about the Cartesian delusion of souls being nestled somewhere in our pineal glands, but instead about biological diversity and the possibility of there actually *being* genuine psychological differences between humans and other animals. It's not a matter of whether other animals, such as chimps, *have* minds or whether they feel emotions deeply. Nobody's really debating that. For any credible scientist at least, it's certainly not a matter of whether humans are "better" or "more evolved" than other species or any such erroneous linear nonsense.

Actually, the only big, juicy question at hand is whether other animals are endowed with a theory of mind. Psycholinguist Derek Bickerton from the University of Hawaii suggests that, were it not politically incorrect and were scientists not unfairly portrayed as foolish little men luxuriating in the delusion of human supremacy, the massive cognitive differences between our species and other animals would be obvious to all. He claims the trouble is that even alluding to the possibility that human beings are unique these days falls "somewhere between Holocaust denial and rejection of global warming."[24]

But after all, a lot has transpired over the past six million years, which is about how long ago it was that we last shared a common ancestor with chimpanzees. Some twenty intermediary human species, from the hairy australopithecines onward, have come and gone over that long time span. Our brains tripled in size, we became striding bipeds (walking fluidly on two legs), and our skulls, pelvic girdles, hands, and feet were dramatically retooled. Certainly this was enough time for natural selection to carve out more or less unique brain-based cognitive properties too—properties that might explain just why our species stands apart so radically today. Perhaps theory of mind can best be understood as a human psychological adaptation similar to other recently evolved physical traits, such as our specialized skulls, hands, and pelvises.

In fact, systematic reconstructions of the human fossil record and painstaking analyses of ancient dwelling sites led cognitive archaeologists Frederick Coolidge and Thomas Wynn to question whether even Neanderthals had a theory of mind. And if chimps are the equivalent of our distant cousins on the evolutionary tree, Neanderthals are something like our fraternal twins. In *The Rise of Homo sapiens: The Evolution of Modern Thinking* (2009), Coolidge and Wynn point out that a conspicuous clue to the Neanderthals' theory-of-mind abilities, or rather their absence, is the fact that they didn't seem to gather socially at the most obvious place for a meeting of the minds:

> *Neanderthals occasionally scooped out a depression for the fire, but only rarely lined the pit with stone, or built the hearth in any significant way. And the hearths were not predictably centered in the living area; they were in fact rather haphazardly placed . . . Neanderthals appear not to have sat around their fires for storytelling, or ritual, keeping the fire intense, and using it as the metaphorical center of the social group. If Neanderthals did not, or could not, maintain shared group attention for purely social purposes, then their lives were very different from our own.*[25]

Some scientists believe that the evolution of theory of mind in humans but not other living primates might be analogous to the evolution of bat echolocation, where this bio-sonar capacity for navigating and hunting in the dark is present in one of the major suborders of bats (Microchiroptera) while almost completely absent in the other (Megachiroptera). And none have toed this line of human uniqueness more so than a charismatic yet cantankerous researcher from Louisiana named Daniel Povinelli. Appearing on the scene in the early 1990s when he established his own chimp research center deep in the heart of the Cajun bayous, Povinelli, then an impressive young anthropologist who had recently earned his doctoral degree from Yale and who had cut his teeth on his school's undergraduate debating team, had become irritated by what he believed was a misguided agenda among comparative psychologists, one in which genuine differences between human beings and other animals were being swept under the rug while researchers instead focused on "narrowing the gap" between our minds. "If we are to make progress toward understanding how humans and chimpanzees can resemble each other so closely in behavior," Povinelli once wrote in his characteristically strident style, "and yet differ so dramatically in psychological functioning, we need to abandon the visual rhetoric of *National Geographic* documentaries."[26] In other words, although anthropomorphizing other animals was increasingly in vogue, and the public had largely grown to distrust scientists who believed humans were "special," this reluctance to focus on differences rather than similarities between humans and other animals wasn't doing us any favors in terms of understanding human nature.

One of the major offenses Povinelli sought to expose was the poetic license that many researchers were taking in interpreting animal behavior in the wild. And contrary to what investigators such as Fouts would have us believe, he pointed out, chimpanzees are not merely hairy, watered-down little humans. Povinelli reasoned that of course a chimp's behavior is similar to our own, because we do in fact share a relatively recent common ancestor with them, as well as 98.4 percent of our DNA. But because we can't help but see and interpret their behaviors through the lens of our own theory of mind (a cognitive trait that Povinelli believes evolved *after* this common ancestor split into two separate ancestral lines, one leading to our own species and the other to modern chimps), we may be seeing more than is actually there. Perhaps we're simply reading into their behaviors by projecting our own psychology onto theirs.

Now, determining whether a chimp has thoughts about others' thoughts is a rather tricky research question. But Povinelli had some ingenious ways of going about it. For example, in a famous series of experiments published as a monograph titled *What Young Chimpanzees Know about Seeing* (1996), Povinelli trained his group of seven apes to come into the lab one at a time, reach their arms through a hole in a Plexiglas partition, and beg for a food reward from one of two human experimenters. There were two holes, one in front of each of the two experimenters, respectively. If the chimps reached out to person A, then person A would hand them the treat. If the chimps reached out to person B, person B would give it to them instead. But the chimps got only one choice between these two experimenters before the next trial began and the chimp next in line made its own selection.

After the animals got the gist of this simple game, the real experiment began. The rules remained the same—again, reach through one of the holes to get that person to fetch your treat—but now when the chimp entered the lab, it saw one of the experimenters wearing a blindfold, or with her back turned, her eyes closed, or even wearing a bucket over her head. The other experimenter, meanwhile, had her eyes wide open and was watching the chimp attentively.

If you're thinking like an experimental psychologist, then the purpose of the study should at this point be jumping out at you. Povinelli hypothesized that if chimpanzees have a theory of mind, well then they should quite clearly pick the person who can see them over the one who can't. After all, picking the unsighted experimenter would leave the chimp without its prize because—being unable to see the chimp's gesture toward her—this person can't possibly *know* she has been chosen. The point is that to avoid making the wrong choice, the animal must take the perspective of the person, or at least attribute the mental state of "not seeing" to her.

Povinelli and his coauthor, Timothy Eddy, surprised almost everyone when they found that the chimps failed to show a preference between the two experimenters.[27] By contrast, in a similar game, even two-year-old children showed a clear preference for the sighted person. Other cleverly designed studies followed, by both Povinelli and others, all presumably showing that, contrary to what we had been led to believe by the "visual rhetoric" of those Goodall-esque documentaries, chimps aren't entirely like us after all; in particular, they lack a theory of mind and fail to reason about what others see, know, feel, believe, or intend.

These studies, along with Povinelli's persuasive arguments for human uniqueness, convinced many at the time, but they certainly didn't convince all. In fact, soon the tables turned again, and just like those he had criticized before, Povinelli now found himself to be the subject of scathing criticism. He was excoriated by the "Darwinian continuity theorists" for his contrived laboratory approaches to such a complex question—ones in which chimps were asked to reason about the mental states of humans rather than those of their own kind. And that's not even to mention, others pointed out, the fact that Povinelli's Louisiana apes were raised in concrete-and-steel cages and therefore could hardly be regarded as the best and brightest of their species—or even representative of their species, for that matter, because their cognitive potential had probably been stultified under such poor, restricted conditions. Making a comparison to the "biological ignorance" likely to be found in an average human group of stuffy, Western suburbanites whose knowledge of the natural world hadn't blossomed under the jungle canopy (their natural capacity to acquire such a biological understanding instead being starved by interminable deserts of strip malls, gabled houses, and Starbucks), German primatologist Christophe Boesch surmises in the *Journal of Comparative Psychology,*

> [Chimpanzees] need a phase during their up-bringing dur-
> ing which they face conditions that challenge them for any
> experience-based ability to develop . . . If the situations are never
> or infrequently encountered, [such] abilities will remain absent
> or develop only impartially . . . Thus, what has been presented
> as "comparisons between humans and chimpanzees" has really

represented "comparisons between Western Middle Class *humans and* captive *chimpanzees."*[28]

In fact, another team of researchers, this one led by psychologists Michael Tomasello and Josep Call at the Max Planck Institute for Evolutionary Anthropology in Leipzig, Germany, reported that their chimps demonstrated some degree of theory of mind, especially when competing for food against other chimps. In a widely publicized 2000 study conducted in Leipzig and spearheaded by one of their colleagues, Duke University psychologist Brian Hare, a group of chimps was divided into pairs of two, in which (on the basis of previous competitive games) one animal was known to be clearly dominant in the group and the other one clearly subordinate. The two animals faced each other in opposite cages separated by a middle, empty cage, while an experimenter baited this center area with a desirable food reward. For example, the experimenter might put the food reward behind a large tire swing on the side of the subordinate so that the dominant animal couldn't see it. In some cases, this baiting was done while the dominant wasn't present in its cage; in others, both animals saw where the experimenter placed the coveted food.

After the baiting, the middle area was opened and the two chimps were observed. One of the main hypotheses in this study was that, if the subordinate understood that the dominant didn't *see* where the food reward was hidden, then it didn't *know* where the food was, and therefore the subordinate shouldn't give the hiding location away by directing the dominant's attention to this spot. (If it did, the dominant would surely rush in and strong-arm this delicious cache away from the subordinate.) And, sure enough, Hare and his coauthors found precisely this effect. Under such conditions, the subordinate acted as though it knew nothing of the food's whereabouts, instead waiting until the dominant left the scene before gathering up its loot.[29]

On the basis of such findings, Call and Tomasello recently wagged a finger of disapproval at Povinelli and other "killjoy skeptics" of nonhuman theory of mind: "It is time for humans to quit thinking that their nearest primate relatives only read and react to overt behavior."[30] Yet Povinelli attempted to replicate Hare's findings and failed to do so. He therefore remains unrepentant and unconvinced, arguing instead that all social behaviors in chimpanzees can still be understood without invoking a theory-of-mind interpretation and claiming that it's the smoke and mirrors from our own theory of mind that's occluding our view of other animals' psychology.

It seems a debate unlikely to be settled anytime soon. In one of his latest comments regarding the subject, a 2007 position piece published in the *Philosophical Transactions of the Royal Society*, Povinelli and coauthor Derek Penn provocatively titled their article: "On the Lack of Evidence that Non-human Animals Possess Anything Remotely Resembling a 'Theory of Mind.'" (Some comparative psychologists believe that the best evidence lies not in chimps, but rather dogs, dolphins, or even scrub jays.)

Despite the stalemate, even the most unwavering continuity theorist demurs that with the possible, qualified exception of a few other species of great apes, there's indeed no clear evidence that any primate species but our own possesses "anything remotely resembling a theory of mind."[31] And although the jury is still out on whether we're *entirely* unique in being able to conceptualize unobservable mental states—chimps may well have some *degree* of theory of mind that eludes all but the most sensitive experiments—there's absolutely no question that we're uniquely good at it in the whole of the animal kingdom. We are exquisitely attuned to the unseen psychological world. Theory of mind is as much a peculiar trademark of our species as is walking upright on two legs, learning a language, and raising our offspring into their teens.

In fact, once we assume the intentional stance, we can't shut it off. If I were to extend my arm at a ninety-degree angle, pointing at the sky by uncoiling just my index finger, with the rest of my digits drawn into my palm and my eyes fixed upon some apex at the end of an invisible trajectory, you would almost certainly perceive this action as a communicative act. Perhaps I'm attempting to direct your *attention* to, say, the large seagull that's threatening to release its bowels on your recently shampooed head, or the hot-air balloon that's spiraling out of control into the open sea. Even if I were to admonish you not to perceive this set of my concrete behaviors in such a manner, but instead to look upon these actions as only my arm and hand and eyes moving about in some stereotyped way, your brain would resist following the rules—you would want to turn around and look, to see what I'm seeing. As any good magician knows, pointing is an extraordinarily effective means of inconspicuously diverting the audience's attention.

As a human being, you're even prone to overextending your theory of mind to categories for which it doesn't properly belong. Many people remember fondly the classic film *Le Ballon Rouge* (*The Red Balloon*, 1956) by French filmmaker Albert Lamorisse, in which a sensitive schoolboy—in reality Lamorisse's own five-year-old son, Pascal—is befriended by a good-natured, cherry-red helium balloon. Absent dialogue, the camera follows the joyful two, boy and balloon, through the somber, working-class streets of the Ménilmontant neighborhood of Paris, the glossy red balloon contrasting sharply with the bleak old-Europe atmosphere while adults, oblivious to the presence of an inanimate object that has apparently been ensouled by an intelligent gas, are largely indifferent, even hostile, to the pair. Eventually, a mob of cruel children corners the boy and begins pelting the "kindhearted" balloon with stones, ultimately popping it. There's something of a happy ending, though, with the smiling boy being hoisted off to an unknown destiny by the other resident helium souls of Ménilmontant, sympathetic balloons that, we can only assume, have been inspired by the "death" of their persecuted red brother to untangle themselves from their heartless captors and rescue Pascal.

The plot of *Le Ballon Rouge* exemplifies how our evolved brains have become hypersocial filters, such that our theory of mind is applied not only to the mental innards of other people and animals, but also, in error, to categories that haven't any mental innards at all, such as ebullient skins of elastic stretched by an inert gas. If it weren't for our theory of mind, we couldn't follow the premise of the movie, let alone enjoy Lamorisse's particular oeuvre of magical realism. When the balloon hovers outside Pascal's flat after his grandmother tries to rid herself of this nuisance, we perceive a charismatic personality in the balloon that "wants" to be with the boy and is "trying" to leverage itself against the windowpanes; it "sees" Pascal and "knows" he's inside. Our theory of mind is so effortlessly applied under such conditions that it's impossible to see the scene any other way. In fact, part of the reason the movie may have been so effective was that the lead role, the young boy, genuinely believed that the balloon was alive. "The Red Balloon was my friend," recalled a much-older Pascal Lamorisse in a 2007 interview. "When you were filming it, did you really feel that way?" asked the reporter. "Yes, yes, he was a real character with a spirit of his own."[32]

As a direct consequence of the evolution of the human social brain, and owing to the weight of selective importance placed on our theory-of-mind skills, we sometimes can't help but see intentions, desires, and beliefs in things that haven't even a smidgeon of a neural system there to generate the psychological states we perceive—just as we do for the Red Balloon. In particular, when inanimate objects do unexpected things, we sometimes reason about them just as we do for oddly behaving—or misbehaving—people. More than a few of us have kicked our broken-down, "untrustworthy" vehicles in the sides and have verbally abused our "incompetent" computers. Most of us stop short of actually believing these objects possess mental states—indeed, we would likely be hauled away to an asylum if we genuinely believed that they held malicious intentions toward us—but our emotions and behaviors toward such objects seem to betray our primitive, unconscious thinking: we act as though they're morally culpable for their actions.

Some developmental psychologists even believe that this cognitive bias to see intentions in inanimate objects—and thus a very basic theory of mind—can be found in babies just a few months out of the womb. For example, Hungarian psychologists György Gergely and Gergely Csibra from the Central European University in Budapest have shown in their work that babies, on the basis of their staring response, act surprised when a dot on a computer screen continues to butt up against an empty space on the screen after a computerized barrier blocking its path has been deleted. It's as if the baby is staring at the dot trying to figure out why the dot is acting as though it "thinks" the barrier is still there. By contrast, the infants are not especially interested—that is, they don't stare in surprise—when the dot stops in front of the block, or when the dot continues along its path in the absence of the barrier.[33]

The most famous example of this cognitive phenomenon of seeing minds in nonliving objects, however, is a 1944 *American Journal of Psychology* study by Austrian researchers Fritz Heider and Mary-Ann Simmel. In this very early study, the scientists put together a simplistic animated film depicting three moving, black-and-white figures: a large triangle, a small triangle, and a small circle. Participants watched the figures moving about on the screen for a while and then were asked to describe what they had just seen. Most reported using a human social behavioral narrative—for example, seeing the large triangle as "bullying" the "timid" smaller triangle, both of "whom" were "seeking" the "affections" of the "female" circle.[34]

———◆———

So it would appear that having a theory of mind was so useful for our ancestors in explaining and predicting other people's behaviors that it has completely flooded our evolved social brains. As a result, today we overshoot our mental-state attributions to things that are, in reality, completely mindless. And all of this leads us, rather inevitably, to a very important question—one that's about to launch us into an official inquiry spanning the remainder of this book. What if I were to tell you that God's mental states, too, were all in your mind? That God, like a tiny speck floating at the edge of your cornea producing the image of a hazy, out-of-reach orb accompanying your every turn, was in fact a psychological illusion, a sort of evolved blemish etched onto the core cognitive substrate of your brain? It may feel as if there is something grander out there . . . watching, knowing, caring. Perhaps even judging. But, in fact, that's just your overactive theory of mind. In reality, there is only the air you breathe.

After all, once we scrub away all the theological bric-a-brac and pluck out the exotic cross-cultural plumage of strange religious beliefs all over the world, once we get under God's skin, isn't He really just another mind—one with emotions, beliefs, knowledge, understanding, and, perhaps above all else, intentions? Aren't theologians really just playing the role of God's translators, and every holy book ever written is merely a detailed psychoanalysis of God? That strangely sticky sense that God "willfully" created us as individuals, "wants" us to behave in particular ways, "observes" and "knows" about our otherwise private actions, "communicates" messages to us in code through natural events, and "intends" to meet us after we die would have also been felt, in some form, by our Pleistocene ancestors.

Consider, briefly, the implications of seeing God this way, as a sort of scratch on our psychological lenses rather than the enigmatic figure out there in the heavenly world that most people believe Him to be. Subjectively, God would still be present in our lives. (For some people, rather annoyingly so.) In this way of perceiving, He would continue to suffuse our experiences with an elusive meaning and give the sense that the universe is communicating with us in various ways. But this notion of God as an illusion is a radical and, some would say, even dangerous idea because it raises important questions about whether God is an autonomous, independent agent that lives outside human brain cells, or instead a phantom cast out upon the world by our species' own peculiarly evolved theory of mind.

Since the human brain, like any physical organ, is a product of evolution, and since natural selection works without recourse to intelligent forethought, this mental apparatus of ours evolved to think about God quite without need of the latter's consultation, let alone His being real. Then again, one can never rule out the possibility that God microengineered the evolution of the human brain so that we've come to see Him more clearly, a sort of divine LASIK procedure, or scraping off the bestial glare that clouds the minds of other animals.

Either way, we're about to discover just how deeply this one particular cognitive capacity, this theory of mind, has baked itself into our heads when it comes to our pondering of life's big questions. Unlike any science-literate generation that has come before, we now possess the intellectual tools to observe our own minds at work and to understand how God has come to be there. And we alone are poised to ask, "Has our species' unique cognitive evolution duped us into believing in this, the grandest mind of all?"

2 | A LIFE WITHOUT PURPOSE

Much to the chagrin of those faithful evolutionists who like to think they've cast off the lodestone of God altogether, the father of evolutionary theory himself, Charles Darwin, was a far cry from the full-blooded scientific atheist he is often portrayed to be. In trying to conceptualize the natural world without God, Darwin repeatedly stumbled over a major psychological hurdle. His writings hint at a mysterious Creator that had purposefully geared up the apparatus of natural selection. In his 1876 autobiography, Darwin does more than just allude to these godly leanings. He admits that while writing *On the Origin of Species* (1859), he experienced

> *the extreme difficulty or rather impossibility of conceiving this immense and wonderful universe, including man with his capacity of looking far backwards and far into futurity, as the result of blind chance or necessity. When thus reflecting I feel compelled to look to a First Cause having an intelligent mind in some degree analogous to that of man; and I deserve to be called a Theist.*[1]

Actually, given this description, and knowing what we do of his other ideas, Darwin might properly be called a "deist," someone who believes that an intelligent God created the world but exerts no causal influence over natural phenomena. But Darwin didn't know about theory of mind. It would be another century still before the researchers we met in the previous chapter would first identify theory of mind as an evolved cognitive capacity, a psychological specialization of the human brain. So, what if Darwin's inability to conceptualize such mindless origins was due not to some inexorable truth of an intelligent First Cause, but instead to the distorting forces of the evolved cognitive apparatus by which he perceived the universe—his own theory of mind? That is to say, perhaps it was only through the lens of his theory of mind that all the heavens and earth, including human existence, appeared purposeful and meaningful, as the product of intelligent design.

———•———

Curiously enough, a very non-evolutionary-minded thinker came a lot closer than Darwin ever did to unraveling our species' insuperable tendency to reflect on God's creative intentions. Just behind the old stone wall encircling Montparnasse Cemetery in the north end of Paris, not far from the main entrance, lie the bodies of Jean-Paul Sartre and his longtime companion, Simone de Beauvoir. Here, under a conspicuously frugal headstone, this famous duo cannot see the many mourners who trudge daily through rain and snow or shield their eyes from the heavy French sun to leave offerings of flowers, business cards, and, of course, cigarettes, to which Sartre suffered an unabashed addiction.

Throughout much of the twentieth century, this affable genius— a prolific philosopher, writer, and playwright—made his living as the world's most notorious (and arguably its most beloved) atheist. Sartre was a true public intellectual. When he died in 1980 at the age of seventy-four, thousands thronged the already congested streets of Paris's fourteenth arrondissement to march in solidarity with his casket during the two-hour funeral cortege from the hospital where he had expired. Simone de Beauvoir, whom Sartre affectionately called "The Beaver," was a leading thinker in her own right, still regarded by many as the grand dame of modern feminism.

In his autobiography *The Words* (1964), Sartre writes about his alleged falling out with God while still a very young child:

> *Only once did I have the feeling that [God] existed. I had been playing with matches and burnt a small rug. I was in the process of covering up my crime when suddenly God saw me. I felt His gaze inside my head and on my hands. I whirled about in the bathroom, horribly visible, a live target. Indignation saved me. I flew into a rage against so crude an indiscretion. I blasphemed. I muttered like my grandfather: "Sacré nom de Dieu de nom de Dieu de nom de Dieu." ["God damn it, God damn it, God damn it."] He never looked at me again.* [2]

If we are to believe Sartre's autobiographical reflections, then he held a precocious and unflinching atheistic worldview. Indeed, he first rejected God around the same time his classmates were just learning their basic arithmetic. [3] And what Sartre came to dislike most about God was what he saw as the crippling notion that God created man for His own selfish ends. Sartre later railed against the infectious complacence of the middle class in its accepting as fact the erroneous premise that God creates the individual person with a specific purpose in mind, thus delimiting one to a particular function—or, in Sartre's view, a burden—in life.

It was during a 1945 lecture at the Club Maintenant in Paris that

Sartre first offered the following useful metaphor of this lay concept of God the Creator—one he repeated often:

> *When we think of God as the Creator, He is generally thought of as a superior sort of artisan. Whatever doctrine we may be considering . . . we always grant that will more or less follows understanding or, at the very least, accompanies it, and that when God creates he knows precisely what he is creating. Thus, the concept of man in the mind of God is comparable to the concept of paper-cutter in the mind of the manufacturer, and, following certain techniques and a conception, God produces man, just as the artisan, following a definition and a technique, makes a paper-cutter. Thus the individual man is the realization of a certain concept in the divine intelligence.*[4]

This is nonsense, said Sartre. In reality, we simply come to exist as individuals, just as beads of condensation form on a glass of water or spores of mold appear on old bread. And if there is no God, as Sartre believed, then metaphysical meaning—applied to the individual's raison d'être, as well as to life itself—is only a mirage. But Sartre cautions us not to fall into the Christian trap of seeing this startling truth of God's nonexistence as being reason to experience a crumbling sense of despair. Rather, says Sartre, we should rejoice in this divine absence, because now we are free to define ourselves as we please. That is to say, because God hasn't fettered any of us with a particular function in mind, selfishly obligating us to preordained tasks in this fleeting existence of ours, we've no legitimate grounds to stew over our incorrigible and immovable fates. Instead, our purpose is entirely our own affair: *we* decide who we are, not God. Indeed, this latter point was enough to persuade Sartre that his humanistic principles would apply even if God did exist.

Sartre believed that if people truly appreciated this logic, and were true to their "authentic selves" rather than to what others thought they ought to be, then they would ultimately choose good over evil. This rather optimistic view of atheism was the theme of Sartre's famous essay "Existentialism Is a Humanism" (1946), but even in his earlier, very dense, philosophical treatise *Being and Nothingness* (1943), we can begin to hear the unarticulated rumblings of Sartre's simple and powerful mantra: *l'existence précède l'essence* ("existence precedes essence"). This rather tidy proposition neatly turned the church on its head, capturing Sartre's explosive logic that individual human nature is a product of the human mind, not of God's. God doesn't endow each man with an "essence"—or prewritten, underlying purpose—said Sartre. Purpose is a human construct.

As an admirer, it pains me to say this, but Sartre's version of affairs wasn't entirely accurate either. He downplayed the role of biology in the evolution and development of human behavior and decision making. One person may indeed be freer than another to be "good" instead of "evil," given their inherited individual differences (such as in temperament and general intelligence) in combination with their prior experiences. In reality, we're only as free as our genes are pliable in the slosh of our developmental milieus.[5]

Still, as a secular humanist, in his day, Sartre almost succeeded in single-handedly shooing the faithful out of their pews in the French cathedrals. Unfortunately for him, this notion of God the Creator is nearly as rampant in the world today as it was when the first prophet sat down to put words in God's mouth. For example, although scientists and skeptics might scoff and rankle at the unprecedented commercial success of pastor Rick Warren's "spiritual manual," *The Purpose Driven Life: What on Earth Am I Here For?* (2002), the author's central message—that God created you, and you alone, to serve a special function for His intended desires—resonates deeply with hordes of readers from all walks of life. Warren tells his (mostly Christian) audience,

> *You must begin with God, your Creator. You exist only because God wills that you exist. You were made by God and for God—and until you understand that, life will never make sense. It is only in God that we discover our origin, our identity, our meaning, our purpose, our significance, and our destiny. Every other path leads to a dead end.*[6]

In fact, it is only Warren's evolved theory of mind that enables him to preach to us about the contents of God's mind. And in reality, you exist largely because a particular spermatozoon—one of approximately forty million others contained in just one of your father's ejaculations—shouldered its way past its sibling sperm and, in the wake of a photo finish win with thousands of other competing cells, burrowed headfirst into your mother's fertile ovum. Consider that even the slightest, virtually imperceptible tic on this particular occasion of your parents' act of coitus—say, an immeasurable lag in the duration of that final pelvic thrust, or a distracting thought interfering with your father's arousal—would have reduced the probability of your having been conceived to next to nil by perturbing the seminal alchemy. You may well owe your exquisitely singular existence to the fact that one of your father's testicles happened to descend some midsummer's evening by a hairsbreadth, or that your mother had a sudden cramp in her calf and changed her position in the few milliseconds leading up to your conception.

But why do we attribute more to our particular being than such sundry reproductive facts? Warren's theistic answer is almost certainly a fairy tale but, again, it strikes a strangely common chord with most people. And it's a chord that we can hear only with our evolved theory of mind: What did God have in mind when creating us?

Whereas Sartre refuted such traditional "arguments" on the basis of his existential philosophy, the zeitgeist of today's atheists is science. And, usually, this means that they turn to the mechanistic principles of evolution when countering the religious majority, principles that can silence the strong tendency to invoke God—or rather God's mind—in explaining origins.

———

In his best seller *The God Delusion* (2006), evolutionary biologist and writer Richard Dawkins attacks everyday creationist ideas, such as those of Rick Warren, with great verve and clarity. Dawkins and other scientific atheists aren't claiming that science presents us with an alternative way of deciphering the mysterious purpose of life; rather, they argue that, in fully comprehending Darwin's basic idea of natural selection, we can begin to understand why there's really no riddle at all. In an interview with *Salon* magazine conducted shortly after the release of his book, Dawkins was asked, "What is our purpose in life?" He responded,

> *If you happen to be religious, you think that's a meaningful question. But the mere fact that you can phrase it as an English sentence doesn't mean it deserves an answer. Those of us who don't believe in a god will say that is as illegitimate as the question, why are unicorns hollow? It just shouldn't be put. It's not a proper question to put. It doesn't deserve an answer.*[7]

Dawkins clearly believes that there isn't an answer to the purpose-of-life question, because the question implies, unnecessarily, an intelligent Creator that had a *purpose in mind*. Natural selection, as

Dawkins tells us, is indeed "blind." But we can also begin to see here how theory of mind becomes directly relevant to our species' ability to reason about its own origins. Without it, this type of purpose-of-life question couldn't even be entertained, not to mention obsessed over.

We would be justified in disagreeing with Dawkins on one crucial point, however, which is that this ubiquitous and timeless nonquestion does deserve an answer, or at least a closer look. The theory of natural selection should have vanquished God (or at least a God concerned with human affairs), just as Dawkins so elegantly shows us in his works time and again—except it hasn't, even among those who claim to understand it deeply.[8]

In philosophical terms, asking about the purpose of life may indeed be analogous to asking why unicorns are hollow. But in psychological terms, that's an anemic comparison. People aren't normally very preoccupied with uncovering the secret attributes of unicorns; we accept that unicorns don't exist and, as a consequence, whether they're hollow or solid doesn't exactly weigh on our thoughts. The same doesn't necessarily hold true for God, however. Many people don't believe in God, yet they still ask themselves about the purpose of life and can't easily shake their curiosity about this seemingly grand and obscure mystery. Even though we know our biological facts and have managed to emotionally disencumber ourselves from the strappings of the Cross, or flung off our yarmulkes, turned our hijabs into throws, and all the rest, the question of why we're here still occasionally rises up in our thoughts like a case of hives—and it's an itchy rash that science just can't seem to scratch. So the real mystery lies not in why we are here on this earth, each as distinct individuals; instead, the real mystery is why this purpose-of-life question is so seductive and recalcitrant in the face of logical science.

In fact, there's reason to believe that, even for the committed atheist, the voice of God is still annoyingly there, though perhaps reduced to no more than a whisper. I suspect Dawkins would be reluctant to tell us if ever he felt strangely "called" to be the proselytizing atheist he has become—that this is ironically what he feels meant for, much as I sometimes feel that my purpose in life is to explain to others why such feelings of purpose are cognitive illusions. But we do know that Sartre, at least, had precisely these types of fleeting theistic inclinations.

We are privy to these secret ruminations only because Sartre's partner, Simone de Beauvoir, had the good sense to keep a meticulous diary of her conversations with Sartre in the few years leading up to his death, a collection of personal, sometimes startlingly frank exchanges that she published as an anthology shortly before her own death. And what Beauvoir discovered between coffee and cigarettes at the famed café Les Deux Magots and in Sartre's cluttered apartment was an especially lucid mind, a man who was unusually aware of his own contradictions in thought and willing to acknowledge the niggling sense that, at least in the theater of his own consciousness, there was a lingering, strange tension between his explicit beliefs and a very subtle, very particular type of creationist cognition.

Below is Sartre's inward glimpse of how, despite his atheistic convictions, there was all along a certain conceptual impotence in his "existence precedes essence" formula when applied to his own subjective consciousness. "I don't see myself as so much dust that has appeared in the world," he confessed to Beauvoir,

> but as a being that was expected, prefigured, called forth. In short, as a being that could, it seems, come only from a creator ... It contradicts many of my other ideas. But it is there, floating vaguely. And when I think of myself I often think rather in this way, for want of being able to think otherwise.[9]

This is a rather amazing admission from someone who claimed to have rid himself of God back as a naughty schoolboy secretly playing with matches in the bathroom. But there's no hypocrisy here. Unlike most people, Sartre didn't allow this glandular feeling to persuade him that God actually existed. Rather, he considered it to be a trick of the mind. And what we can say now about this trick was that it was rendered by Sartre's own very human theory of mind. Like so many others, Sartre couldn't help but attribute some inherent purpose to his life—to see a grand mind at work behind the scenes.

Sartre wasn't alone in experiencing this puzzling juxtaposition of his atheistic beliefs and his private illusions. Other astute thinkers and writers have noticed a similar disconnect; and often we find it in the voice of their fictional characters. In Albert Camus' *The Fall* (1956), for example, the protagonist is Jean-Baptiste Clamence, an eccentric, ex-Parisian lawyer who embarks on a brooding journey to dissect the artifice of meaning. For Clamence, meaning is an illusion that embeds individuals in preposterous self-narratives leading to "absurd" human conventions. Ultimately, he concludes that human existence itself is an affliction of epic proportions, so cosmically irrelevant is our hidden suffering.

But Clamence wasn't always like this. It was only after a series of calamitous events in his personal life (namely, a lingering guilt about deciding not to try to rescue a woman who leapt to her death from a bridge as he happened to stroll past her) that he became such a cynical misanthrope. Before this, the atheistic Clamence saw himself, oddly, as a metaphysically privileged entity—a secular angel who, upon reflecting on his own seemingly blessed station in life, felt the shadowy hand of a benevolent Creator who had designed him:

> *As a result of being showered with blessings, I felt, I hesitate to admit, marked out. Personally marked out, among all, for that*

*long uninterrupted success . . . I refused to attribute that success
to my own merits and could not believe that the conjunction in a
single person of such different and such extreme virtues was the
result of chance alone. This is why in my happy life I felt somehow that that happiness was authorized by some higher decree.
When I add that I had no religion, you can see even better how
extraordinary that conviction was.*[10]

Clamence realizes that he once was ensnared by the very illusion
he had since come to discover and expose as a seductive artifice of
human thought. Such self-surprising insights about the atheist's rather
embarrassing vulnerability to feel as though he were the product of
intelligent design would seem to suggest that logical thought in this
domain runs against the grain of our natural psychology.

An objection to this "nativist" view of an intentional, creative God,
however, is that even atheists have been polluted by cultural residue,
including the idea that God creates man and infuses him with a special
essence or spirit—what many Christians call "ensoulment." The concept of God as creator of souls certainly wasn't confined to Sartre's
twentieth-century French bourgeoisie. In his book *The Soul of the
Embryo* (2005), University of Surrey bioethicist David Albert Jones
reveals how this line of thought stretches back to the very earliest
days of Christian theology, with liberal evidence of such creationist
reasoning even in the Hebrew scriptures. "The molding of the body
in the womb, the gift of life and the call from God are coterminous,"
summarizes Jones of these precanonical writings.[11] And although
you may not like Sartre's particular image of God as a brusque tinker hammering out soul after soul like a sweaty smithy knocking off
cheap metal goods, in the book of Job we can see how this analogy
isn't much of a leap from traditional Christian thought. "Remember
that you fashioned me like clay," says Job to the Lord. "Did you not

pour me out like milk and curdle me like cheese? You clothed me with skin and flesh, and knit me together with bones and sinews."[12]

When growing up hearing tales such as these, is it any wonder that so many people believe that there is some intelligent, "higher" purpose to human life? Many contemporary atheists, for example, believe that such religious ideas amount to a sort of cultural virus, the human brain being parasitized by virulent concepts that children catch like a bug from infected adults, and that are especially potent in a climate of fear and ignorance. And atheists and believers alike see children generally as acquiring religion from outside sources. But are children's minds really the religious tabula rasa we make them out to be? Or rather, are human beings, in some sense, born believers?

———◆———

Scientists would be hard-pressed to find and interview feral children who've been reared in a cultural vacuum to probe for aspects of quasi-religious thinking. In reality, the closest we may ever get to conducting this type of thought experiment is to study the few accounts of deaf-mutes who, allegedly at least, spontaneously invented their own cosmologies during their prelinguistic childhoods. In his book *The Child's Religion* (1928), the Swiss educator Pierre Bovet recounted that even Helen Keller, who went deaf and blind at nineteen months of age from an undiagnosed illness, was said to have instinctively asked herself, "Who made the sky, the sea, everything?"

Such rare accounts of deaf-mute children pontificating about Creation through some sort of internal monologue of nonverbal thought—thought far removed from any known cultural iterations or socially communicated tales of Genesis—are useful to us because they represent the unadulterated mind at work on the problem of origins. If we take these accounts at face value, the basic existential problem of reasoning about our purpose and origins would appear not to be the mental poison of religion, society, or education, but rather an insuppressible eruption of our innate human minds. We're preoccupied with why things are. Unlike most people, these deaf-mute children—most of whom grew up before the invention of a standardized symbolic communication system of gestures, such as American Sign Language (ASL)—had no access to the typical explanatory balms of science and religion in calming these bothersome riddles. Without language, one can't easily share the idea of a purposeful, monotheistic God with a naive child. And the theory of natural selection is difficult enough to convey to a normal speaking and hearing child, let alone one who can do neither. These special children were therefore left to their own devices in making sense of how the world came to be and, more intriguingly, in weaving their own existence into the narrative fabric of this grand cosmology.

In an 1892 issue of *The Philosophical Review*, William James, brother to the novelist Henry James and himself arguably the world's most famous psychologist of his era (some years later, he would write the classic *Varieties of Religious Experience*), penned an introduction to the autobiographical account of one such deaf-mute, Theophilus Hope d'Estrella. "I have Mr. d'Estrella's permission," James tells us, "to lay before the readers of *The Philosophical Review* a new document which is most interesting by its intrinsic content."[13] For uncertain reasons (perhaps literary), D'Estrella writes of his early childhood in the third person, but it's indeed a remarkably eloquent and beautifully composed piece of work. Born in 1851 in San Francisco to a French-Swiss father he never met and a Mexican mother who died when he was five years old, D'Estrella grew up as an orphan raised by his mother's short-tempered best friend—another Mexican woman who, judging by her fondness for whipping him over the slightest misdeeds, apparently felt burdened by his frustratingly incommunicative presence.

With no one to talk to otherwise, and only wordless observations and inborn powers of discernment to guide his naive theories of the world, D'Estrella retreated into his own imagination to make sense of what must have been a very confusing existential situation. For example, he developed an animistic theory of the moon that hints at the egocentric nature of children's minds, particularly with respect to morality:

> He wondered why the moon appeared so regularly. So he thought that she must have come out to see him alone. Then he talked to her in gestures, and fancied that he saw her smile or frown. [He] found out that he had been whipped oftener when the moon was visible. It was as though she were watching him and telling his guardian (he being an orphan boy) all about his bad capers.[14]

D'Estrella writes also about his notions of the origins of natural objects and events in the world—namely, the sun, the stars, the wind, and the ocean. In these observations we see something like a natural creationist bent, one that reflexively imbues objects in the world with pragmatic functions and clear purposes:

> One night he happened to see some boys throwing and catching burning oil-soaked balls of yarn. He turned his mind to the sun, and thought that it must have been thrown up and caught just the same—but by what force? So he supposed that there was a great and strong man, somehow hiding himself behind the hills (San Francisco being a hilly city). The sun was his ball of fire as a toy, and he amused himself in throwing it very high in the sky every morning and catching it every evening.
> He supposed that the god lit the stars for his own use as we do

gas-lights in the street. When there was wind, he supposed that it was the indication of his passions. A cold gale bespoke his anger, and a cool breeze his happy temper. Why? Because he had some-times felt the breath bursting out from the mouth of angry people in the act of quarreling or scolding.

Let me add as to the origin of the ocean. One day he went with some boys to the ocean. They went bathing. He first went into the ocean, not knowing how it tasted and how strong the waves rolled. So he was knocked around, with his eyes and mouth open. He came near to being drowned. He could not swim. He went to the bottom and instinctively crawled up on sand. He spit the water out of his mouth, and wondered why the water was so salty. He thought that it was the urine of that mighty god.[15]

It's worth cautioning that D'Estrella would have been about forty years old when he wrote about these early childhood experiences—experiences that were retrospectively given voice by a mind that had since learned language. In fact, by the time he authored these personal accounts, D'Estrella had become an accomplished artist and was employed as the drawing instructor at the unfortunately named California Institution for the Deaf and Dumb.[16] But regardless of the inevitable failings of memory, D'Estrella's recollections were still convincing enough for William James to argue that the human mind, even without language, is predisposed to engage in abstract, metaphysical reflection. "It will be observed," James summed up authoritatively at the end of the essay in *The Philosophical Review,* "that [D'Estrella's] cosmological and ethical reflections were the outbirth of his solitary thought."[17]

A few decades later, another psychologist—this time the influential cognitive developmentalist from Geneva, Jean Piaget—elaborated on this innate cosmological penchant by postulating that all school-age children tend to think in "artificialist" terms. To Piaget, young children weren't simply less knowledgeable than older children and adults, but they were qualitatively different types of thinkers operating under cognitive constraints—constraints that were systematically shed with age and over discrete stages of development. In Piaget's stage theory of cognitive development, "artificialism" referred to young children's seeing aspects and features of the natural world as existing solely to solve human problems, or at least meant for human use. Like Sartre, however, Piaget was skeptical of atheists' claims of entirely escaping this psychological bias of seeing the workings of the natural world in intentional, human-focused terms. Rather, he suspected that artificialist beliefs never really went away; instead, they would continue cropping up in the nonbeliever's mental representations in very subtle ways. "A semi-educated man," wrote Piaget, "may very well dismiss as 'contrary to science' a theological explanation of the universe, and yet find no difficulty in accepting the notion that the sun is there to give us light."[18]

———◆———

Piaget's central argument has continued to hold up under controlled experimental conditions. This is the finding that children, and to some extent even science-literate adults, are compelled to reason in terms of an inherent purpose when deliberating about origins—that objects, artifacts, events and even whole animals exist "for" a certain reason. That is to say, our minds are heavily biased toward reasoning as though a designer held a conception in mind. In fact, contrary to what many atheists tend to believe, recent findings from the cognitive sciences suggest that, just like a crude language sprouting up, at least some form of religious belief and behavior would also probably appear spontaneously on a desert island untouched by cultural transmission, particularly beliefs involving purpose and origins.

Underpinning purpose-based thinking is what's called "teleo-functional reasoning," which sounds more complicated than it really is. Actually, you do it all the time—at least, every time you walk into your local Brookstone store or stand before a museum display case scratching your head over some baroque contraption for, say, cleaning cow hooves or extracting molars. In fact, "teleo-functional reasoning" is just a fancy philosophical expression that refers to people's thinking that something *exists for a preconceived purpose* rather than simply came to be as a functionless outgrowth of physical or otherwise natural processes.

It's entirely logical to say that a showerhead sprays clean, plumbed-in water over dirty bodies because it's designed for such a purpose. But it would sound absolutely bizarre to say that a natural waterfall is "for" anything in particular, even though, if one were standing beneath a waterfall, it might well do the very same thing the showerhead does. As an artifact, the showerhead is the product of human intentional design, and thus it has an essential purpose that can be traced back to the mind of its creator (in this case, some long-forgotten and vastly underappreciated Athenian inventor working on the athletic stadiums in ancient Greece). Without a theory of mind, we couldn't easily reflect on the purpose of this object, because "purpose," in this sense, implies a purposeful *mental agent* as creator. By contrast, the waterfall is just there as the result of a naturally occurring configuration of the geographic landscape.

Yet, as Boston University psychologist Deborah Kelemen has found in study after study, young children erroneously endow such natural, inanimate entities—waterfalls, clouds, rocks, and so on—with their own teleo-functional purposes. Because of this tendency to over-attribute reason and purpose to aspects of the natural world, Kelemen refers to young children as "promiscuous teleologists." For example, Kelemen and her colleagues find that seven- and eight-year-olds who are asked why mountains exist overwhelmingly prefer, *regardless of their parents' religiosity or irreligiosity,* teleo-functional explanations ("to give animals a place to climb") over mechanistic, or physical, causal explanations ("because volcanoes cooled into lumps").[19] It's only around fourth or fifth grade that children begin abandoning these incorrect teleo-functional answers in favor of scientifically accurate accounts. And without a basic science education, promiscuous teleology remains a fixture of adult thought. In studies with uneducated Romany adults, Kelemen and psychologist Krista Casler revealed the same preference for teleo-functional reasoning that is seen in young children;[20] it also appears in Alzheimer's patients, presumably because their scientific knowledge has been eaten away by disease, thus allowing the unaffected teleo-functional bias to recrudesce.[21]

There is, of course, a type of purpose in the natural world—just not teleo-functional purpose. Many biological traits are "for" specific purposes, even though they owe their existence entirely to the mindless machine of natural selection. These are evolutionary adaptations. It's perfectly reasonable to say that a turkey vulture's small, diamond-shaped, featherless head is "for" rooting around inside the meaty looms of carcasses.

It's a different story with artificial selection, where human beings domesticate and selectively breed plants and animals to accentuate particular traits for either pragmatic or aesthetic ends. Here, teleo-functional reasoning is logical because selective breeding is done with an end product in mind. My dog, Gulliver, has the typically shaped head of a border terrier, a hunting breed whose streamlined cranium resembles that of an otter. This skull design is the product of generations of Scottish breeders whittling away at the basic cranial morphology using selective breeding, to better allow "for" furrowing deep into holes and flushing out foxes.

So with artifacts and some biological features (those modified by human beings), we're on solid ground using teleo-functional reason-ing. Again, however, young children and adults lacking a basic sci-entific education overdo it; they're promiscuously teleological when reasoning about happenstance properties of nonbiological, inanimate objects. For example, when asked why rocks are pointy, the seven- and eight-year-olds in Kelemen's studies endorse teleo-functional accounts, treating rocks as something like artifacts ("so that animals could scratch on them when they get itchy") or as though the rocks were organisms themselves with evolved adaptations ("so that animals wouldn't sit on them and smash them").

If you think this type of response is just the result of what kids hear on television or from their parents, Kelemen is one step ahead of you, at least with respect to parental input. In looking at spontaneous dialogues occurring between preschoolers and their parents—particularly with respect to "why" and "what's that for" questions—Kelemen and her colleagues showed that parents generally reply with naturalistic causal answers (that is, scientific) rather than teleo-functional explanations. And even when they're given a choice and told that all-important adults prefer nonfunctional explanations over teleo-functional ones, children still opt strongly for the latter. "So current evidence suggests the answer does not lie there," says Kelemen. "At least, not in any straightforward sense."[22]

Furthermore, not only do children err teleologically about inani-mate natural entities like mountains, or about the physical features of inorganic objects like the shapes of rocks; they even display teleo-functional reasoning when it comes to the existence of *whole organ-isms*. One wouldn't (at least, one shouldn't) say that turkey vultures as a whole exist "for" cleaning up roadkill-splattered interstates. Dogs, as a domesticated species, may have been designed for human pur-poses, but, like buzzards, canines as a group aren't "for" anything either. Rather, they simply are; they've come to exist; they've evolved.

And yet, again, Kelemen has found that when children are asked why, say, lions exist, they prefer teleo-functional explanations ("to go in the zoo").

All of this may sound silly to you, but such findings, and the distorting lens of our species' theory of mind more generally, have obvious implications for our ability to ever truly grasp the completely mindless principles of evolution by random mutation and natural selection. In fact, for the past decade University of Michigan psychologist Margaret Evans has been investigating why creationist thinking comes more easily to the human mind than does evolutionary thinking. "Persistence [of creationist beliefs] is not simply the result of fundamentalist politics and socialization," writes Evans. "Rather, these forces themselves depend on certain propensities of the human mind."[23]

According to Evans, the stubborn preponderance of creationist beliefs is due in large part to the way our cognitive systems have, interestingly enough, evolved. Like Kelemen, Evans has discovered that irrespective of their parents' beliefs or whether they attend religious or secular school, when asked where the first member of a particular animal species came from, five- to seven-year-old children give either spontaneous generationist ("it got born there") or creationist ("God made it") responses. By eight years of age, however, children from both secular and religious backgrounds give more or less exclusively creationist answers. Usually these answers predictably manifest as "God made it," but otherwise Nature is personified, seen as a deliberate agent that intentionally made the animal for its own ends. It's at eight years or so, then, that teleo-functional reasoning seems to turn into a full-blown "design stance," in which children envisage an actual being as intentionally creating the entity in question for its own personal reasons.

Only among the oldest children she has studied, the ten- to twelve-year-olds, has Evans uncovered an effect of developmental experience, with children of evolutionary-minded parents finally giving evolutionary responses and those of evangelical parents giving creationist answers to the question of species origins. And even the "evolutionary" responses are often corrupted by culturally based misunderstandings. For example, Japanese fifth-graders tend to believe that human beings evolved directly from monkeys, probably because macaque monkeys are prodigious in Japan.[24] In other words, all of this suggests that thinking like an evolutionist is hard work because, ironically, our psychological development—and, in particular, our theory of mind—strongly favors the purposeful-design framework. Evolutionists will probably never outnumber creationists, because the latter have a paradoxical ally in the way natural selection has lent itself to our species' untutored penchant for reasoning about its own origins.

Even if one acknowledges that the teleo-functional bias distorts our perception of origins by creating the illusion of a creative mind that isn't there, a sticking point for many agnostics and lukewarm believers—including, as we saw at the opening of this chapter, Darwin himself—is the problem of ultimate origins. Natural selection may explain the great variability of life on earth today, many argue, but it doesn't explain why there is life to begin with. In other words, something mindful must have wound up the cosmos at its inception, sparked the Big Bang, devised the algorithms of evolution, materialized ether, and so on.

But our overzealous theory of mind can have us easily falling prey to flawed reasoning on this subject as well. Think a bit deeper and you'll notice a few unwarranted inferences in this line of thought. To begin with, let's assume for the moment that "being" (versus "nonbeing") does imply an intelligent Creator. Intelligent beings don't always do intelligent things. There may well be a God, even one who caused Creation. But for all we know, He did so accidentally rather than intentionally. In fact, in many ways, this still-godly account of our ultimate origins—the theistic equivalent of slapstick or a clumsy God or perhaps one sneezing or kicking up a pebble—can account considerably better for our present situation than can an intentional act of Creation. The humanlike God we're prone to worshipping could be a long-dead intergalactic sea horse that, rooting through an ancient seabed for plankton in some unknown dimension, incidentally dislodged the one grain of sand that held all of our own infinite cosmos intact. Philosophers and theologians are quick to point out the untenable assumptions of atheism, noting that the nonexistence of an intentional God is not a scientific hypothesis, because it cannot be proved or disproved. But, in spite of its philosophical soundness and explanatory relevance, and the fact that it also cannot be proved or disproved, few would equally strenuously defend this type of accidental-origin hypothesis.

———◆———

Our species' overabundant theory of mind has clear repercussions for our ability to reason logically about the origins of species, because creationist appeals, however they may vary from one another on the surface, invariably involve an intelligent first "agent" as cause (the "Prime Mover" in cosmological terms). "Someone" or "something" is seen as having engaged deliberately—*mindfully*—in the act of Creation.

Yet how exactly does theory of mind spill over into our thinking about our own individual creation, as unique members of our species? When it comes to religion, most believers reason that human beings are here "for" some divine purpose. And if they're not particularly religious, then you'll often hear people referencing a vaguely spiritualized purpose to human existence, such as "to be happy" or "to love one another." As Camus wrote, "Revolt against man is also directed against God."[25] But many of us go even one step further than this in teleo-functional absurdity, saying that individual members of our species also exist "for" a special reason. This is what the concept of destiny implies and what Sartre was trying to get at all those years ago: that each of us feels as if we're here to satisfy our own unique purpose, one crafted specially for us by intentional design. In our heads, not only are "we" (as in "we humans") here for a reason, but also "we" (me, you, the lady next door, the clerk behind the counter, and every single one of the billions of individuals on this planet) are each here for an even subtler shade of this overall purpose. At least, that's what people like Rick Warren would have you believe. "God broke the mold when he made you," the expression goes.

To see how fantastically odd this highly focused degree of teleo-functional reasoning actually is, imagine yourself on a nice sunny farm. Now have a glance around at the landscape. See that horsefly over there, the one hovering about the rump of that Arabian mare? Good. Now compare its unique purpose in life to, say, that other horsefly over there, the one behind the barn, waltzing around the pond algae. And don't forget about the hundreds of larvae pupating under that damp log—each of which also needs you to assign it a special, unique purpose in life. It's hard enough to come up with a teleo-functional purpose for horseflies as a whole, such as saying that horseflies exist to annoy equestrians or to make the rear ends of equines shiver in anticipation of being stung. Just as American poet Ogden Nash famously penned, "God in His wisdom made the fly / And then forgot to tell us why." But to suggest that each *individual* horsefly is here for a special, unique reason—one different from that of every other horsefly that has ever lived or will live—by using our theory of mind to reflect on God's intentions in crafting each its own destiny, may get us institutionalized. (If horseflies don't do it for you, simply replace the nominal species with another nonhuman species of your choice; perhaps goats, elm trees, or wild boars may suit your imagination better.) Yet this is precisely what we do when it comes to reasoning about individual members of our own species; and, curiously, the concept of destiny doesn't strike most of us as being ridiculous, insane, or conceptually flawed at all.

In fact, by all appearances, it feels quite natural. Just ask Fergie, one of the lead vocalists for the hip-hop group the Black Eyed Peas, who, upon reflecting on critics' rather sour reaction to some of her recent performances, fired back, "Singing is a gift from God, and when people say I can't sing, it's kind of like insulting God."[26] The Fox television correspondent and political pundit Bill O'Reilly feels similarly as though his career were tailor-made by God. O'Reilly believes that God personally crafted his bare-knuckle debating skills, cutthroat journalistic style, and generally feisty persona especially for this self-proclaimed "culture warrior." In O'Reilly's autobiography, *A Bold Fresh Piece of Humanity* (2008)—an unwieldy moniker given to him in the third grade by what he looks back on now as an especially perspicacious nun—O'Reilly sees a benevolent thumbprint in his rags-to-riches story:

> *Every one of us is on the planet for a purpose. I was lucky enough to find mine fairly young in life, but understanding the full extent of my purpose took much longer.*[27]
>
> *I say prayers of thanks for the miracle of life that I have lived . . . Next time you meet an atheist, tell him or her that you know a bold, fresh guy, a barbarian who was raised in a working-class home and retains the lessons he learned there. Then mention to that atheist that this guy is now watched and listened to, on a daily basis, by millions of people all over the world and, to boot,*

sells millions of books. Then, while the nonbeliever is digesting
all that, ask him or her if they still don't believe there's a God![28]

If the universe had a sense of humor, we would find the deistic
ghost of Charles Darwin as a guest on *The O'Reilly Factor*, staring
bewilderedly at O'Reilly as the latter struggled to make his case in a
red-faced tête-à-tête about the meaning of life. But because it doesn't,
we can just use our imaginations. And fortunately, it's not a huge
stretch to imagine what Darwin would probably say either. In a letter
dated July 3, 1860, and written to his close confidante (and religious
apologist), the botanist Asa Gray, Darwin opined,

> One more word on "designed laws" and "undesigned results."—
> I see a bird which I want for food, take my gun and kill it, I do
> this designedly.—An innocent and good man stands under a tree
> and is killed by a flash of lightning. Do you believe (& I really
> should like to hear) that God designedly killed this man? Many
> or most persons do believe this; I can't and don't.—If you believe
> so, do you believe that when a swallow snaps up a gnat that God
> designed that that particular swallow should snap up that particu-
> lar gnat at that particular instant? I believe that the man and the
> gnat are in the same predicament. If the death of neither man nor
> gnat are designed, I see no good reason to believe that their first
> birth or production should be necessarily designed.[29]

The idea of destiny and essential purpose might seem harmless
enough, but applying teleo-functional reasoning to our personal
being can sometimes go monstrously awry too. For instance, it's arguably one of the core tactics employed in luring unsuspecting young
military recruits into dangerous service. Nobody in his right mind

would believe that God created him for the purpose of hideously maiming an arthritic grandmother or that God designed him, and him alone, especially for flaying the flesh off a cooing baby's tender skeleton with homemade shrapnel. Yet the teleo-functional brain sees things in a curious way. Suppose you're a young Muslim whose neurons have been bathing in the rich, sensory atmosphere of warfare, radical Islam, and instability from the time you were gastrulating in the womb, from which you shimmied out into a world of baroque violence where the staccato sounds of Apache helicopter blades has become as familiar to you as your mother's voice. Handpicked by a charismatic political leader, whose particular God, orthodoxy, and history you happen to share, you're told you've been specially chosen, as God's will, to carry out a secret and holy act of martyrdom for all of Islam. Yes, the shrapnel you're brandishing will destroy a poor arthritic old woman and obliterate an infant who happens to be in the crowded marketplace where your destiny is to be played out, but all is as it should be. "God works in mysterious ways."

What's important to notice here is how teleo-functional reasoning, when applied to this strange quest to uncover the purpose of our lives, can lead to acts of epic devastation when the socioecological conditions are just right—or, rather, just wrong. The trouble is that the terrorist doesn't think he's a terrorist, for God doesn't create terrorists. In 1997, Osama bin Laden, who was already cooking up his egomaniacal plans for his own political ascendancy in the Arab-speaking world, granted a rare interview to an American television reporter, who asked Bin Laden about the increasingly frequent, disturbing strategy of training radical young Muslims to blow up themselves and others in service to Al-Qaeda. Bin Laden responded, "We believe that no one can take out one breath of our written life as ordained by Allah. We see that getting killed in the cause of Allah is a great cause as wished for by our Prophet."[30] So playing on the idea of destiny, teleo-functional thinking can be an insidiously effective trap, abused (either intentionally or unintentionally) by authority figures in their narcissistic manipulations of subordinates. According to one chilling study of Palestinian children, 36 percent of boys and 17 percent of girls between the ages of twelve and fourteen said that they wanted to die a martyr.[31]

This isn't to say that the concept of destiny—or believing, more generally, that God has something specific in mind for us as individuals—is always such a bad thing. In fact, research by Northwestern University psychologist Dan McAdams suggests that people who attribute meaning to their misfortunes tend to become sympathetic older adults, prone to lending a hand to younger individuals who are still going through their own painful "life lessons." Indeed, when now-President Barack Obama was campaigning for the Illinois senate in 2004, he was interviewed by Cathleen Falsani, a religion columnist for the *Chicago Sun-Times*. Falsani was collecting stories for her book *The God Factor* (2007). When she asked whether he ever prayed or meditated, Obama replied:

> *It's much more sort of as I'm going through the day trying to take stock and take a moment here and a moment there to ask, why am I here, how does this connect with a larger sense of purpose . . . the biggest challenge, I think, is always maintaining your moral compass. Those are the conversations I'm having internally. I'm measuring my actions against that inner voice that for me at least is audible, is active, it tells me where I think I'm on track and where I think I'm off track.*[32]

As we've seen, consciously rejecting the idea of destiny doesn't mean we've stopped portraying ourselves as characters in some shadowy personal fable. But understanding destiny for what it is—a cognitive illusion that, given the naturalness of both human egoism and theory of mind, can be both alluring and deadly—we're at least able to resist those unctuous figures that would corrupt us into believing they possess some privileged knowledge about what God has in store for us.

And it's not just warmongers and religious con artists that tempt the young and gullible into unwise fatalistic thinking either. In fact, although their intentions are usually more innocuous than the foregoing, parents and teachers also tend to unwittingly exacerbate the illusion of destiny. Our social environments are blanketed by a thick vocational wilderness in which one's job title serves, often sadly, to identify the essential purpose of that individual. From the earliest ages, children are asked by adults "what they want to be" when they grow up, as though one is not a real person—that is, is *without essential purpose*—until one has a career that serves a function.

As a college professor, I've seen my share of students for whom the future represents an enticing and inscrutable promise, one that they might divine here and there in the form of others' praise or recognition of their talents. We expect young people to "discover themselves," like sleuths working on a case. An implicit assumption in this lock-and-key approach to education is that, with enough self-knowledge, and especially with enough failures and rejections by trying their fit in too many wrong doors, students will eventually find the door that gives them the least resistance, thus realizing what it is they are "meant" to be doing with their lives. Standardized testing is used as a process of elimination, allowing students to whittle down their fates. And for students who read their test results like tea leaves, or take critical evaluations of their potential as inherent truths, this approach often means sacrificing their possible best future selves.

Furthermore, after "seeing" their prewritten purpose, people are prone to feeling cheated, as though they are "living someone else's life" or "not doing what they're meant for" when they find themselves later shackled to the utilitarian realities of having to pay the bills, raising their children, and honoring their rather drab and unromantic commitments. My father, a successful salesman, earned his under-graduate degree in English literature and always felt—largely because of comments from one supportive faculty member during his col-lege years—that he was meant to have been a tea-sipping professor romancing wide-eyed students about Robert Frost on some idyllic liberal arts college campus. But, it didn't quite happen that way. Like Franz Kafka stuck in the mole holes of a labyrinthine bureaucratic absurdity, he instead spent his entire adult life selling wood glue to wholesale suppliers and chairing soporific board meetings on how the present market conditions were affecting the sale of home office goods.

The teleo-functional bias may also influence our self-esteem in subtle, but potentially life-altering, ways. Even for those who believe that "God doesn't make mistakes," our interactions with other people can still sometimes instill in us the vague, unsettling sense that we are human design flaws. When we think about the child who's told everyday by his mother or father that he's useless or "can't do any-thing right," an evolved cognitive penchant for reasoning as though we're artifacts can turn rather tragic. And this sort of strangling effect of teleo-functional reasoning on our self-esteem doesn't necessarily require verbal abuse either. Sometimes it's simply a matter of vicarious learning—learning from the experiences of ostracized others what it is that society feels makes a person defective, and then hiding this part of our own nature so as to avoid the same stereotypical, much maligned destiny.

It's a bit embarrassing for me to recall now, for instance, but when I was about eight years old, I was convinced that a routine bloodletting at the doctor's office would expose me as being secretly gay—that, perhaps by holding the vial up to a ray of sun-filtered light, the doctor would surely detect some homosexual essence floating about in my plasma that would betray my true identity, which was vaguely rotten, a design flaw. The reason I believed this was that I had seen how gay men in my society were treated with disdain, and in fact this was the reason it took a very long time for me to overcome my own antigay prejudices. I was so busy avoiding the fatalistic "story of a gay man" that had been scripted for me by my own homophobic culture, that instead of investing in my own development as an individual person, I invested too much energy in avoiding that already authored destiny of a derogated class.

Research on a related problem in the domain of thinking about artifacts—a problem called "functional fixedness" by developmental psychologists—shows just how detrimental to our personal growth teleo-functional reasoning may actually be. This work on functional fixedness suggests, at least indirectly, that viewing ourselves as having an essential purpose can shape our self-concepts in ways that make us complacent to our less-than-desirable present realities. Direct research on this topic has yet to be done, but if we do indeed reason about ourselves—or at least our purpose in life—much in the same manner as we do for artifacts, such reasoning may well be why our self-concepts are especially vulnerable to what others tell us we are. It may also be why it's so difficult to reinvent ourselves by seeing our own unexplored potential, instead of complacently telling ourselves that if it's meant to happen, it will happen.

Functional fixedness is a cognitive bias, found across human cultures, in which our ability to "think outside the box" when dealing with an artifact is severely hampered by the most obvious and apparent function of that artifact. In other words, our ability to generate fertile, atypical, creative insights into the multitudinous uses of a given object—such as a lampshade being turned into a cowboy hat, or a defunct gravestone into a decorative walkway—becomes increasingly constrained by what we believe the designer of that object intended it to be used for.

In one revealing experiment on functional fixedness by Tim German and Clark Barrett, for example, participants heard about a pair of friends, Bear and Rabbit, who were out playing but suddenly became separated by a fast-moving river (which the experimenter indicated by sweeping his hand across an area of the table before the participants, with the characters separated by a pair of Styrofoam blocks). It was too dangerous for either to swim across, said the researcher, but nevertheless Bear had a couple of handy objects that could be used to help his friend Rabbit get back to the other side—namely, a cup filled with rice, a spoon, a smaller plastic cup, a popsicle stick, a Ping-Pong ball, and an eraser. There were two groups of participants in this study. Each heard exactly the same story and was confronted with exactly the same task—to help Bear help Rabbit get across—but one group was presented with the spoon *inside* the rice-filled cup, and the other half saw the spoon lying on the table *outside* the rice-filled cup. The solution? The distance between the two Styrofoam blocks was precisely the length of the spoon, so the answer was simply to use the spoon to bridge the river. Those who saw the spoon outside the cup solved the challenge significantly faster than those who saw it inside. The spoon-inside-the-cup group was conceptually tethered to this apparent scooping function of the spoon and was forced to first escape cognitively from this purpose-constraining setup.[33]

As with any other psychological trait, there appear to be meaningful individual differences in the constraint imposed by functional fixedness on any given human brain. In other words, there are exceptions to the rule. And sometimes these exceptions make history. In 2001, for example, a Malawian teenager named William Kamkwamba saw a bunch of discarded bicycle tires, rusty old car parts, and blue gum trees as being potential building material for solar-powered windmills, and eventually he brought free electricity to his rural village in Africa. Yet when it comes to the development of our self-concepts, other people's definitions of us, as inferred by their actions and reactions toward us as children, may cast us in something like the role of the spoon in the cup. Sartre believed that this is what happened to the celebrated criminal and playwright Jean Genet (author of *The Maids* and *Our Lady of the Flowers,* among other works). Upon allegedly stealing from a nun as a child, Genet was branded a degenerate by society, and then conformed to be this, his inescapable, essential, rotten identity—but this identity was in fact one that had only been imposed on him by others. Still, Genet saw an inherent purpose in such a life. Amid many colorful, licentious years as a pimp, petty thief, and homosexual prostitute, Genet spent almost two decades as a cog in the French penal system. Yet he pointed out, and reasonably so, that criminals were just as important to society as were those who despised them. After all, said Genet, an entire industry of people—lawyers, judges, jailers, clerks, guards, legislators, psychiatrists, counselors, and so on—were able to pay their taxes, feed their children, and furnish their homes only through the tireless labors of criminals.[34]

—•—

Teleo-functional reasoning isn't just a quirky way of thinking, therefore. It has real consequences for how we come to live our lives. It also plays an important role in the evolution of morality because it relates closely to another important error in our social reasoning, one that tempts us into thinking that we *should* and *ought to* behave a certain way because that is what we are made to do. This notion of God's moral intentions in manufacturing our minds and bodies is connected to the philosophical construct of the "naturalistic fallacy," which is the conceptual error made in claiming that what is natural is also inherently good, proper, or right. Again, without theory of mind, we couldn't very well ponder, squabble about, and kill each other over what God intended or didn't intend for us to be doing.

The naturalistic fallacy plagues especially the discipline of evolutionary psychology, because researchers in this field often uncover aspects of the human psyche that are "natural" (unlearned and largely invariant across cultures) but hardly desirable in terms of social mores. Typical examples are unwelcome sexual proclivities, such as men's tendency to sexually coerce unwilling women, or their carnal desires for legally underage, reproductively viable girls, who, because of their comparative remaining years of fertility, combined with the fact that virginity ensures paternity, are especially high in adaptive value. Showing such desires to be natural, critics argue, equates to giving people permission to unleash these lascivious impulses. "It's only natural," we hear people say—and usually to justify thoughts that inspire guilt and shame, staking them out as being normal and therefore okay. So evolutionary psychology is continually embattled by emotion-fueled claims that tug at people's moralistic penchant for design reasoning, and it must repeatedly defend itself against such misunderstandings by clarifying through ever more creative language that what is natural is neither good nor bad, but simply is.

Another hot-button issue that frequently invokes the naturalistic fallacy, and one that evolutionary psychology has historically brooded over, is the subject of homosexuality. The rather ugly business of homophobia is often smugly wrapped up in a corrosive teleo-functional sentiment involving gender roles. For example, in the 2009 Miss USA pageant, gay celebrity blogger and panel judge Perez Hilton asked Miss California, Carrie Prejean, whether she believed that all states should follow the progressive lead of Vermont in legalizing same-sex marriage. The blonde, statuesque Prejean, a pretty but not much else twenty-one-year-old studying special education at a small evangelical college in San Diego, quickly weighed the question in her

71

head, blinked once, and then polarized the nation by offering through a Vaseline-gummed smile this rambling response:

> *Well I think it's great that Americans are able to choose one or the other, um, we live in a land that you can choose same-sex marriage or opposite marriage, and . . . [here's where she begins answering the question honestly] You know what, in my country and in my family I think that I believe that a marriage should be between a man and a woman, no offense to anybody out there but that's how I was raised and that's how I think that it should be, between a man and a woman.*[35]

Pageant watchers still contend that the bluntness of her answer cost Prejean the crown; she ended up as runner-up to an allegedly more tolerant Miss North Carolina. Another drama unfolded in the lobby after the show, where Miss New Mexico's mother lapsed into a tirade of even more obvious design-stance language, shouting at one outraged audience member the old refrain, "In the Bible it says that marriage is between Adam and Eve, not Adam and Steve!"[36]

Tempting as it may be, however, we mustn't just take the easy road of picking on beauty pageant contestants and their Bible-blinded mothers. In doing so, we would miss psychological clues that run deeper than scripture. In fact, as medical interventionist approaches to "correcting" homosexuality have attested in even recent decades, it's not uncommon for scientific atheists to demonstrate passionate antigay attitudes, and these prejudices are at least partially rooted in the teleo-functional bias. This nonreligious maligning of homosexuality is something often mistaken for religious intolerance. In *The God Delusion* (2006), for example, Richard Dawkins asks us to consider the case of Alan Turing, the doomed British mathematician and German Enigma code breaker who crimped Nazi intelligence efforts and singularly helped end the Second World War. Turing was famously convicted in 1952 under British sodomy laws for an exposed tryst with a young man, and forced by psychiatrists to undergo chemical castration by a series of injections of female hormones—which caused him, sadly, embarrassingly, to grow breasts. Faced with the prospect of continued injections of these hormones or a lengthy prison sentence, Turing escaped both nightmares by biting into a cyanide-laced apple and committing suicide. Dawkins sees Turing, wrongly, as an example of gays being persecuted because of religiously motivated moralistic beliefs. He writes,

> After the war, when Turing's role was no longer top secret, he should have been knighted and fêted as a savior of his nation. Instead, this gentle, stammering, eccentric genius was destroyed, for a "crime," committed in private, which harmed nobody. Once again, the unmistakable trademark of the faith-based moralizer is to care passionately about what other people do (or even think) in private.[37]

In fact, the British government, especially its legislative arm, was among the most secular regulating establishments in the world at that time, and although the legislation of sodomy laws may have occurred against a general backdrop of religious belief in England (and even this was considerably less noticeable compared to other Western nations), the truth is that the 1950s psychiatric community, wholly independent of religious sentiments, regarded homosexuality as a medical disorder mandating curative treatment. So although Dawkins is right to condemn Turing's unspeakable sentence at the hands of the British elite, it is in fact scientists (conducting flawed science, but science nonetheless) who were more to blame for this man's demise than that era's "faith-based moralizers."

There is, needless to say, a genuine adaptive purpose in heterosexual intercourse, which is a very direct route to reproductive success. But we must continually remind ourselves that adaptive biological design offers no intrinsic directives, or prescriptions, for moral behavior. One wouldn't normally say that men *should* be promiscuous because, after all, the pulpy underflaring of their penises' coronal ridges is specially tailored by God for excessive use with multiple women, retracting competitors' sperm. Likewise, one wouldn't usually be concerned about the unnaturalness of masking our body odors by drowning our glands in a factory-derived effluvium, even though the use of deodorant and perfume clearly also goes against the natural order of things.

Another modern example of how teleo-functional thinking intersects with moral reasoning is the issue of medically assisted suicide. Those who believe that one's life is owned by God are more likely to view medical euthanasia—as well as abortion and capital punishment—as being morally wrong. If a person's essence is created by God, as many believe it to be, then it follows that individuals haven't the right to purposefully cause their own death, because that right is seen as being God's alone. Suicide therefore becomes a form of intellectual theft; the self redesigns its end in an act of mutiny against its creator. As an angst-ridden Fyodor Dostoyevsky wrote in his *Diary of a Writer* (1873), "I condemn that nature which, with such impudent nerve, brought me into being in order to suffer—I condemn it in order to be annihilated with me."[38]

———◆———

To see an inherent purpose in life, whether purpose in our own individual existence or life more generally, is to see an intentional, creative mind—usually God—that had a reason for designing it this way and not some other way. If we subscribe wholly and properly to Darwin's theory of natural selection, however, we must view human life, generally, and our own lives, individually, as arising through solely nonintentional, physical means. This doesn't imply that we are "accidents," because even that term requires a mind, albeit one that created by mistake. Rather, we simply *are*. To state otherwise, such as saying that you or I exist for a reason, would constitute an obvious category error, one in which we're applying teleo-functional thinking to something that neither was designed creatively nor evolved as a discrete biological adaptation.

Yet owing to our theory of mind, and specifically to our undisciplined teleological reasoning, it is excruciatingly difficult to refrain from seeing human existence in such intentional terms. To think that we are moral because morality works in a mechanistic, evolutionary sense is like saying that we are moral because we are moral; it's unfulfilling in that it strips the authority away from a God that created us to act in specific ways because He knew best, and He would become disappointed and angry if we failed to go along with His rules for human nature. But peeling back the cognitive illusion of the purpose of life as we have done in this chapter gives us our first glimpse into the question asked at the outset of the book: Has our species' unique cognitive evolution duped us into believing in this, the grandest mind of all? So far, the answer is clearly "yes."

3 | SIGNS, SIGNS, EVERYWHERE SIGNS

JUST AS WE see other people as more than just their bodies, we also tend to see natural events as more than natural events. And again, this seeing beyond the obvious is the consequence of the very peculiar way our brains have evolved, with a theory of mind. At every turn, we seem to think there are subtle messages scratched into the woodwork of nature, subtle signs or cues that God, or some other supernatural agent, is trying to communicate a lesson or idea to us—and often to us alone. Usually, it's about how we should behave. So we listen attentively, effortlessly translating natural events into divine or supernatural messages.

The best examples of seeing God's mind at work in nature tend also to be the most laughable, but from them we can see just how people's religious and spiritual views articulate with our species' evolved theory of mind. The outspoken African American mayor of New Orleans, Ray Nagin, suggested to reporters in 2005 that Hurricane Katrina, one of the most savage and destructive storms ever to strike North American shores, was in fact a climatological testament to God's vitriolic fury at the drug-addled city, the country's military incursion in Iraq, and "black America" all rolled into one:

> *Surely God is mad at America. Surely He's not approving of us being in Iraq under false pretense. But surely He's mad at black America, too. We're not taking care of ourselves.*[1]

This comment drew sharp criticism from all sides and eventually led to Nagin's offering an awkward apology in which he promised to be more sensitive the next time around. But the outrage sparked by the mayor's pulpit rhetoric wasn't due to people's inability to comprehend Nagin's basic point. Rather, it was just that most people didn't believe that their God, whom they viewed as being a loving, nonwrathful God, would communicate to us poor human beings in this particular way. As Einstein once allegedly remarked to a friend, "God is slick, but he ain't mean."[2]

Of course, Nagin was only reinventing the well-treaded fire-and-brimstone wheel in suggesting that our God is a testy and vengeful one. Just a year before he made his political gaffe, other reflective people from all corners of the globe borrowed from the same barrel of explanation and offered commentary on the "real" reason for the Indonesian tsunami that killed nearly a quarter of a million people in Southeast Asia in 2004. (Never mind the sudden shifting of tectonic plates on the Indian Ocean floor.) All similarly saw that catastrophe, too, as a sort of enormous, Vegas-style, blinking marquee meant to convey an unambiguous message to us superficial, fallen, and famously flawed human beings. Here are a few anonymous samples from some online discussion forums just a few days after the tsunami disaster:

> *As God says, I send things down on you as a warning so that you may ponder and change your ways.*

A lot of times, God allows things like this to happen to bring people to their knees before God. It takes something of this magnitude to help them understand there is something bigger that controls this world than themselves.

It might just be God's way to remind us that He is in charge, that He is God and we need to repent.

The calamity—so distressing for those individually involved—was for humanity as a whole a profoundly moral occurrence, an act of God performed for our benefit.

The important thing to notice with all of these examples, or any case in which a natural event is taken as a sign, omen, or symbol, is the universal common denominator: theory of mind. In analyzing things this way, we're trying to get into God's head—or the head of whichever culturally constructed supernatural agent we have on offer. Consider, however, that without our evolved capacity to reason about unseen mental states, hurricanes and tsunamis would be just what they are for every other animal on earth—really bad storms. That is to say, just like other people's surface behaviors, natural events can be perceived by us human beings as being *about* something other than their surface characteristics only because our brains are equipped with the specialized cognitive software, theory of mind, that enables us to think about underlying psychological causes.

Of course, in reality there probably aren't any such psychological causes, but our brains don't mind that. Our theory of mind goes into overdrive, jump-started in the very same way it's provoked by another person's unexpected social behavior. It's a bit like if you went to shake your best friend's hand and he punched you in the face. It may not be immediately apparent, but there must be some reason for him to have acted in this way. Except here, it's not other people's behaviors we're trying to understand; it's God's "behaviors," or otherwise the universe acting as if it were some vague, intentional agent.

In his book *Acts of Meaning* (1992), Harvard University psychologist Jerome Bruner argues that we tend to search for meaning whenever others' behaviors violate our expectations, or when they don't adhere to basic social norms. For instance, breaches of linguistic rules—what language theorists call "conversational implicatures"—often encourage a frenzied search for the speaker's intentions. If someone responds with "a whiskey sour, please" after being asked what the weather forecast is for tomorrow, most listeners will automatically think about the causes for this inappropriate—or at least unexpected—social response. Perhaps the person doesn't speak English and didn't understand the question; perhaps the person is mentally ill; or maybe he's angry and is trying to frustrate the listener; perhaps the person is being sarcastic, playful, is hard of hearing—or maybe he's just really thirsty. Although each of these explanations invokes different theories for the cause of the speaker's strange response, they all share an appeal to his mental state. By contrast, it's unlikely a similar search for meaning would occur if he had made an appropriate response, such as, "I think it's supposed to rain." Likewise, natural events that are expected or mundane are unlikely to be seen as signs or messages from God, because they fail to trigger our theory of mind. Most of the time, things unfold in a manner consistent with our expectations. It's when they don't that we become such willing slaves to illogical thinking.

———◆———

Without a general cognitive bias to see hidden messages as being embedded in natural events, much of religion as we know it would never have gotten off the ground. This is because such episodes are often taken as confirmation that there are communicative "others"—God, ancestors, whatever—capable of influencing our personal lives through causal interference with the natural world. This perceived feedback from the other side induces the powerful sense for us that we (and perhaps more importantly, our behavior) *matter* to something more than just the here and now. And without the belief that God cares enough about us as individuals to bother sending us a veiled, personalized "just thinking of you" message every once in a while, there's not really much reason to pay attention to Him.[3]

If seeing signs in natural events hinges on the presence of a fully functioning theory of mind, then we might expect people with clinically impaired theory-of-mind abilities to be less susceptible to this type of thinking and so to manifest religion very differently from the rest of us. One such disorder is autism. Individuals along the autistic spectrum, including otherwise high-functioning people with Asperger's syndrome who have very normal (or even high) general IQs, often have tremendous difficulty reasoning about other people's psychological states, particularly the subtle, nuanced aspects of other minds, such as sarcasm, faux pas, and irony. University of Cambridge psychologist Simon Baron-Cohen—who happens to be first cousin to the *Borat* (2006) and *Brüno* (2009) star—has referred to autistics as being "mindblind,"[4] although this characterization is probably a bit strong. A better way to conceptualize people with autism is to view them as having never developed a fully erect intentional stance. Their sensitivity to mental states is probably diluted rather than missing altogether.

In recent years, Baron-Cohen and his colleagues have put forth the rather astonishing hypothesis that, although they tend to have profound difficulties in the social domain, people with autism may actually possess a superior understanding of folk physics when compared to the rest of us. "Folk physics," according to Baron-Cohen, "is our everyday ability to understand and predict the behavior of inanimate objects in terms of principles relating to size, weight, motion, physical causality, etc."[5] In short, autistics are preoccupied with the way things work in terms of *how* they work, not *why*. The parents of many autistic children, for instance, are often startled to see that their sons and daughters display obsessive-compulsive interests clustering around machines and physical systems. These children tend to become thoroughly enamored with what might seem to the rest of us the most eccentric of hobbies: collecting patterned light filaments, systematically dismantling old Polaroid cameras and television remote controls, accumulating encyclopedic knowledge of nineteenth-century railway transport engines. This tendency to become transfixed by surface causes may help us understand why, in families where autism appears to run in the bloodline, professions such as engineering, accounting, and the physical sciences tend to be curiously overrepresented in the genealogy.

In some cases, it seems, this form of physical causal expertise is very practically translated to social problem solving. That is to say, many autistics get by perfectly fine in the real world by exploiting their heightened knowledge of surface-level behaviors, never having to really think about the confusing mental states underlying other people's actions. University of Sheffield psychologist Digby Tantum gives this intriguing example of a woman with Asperger's syndrome trying to navigate her way around the use of a crowded ATM machine:

> She had observed that when people lined up, they left a gap between themselves and the person in front, and that this gap was substantially larger in the case of men standing behind women. She used this information to jump lines, looking for this combination and pushing in behind the woman nearest the front who was followed by a man.[6]

This woman's understanding of the way people work was motivated by a desire to learn how they typically behaved in this particular social setting, not their mental reasons for doing so. Only by assessing and becoming extraordinarily sensitive to the way routines and conventional social rules intersect with people's overt behavior could she enter the social environment, albeit inappropriately in this instance—she still couldn't understand why those waiting patiently in line behind her would get so angry.

Several autobiographical accounts provide fascinating glimpses into the autistic person's view of God. And because, as we've now seen, reasoning about God is fundamentally about using our evolved theory of mind to think about God's mental states, it's perhaps not surprising that these writings appear to reflect a very different kind of God than the conventionally maudlin version most of us are more familiar with. For instance, in her book *Thinking in Pictures: And Other Reports from My Life with Autism* (1996), the autistic scientist and writer Temple Grandin speaks of her lifelong struggle with her belief in God:

It is beyond my comprehension to accept anything on faith alone, because of the fact that my thinking is governed by logic instead of emotion.[7]

In high school I came to the conclusion that God was an ordering force that was in everything. I found the idea of the universe becoming more and more disordered profoundly disturbing.[8]

In nature, particles are entangled with millions of other particles, all interacting with each other. One could speculate that entanglement of these particles could cause a kind of consciousness for the universe. This is my current concept of God.[9]

Another case comes from autistic mathematician and computer programmer Edgar Schneider's *Discovering My Autism* (1999). In chapters devoted to his religious beliefs, Schneider writes,

> *My belief in the existence of a supreme intelligence (or, if you will, a God) is based on scientific factors.*[10]

> *It must be pointed out explicitly that none of this [religious beliefs] has any emotional underpinnings, but is totally intellectual in its nature.*[11]

> *To me, as far as adherence to a religion (or any other type of ideology) is concerned, intellectual conviction is a condition that mathematicians call "both necessary and sufficient." My religious faith, I guess I could say, is not a gift from God, as so many people say; it is a gift I gave to myself. In line with this, I have never felt the emotional exhilaration that people must feel when they have a "religious experience." This is true even when I receive the sacraments. The only thing that has deeply moved me is the reasonableness of it all.*[12]

We can't help but get the distinct impression from such descriptions that theism in autistic people is somehow different from the garden-variety version. It's not that autistic religion isn't theologically sophisticated. On the contrary, these writers' religious views are extraordinary. When I met with Schneider at a public library to discuss his beliefs with him in person, he had a colossal, self-published tome tucked under his arm, a document riddled with complicated mathematical formulas, which he was convinced showed clearly how God was busy at work in the quantum universe. (It may well have been just what he said it was. But given my own shameful impoverishments in the subject of physics, the document was almost entirely incomprehensible to me.)

Yet at least in the autobiographies of autistic individuals, God, the cornerstone of most people's religious experience, is presented more as a sort of principle than as a psychological entity. For autistics, God seems to be a faceless force in the universe that is directly responsible for the organization of cosmic structure—arranging matter in an orderly fashion, or "treating" entropy—or He's been reduced to cold, rational scientific logic altogether. To Schneider, instead of the emotional correlates of church ritual that so often engender the physiology of spiritual awakenings (what University of Oxford anthropologist Harvey Whitehouse calls "sensory pageantry"),[13] Catholicism is more an anxiety-reducing medium with its formal, predictable procedures and the clarity of its canons. It gives almost step-by-step instructions, telling the autistic how to behave in a very threatening, confusing social world and affording them some degree of control.

What is noticeably missing in the preceding accounts is a sense of interpersonal relations between the autistic individual and God. It's almost as if the algorithmic strategies used to deal with other people—such as the lady at the ATM machine—spill over into the authors' religious beliefs as well. Rather than an emotional dependence or rich social relationship with God, deductive logic is used to lay the groundwork for understanding existence and to impose order on a chaotic world. The sense of the *numinous*, or spiritual "otherness," inherent in most people's religious beliefs is conspicuously absent in the autistic.

All this is to say that, for autistics, God may be a behavioral rather than a psychological agent. If this is indeed the case, then people with autism should be less inclined to see natural events as carrying some type of subtle, hidden message. For example, a lonely, single man with autism might pray for a wife but will not be able to decode the symbolic device—a natural event—by which God "responds," such as a female friend's husband leaving her for another woman. A nonautistic, religious observer might interpret this to be God's "wanting" the man to be with this female friend, and thus view God as having intentionally set up this chain of social events as a way to respond to the man's prayer; yet, because of his theory-of-mind impairments, the autistic man wouldn't easily infer God's intentions in this episode. Indeed, one man with Asperger's syndrome inquired on an Internet bulletin board whether others with the disorder were like him, "conscious of no feedback from the divine." If God communicates in the subtle language of natural events, it's no wonder that people on the autistic spectrum would so often fail to pick up on His communicative messages.

On the other side of the clinical coin from autism is the disorder of paranoid schizophrenia, in which the term "paranoid" captures the essence of a theory of mind gone completely wild. These individuals see personal signs and messages in nearly everything. The experience of *apophenia* (seeing patterns of connections in random or meaningless events) that is more or less endemic to the psychology of these patients is especially telling. For example, University of Edinburgh psychiatrist Jonathan Burns writes,

> *Patients with schizophrenia seek meaning in the bizarre phenomena of their psychoses. Theistic and philosophical phenomena populate their hallucinations, while the frantic search for, and misattribution of, intentionality must lie at the heart of symptoms such as thought insertion, ideas of reference and paranoid delusions.*[14]

But even cognitively normal, nonschizophrenic people often have trouble *not* seeing hidden messages in natural events. One of the things that has always intrigued me about human psychology is the fact that our minds so often make decisions without first consulting our knowledge and beliefs. A scientifically headed, otherwise rational person can say with absolute conviction and sincerity, "I do not believe." And yet, when the conditions are just right, the physiology, emotions, even behavior of such individuals would seem to say otherwise. Very often, we're entirely unaware of these contradictions in our thoughts, or at least circumspection is rare. But every now and then, there's something of a collision between the rational and the irrational.

In my case, I tend to become most acutely aware of the fact that my mind has a mind of its own whenever some coincidence of events serves to trigger thoughts of my dead mother. Yes, she "lives in my heart," metaphorically speaking. But whatever is left of Alice Bering—those smiling, laughing eyes that welled up so quickly with giant teardrops; her sense of humor; fingers that would rake gently against the scalp of my feverish head when I was a boy; the worried knot between her brows that reflected unspoken despair; even the cancer that took this all furiously away—has for ten years been turning to dust in a satin-lined, walnut casket buried six feet beneath the Florida sun–soaked earth in the middle of a crowded Jewish cemetery.

Now, I believe, without any tremor of agnostic hesitation, that the whole of my mother's existence is presently encapsulated as a fragile artifact in this lonely tomb. I also believe that her mental life ended before my eyes in one great, exasperated sigh on a grim January evening in 2001, "like the light ash of a butterfly wing incinerated in a forest fire," as Camus said about his long-dead father.[15] On several occasions since then, however, I've caught myself in a rather complicated lie, one in which, at some level, I've leapt to the conclusion that my mom still has a very active mental life—which, of course, I can perceive only by using my theory of mind.

During the long sleepless night that followed in the wake of her death, for instance, my own mind registered the quiet harmony of the wind chimes jingling outside her bedroom window, and I'd be lying if I said that my first thought was not that she was trying to communicate a gentle message to me in the guise of this sweet device. I did not *believe* this to be the case; I knew very well that, at that very instant, her body was probably being fussed over by a coroner's assistant in scrubs miles away. But my beliefs at that moment were irrelevant. My brain happily bypassed them and jumped to translation mode: *she's telling me everything is okay.*

Yale University philosopher Tamar Gendler recently coined the term "alief" to describe just this sort of quasi belief—more primitive than a full-fledged belief or even imagination—in which a mental state is triggered by ambient environmental factors, generating very real emotional and behavioral responses, but the person experiencing that mental state isn't convinced that the trigger reflects something *true.*[16] Another way to say this is that the person's mind is somehow tricked by environmental cues that, in the ancestral past, would usually have been associated with adaptive responses. A clearer example of the experience of alief is offered by University of Oxford psychologist Ryan McKay and philosopher Daniel Dennett in their 2009 *Behavioral and Brain Sciences* article,

> *A person who trembles (or worse) when standing on the glass-floored Skywalk that protrudes over the Grand Canyon does not believe she is in danger, any more than a moviegoer at a horror film does, but her behavior at the time indicates that she is in a belief-like state that has considerable behavioral impact.*[17]

An even simpler explanation for my reaction to the wind chimes than that of alief is merely to say that part of me wanted there to be an afterlife, that we see what we want to see, and so my desire to believe that my mom's spirit somehow survived her bodily death simply short-circuited the rationality of my materialist beliefs. Yet sheer emotionalism is likely an inadequate account in such instances. After all, many animals become emotionally distraught over the death of a loved one.[18] But without theory of mind, human beings could not perceive the dead as intentionally sending them telegrams in the protean shapes of natural events—such messages, after all, are perceived as coming directly from the spirits' minds. My mom *wanted* me to *know* that she had cleared customs in heaven (or some such).

Still another explanation for my reaction to the wind chimes, and the one preferred by cognitive scientists such as Justin Barrett from the University of Oxford and Stewart Guthrie of Fordham University, is that such psychological responses result from the activation of a "hyperactive agency detection device" by unexpected movements in the environment.[19] This position holds that, because of the ever-present threat of animal (and other human) predators in the ancestral past, human minds evolved a sort of hair-trigger device to identify movement or sound as being caused by a dangerous creature (or some other potentially deadly entity), rather than assuming that it's coming from something more innocuous (such as the wind). Often we're wrong—I've mistaken plenty a garden hose for a snake—but from the gene's point of view, erring the other way around would be a much costlier error, and it's better to be safe than sorry. So when it comes to something like wind chimes moving presumably of their own accord, the absence of an actual threatening physical being to explain the cause of the event instinctively conjures up the thought of a nonphysical being, such as a ghost.

But this account, too, is inadequate to explain my reaction to the wind chimes. To begin with, it completely overlooks my theory of mind. This wasn't just my mother's aloof, restless ghost playing around out there because she had nothing better to do. Rather—at least for my secret, illogical twin who had apparently pirated my scientific brain in this instance—she was using the objects to give me a personal message, what appeared to be a peaceful ode, a meaningful whisper, about her safe passage to the other side. In effect I was putting myself in my dead mother's shoes, employing my theory of mind to try to decipher the mental reasons for her actions. Without a theory of mind, there would just be the sound of wind chimes. And with a mere hyperactive agency detection device, it would just be her moving them.

To perceive any event as meaningful, or otherwise "standing for" the unobservable mental states presumed to be causing them, requires a theory of mind. There must be some intentional purpose, some intelligent reason, for the event to transpire. And this is just as true when we perceive meaning in mindless natural events such as hurricanes, plagues, earthquakes, and wind chimes as it is when we're reasoning about other (living) people's everyday social behaviors. "What's this about?" we immediately ask ourselves. "Why is God (or our dead mother) doing this?" It is especially telling that the question of how God acts on the universe—rather than simply why He does so—so seldom arises in people's thoughts. If a believer were diagnosed with cancer, for example, it would be rather unusual for the person to dwell on how God went about causing his or her cells to turn physically malignant. Did He use His hands? Telepathy? And if He used telepathy, does that mean He has a physical brain? That such questions of actual physical causality—how God goes about converting His intentions into palpable events in the physical world—sound so odd to us betrays their psychological unnaturalness. They're hardly the stuff of church sermons anyway.

Our human penchant for seeing meaningful signs in unexpected natural events is something that many New Age belief systems have exploited to great (and profitable) effect. For example, a leading figure in the "angel-oriented therapy" business is a California woman named Doreen Virtue, who at the time of this writing has sold three-quarters of a million copies of her book *Messages from Your Angels* (2003). And if you pay $150 a mortal head to attend one of her all-day workshops, Virtue will tell you that when you simply believe and tune into the ambient static of humdrum life all around you, you, too, will be able to pick up the clear signals of your friendly guardian angels, fairies, chakras, dead folks, and goddesses. Her publicist also advertises that, as a special treat, Virtue's clairvoyant son, Charles (who is curiously leading his own "angel certification program" in Germany), "will teach about a newly discovered archangel who assists you in making powerful and amazing changes in your life."[20] Amazing indeed.

Virtue's books are mostly compendiums of untempered anecdotes: enthusiastic, first-person testimonials from people who are absolutely convinced that invisible beings are in regular contact with them. In Virtue's latest book, *Signs from Above* (2009)—coauthored by her son—an ambivalent woman describes how she deferred to the advice of an angel with a feather fetish in making an important life decision.

I was driving to work one morning, having doubts about moving forward with my plans to reduce work hours so that I could focus on self-employment in my desired area. A moment later, I turned onto the highway. Suddenly, I was surrounded by a cloud of white feathers swirling all around my car. I wondered whether the vehicle ahead had hit a bird, but there was nothing on the road to indicate this. When I looked behind me in the rearview mirror, the feathers were gone! When I arrived at work, I found the purest white feather attached to my car. I've taken this to be a sign that I should move forward with my business and have accordingly reduced my hours.[21]

This woman may well owe her current business success (or perhaps lack thereof) to an unfortunate chicken that tumbled off a loaded poultry truck, but for our purposes that's neither here nor there. And, in fact, we don't have to subscribe to New Age belief systems to find ourselves reasoning in this general way. Although we often pay it very little notice, such thinking is prevalent in the nuances of our everyday lives. It can be as subtle as finding yourself in a bookstore, your fingers lighting inadvertently on the crooked spine of an old book that seemed as though you were *meant* to read it. A frustrating stream of slipups, delays, misplaced documents, or lost luggage at the airport could have even the most skeptical among us asking ourselves whether something—or rather someone—is trying to tell us not to get on that plane.

A year after her younger brother was killed in a tragic car accident, a very intelligent and clearheaded friend of mine confided in me that she had suddenly begun noticing frogs everywhere; she said she couldn't help but see this as a sort of communicative sign from her brother, because after all he had had a thing for frogs when he was alive. I'm not superstitious either, but I once gave a house purchase a split-second thought when I entered as a proud new owner and found a large dead raven lying prominently on the living room floor. And of course, my colorful history of run-ins with my dead mother just adds to the embarrassment of riches. It may be nonsense—all of it. But, owing to our overactive theory of mind, it's also completely natural.

———

The unexpected event that finally compelled me to channel my mom's spirit into an actual psychology experiment happened one day while

I was standing in front of the sink brushing my teeth. I heard a loud crash downstairs, glass shattering on hard floor. "The cat," I thought to myself. But the cat was upstairs on the bed, grinning, squinting, flicking its tail at me. Further inspection revealed that the noise had come from a decorative stained-glass windowpane that I had purchased at an antique store years before and had leaned precipitously against a wall. To this day I have no idea how it happened to fall, but I can tell you that I instinctively inferred that my mom's ghost was behind it, because it happened to be the anniversary of her death and I could have sworn she told me once that she wasn't very fond of the thing.

In any event, the incident finally got me thinking like a psychological scientist: what type of mind does it take to be superstitious, and how can one investigate this in the laboratory? So, in the summer of 2005, my University of Arkansas colleague Becky Parker and I began the first study ever to investigate the psychology underlying the human capacity to see messages—signs or omens—in unexpected natural events.[22] We knew that theory of mind was involved, because again such a capacity requires sleuthing out the mental reasons for the supernatural agent to have acted in such a manner. But because previous research had shown that a fully developed theory of mind does not appear in children's thinking until about four years of age (before this, children still mind-read, but they're just not as good at taking the perspectives of others and they tend to make frequent egocentric errors), we suspected there might be subtle, age-related differences in children's ability to engage in the divination of everyday events.

In these initial experiments, which have come to be known among my students as the "Princess Alice studies," we invited a group of three- to nine-year-old children into our lab and told them they were about to play a fun guessing game. It was a simple game in which each child was tested individually. The child was asked to go to the corner of the room and to cover his or her eyes before coming back and guessing which of two large boxes contained a hidden ball. All the child had to do was place a hand on the box that he or she believed contained the ball. A short time was allowed for the decision to be made but, importantly, during that time the children were allowed to change their mind at any time by moving their hand to the other box. The final answer on each of the four trials was reflected simply by where the child's hand was when the experimenter said, "Time's up!" Children who guessed right won a sticker prize.

In reality, the game was a little more complicated than this. There were secretly two balls, one in each box, and we had decided in advance whether the children were going to get it "right" or "wrong" on each of the four guessing trials. At the conclusion of each trial, the child was shown the contents of only one of the boxes. The other box remained closed. For example, for "wrong" guesses, only the unselected box was opened, and the child was told to look inside ("Aw, too bad. The ball was in the other box this time. See?"). Children who had been randomly assigned to the control condition were told that they had been successful on a random two of the four trials. Children assigned to the experimental condition received some additional information before starting the game. These children were told that there was a friendly magic princess in the room, "Princess Alice," who had made herself invisible. We showed them a picture of Princess Alice hanging against the door inside the room (an image that looked remarkably like Barbie), and we gave them the following information: "Princess Alice really likes you, and she's going to help you play this game. She's going to tell you, somehow, when you pick the *wrong* box." We repeated this information right before each of the four trials, in case the children had forgotten.

For every child in the study, whether assigned to the standard control condition ("No Princess Alice") or to the experimental condition

("Princess Alice"), we engineered the room such that a spontaneous and unexpected event would occur just as the child placed a hand on one of the boxes. For example, in one case, the picture of Princess Alice came crashing to the floor as soon as the child made a decision, and in another case a table lamp flickered on and off. (We didn't have to consult with Industrial Light & Magic to rig these surprise events; rather, we just arranged for an undergraduate student to lift a magnet on the other side of the door to make the picture fall, and we hid a remote control for the table lamp surreptitiously in the experimenter's pocket.) The predictions were clear: if the children in the experimental condition interpreted the picture falling and the light flashing as a sign from Princess Alice that they had chosen the wrong box, they would move their hand to the other box.

What we found was rather surprising, even to us. Only the oldest children, the seven- to nine-year-olds, from the experimental (Princess Alice) condition, moved their hands to the other box in response to the unexpected events. By contrast, their same-aged peers from the control condition failed to move their hands. This finding told us that the explicit *concept* of a specific supernatural agent—likely acquired from and reinforced by cultural sources—is needed for people to see communicative messages in natural events. In other words, children, at least, don't automatically infer meaning in natural events without first being primed somehow with the idea of an identifiable supernatural agent such as Princess Alice (or God, one's dead mother, or perhaps a member of Doreen Virtue's variegated flock of angels).

More curious, though, was the fact that the slightly younger children in the study, even those who had been told about Princess Alice, apparently failed to see any communicative message in the light-flashing or picture-falling events. These children kept their hands just where they were. When we asked them later why these things happened, these five- and six-year-olds said that Princess Alice had caused them, but they saw her as simply an eccentric, invisible woman running around the room knocking pictures off the wall and causing the lights to flicker. To them, Princess Alice was like a mischievous poltergeist with attention deficit disorder: she did things because she wanted to, and that's that. One of these children answered that Princess Alice had knocked the picture off the wall because she thought it looked better on the ground. In other words, they completely failed to see her "behavior" as having any meaningful connection with the decision they had just made on the guessing game; they saw no "signs" there.

The youngest children in the study, the three- and four-year-olds in both conditions, only shrugged their shoulders or gave physical explanations for the events, such as the picture not being sticky enough to stay on the wall or the light being broken. Ironically, these youngest children were actually the most scientific of the bunch, perhaps because they interpreted "invisible" to mean simply "not present in the room" rather than "transparent."[23] Contrary to the common assumption that superstitious beliefs represent a childish mode of sloppy and undeveloped thinking, therefore, the ability to be superstitious actually demands some mental sophistication. At the very least, it's an acquired cognitive skill.

Still, the real puzzle to our findings was to be found in the reactions of the five- and six-year-olds from the Princess Alice condition. Clearly they possessed the same understanding of invisibility as did the older children, because they also believed Princess Alice caused these spooky things to happen in the lab. Yet although we reminded these children repeatedly that Princess Alice would tell them, somehow, if they chose the wrong box, they failed to put two and two together.[24] So what is the critical change between the ages of about six and seven that allows older children to perceive natural events as being communicative messages *about* their own behaviors (in this case, their choice of box) rather than simply the capricious, arbitrary actions of some invisible or otherwise supernatural entity?

The answer probably lies in the maturation of children's theory-of-mind abilities in this critical period of brain development. Research by University of Salzburg psychologist Josef Perner, for instance, has revealed that it's not until about the age of seven that children are first able to reason about "multiple orders" of mental states.[25] This is the type of everyday, grown-up social cognition whereby theory of mind becomes effortlessly layered in complex, soap opera–style interactions with other people. Not only do we reason about what's going on inside someone else's head, but we also reason about what other people are reasoning is happening inside still other people's heads! For example, in the everyday (nonsupernatural) social domain, one would need this kind of mature theory of mind to reason in the following manner:

"Jakob thinks that Adrienne doesn't know I stole the jewels."

Whereas a basic ("first-order") theory of mind allows even a young preschooler to understand the first propositional clause in this statement, "Jakob thinks that . . . ," it takes a somewhat more mature ("second-order") theory of mind to fully comprehend the entire social scenario: "Jakob thinks that [Adrienne doesn't know] . . ."

Most people can't go much beyond four orders of mental-state reasoning (consider the Machiavellian complexities of, say, Leo Tolstoy's novels), but studies show that the absolute maximum in adults hovers around seven orders of mental state. The important thing to note is that, owing to their still-developing theory-of-mind skills, children younger than seven years of age have great difficulty reasoning about multiple orders of mental states. Knowing this then helps us understand the surprising results from the Princess Alice experiment. To pass the test (move their hand) in response to the picture falling or the light flashing, the children essentially had to be reasoning in the following manner:

> *"Princess Alice knows that [I don't know] where the ball is hidden."*

To interpret the events as communicative messages, as being *about* their choice on the guessing game, demands a sort of third-person perspective of the self's actions: "What must this other entity, who is watching my behavior, think is happening inside my head?" The Princess Alice findings are important because they tell us that, before the age of seven, children's minds aren't quite cognitively ripe enough to allow them to be superstitious thinkers. The inner lives of slightly older children, by contrast, are drenched in symbolic meaning. One second-grader was even convinced that the bell in the nearby university clock tower was Princess Alice "talking" to him.

Just think back to your own childhood memories, to the time when your everyday experiences first began bubbling up with rich, symbolic meaning—particularly with messages from "the other side." In one of my earliest diary entries, written when I was nine years old, I describe an encounter with a stray dog in the parking lot of a kerosene supply store where my father was shopping for a new space heater. The dog had approached me in a friendly manner before proceeding to coyly steal my new watch with its teeth and then promptly scurry off with it. The incident apparently made quite an impression on me, because it was the day after my own dog died and I saw the entire episode as a sort of playful, communicative gesture toward me, one emitted by the spirit of that other, decedent canine.

Princess Alice may not have the *je ne sais quoi* of Mother Mary or the fiery charisma of the Abrahamic God we're all familiar with, but she's arguably a sort of empirically constructed god-by-proxy in her own right. The point is, the same basic cognitive processes—namely, a mature theory of mind—are also involved in the believer's sense of receiving divine guidance from these other members of the more popular holy family. When people ask God to give them a sign, they're often at a standstill, a fork in the road, paralyzed in a critical moment of existential ambivalence. In such cases, our ears are pricked, our eyes widened, our thoughts ruminating on a particular problem—often "only God knows" what's on our minds and the extent to which we're struggling to make a decision. It's not questions like whether we should choose a different box, but rather decisions such as these: Should I stay with this person or leave him? Should I risk everything, start all over in a new city, or stay here where I'm stifled and bored? Should I have another baby? Should I continue receiving harsh treatment for my disease, or should I just pack it in and call it a life? Just like the location of the hidden ball inside one of those two boxes, we're convinced that there's a right and a wrong answer to such important life questions. And for most of us, it's God, not Princess Alice, who holds the privileged answers.

God doesn't tell us the answers directly, of course. There's no nod to the left, no telling elbow poke in our side or "psst" in our ear. Rather, we envision God, and other entities like Him, as encrypting strategic information in an almost infinite array of natural events: the prognostic stopping of a clock at a certain hour and time; the sudden shrieking of a hawk; an embarrassing blemish on our nose appearing on the eve of an important interview; a choice parking spot opening up at a crowded mall just as we pull around; an interesting stranger sitting next to us on a plane. The possibilities are endless. When the emotional climate is just right, there's hardly a shape or form that "evidence" cannot assume. Our minds make meaning by disambiguating the meaningless.

Oddly enough, each of us is also soundly convinced that God shares our opinions and points of view, so it makes sense that He would be motivated to help us by giving us hints here and there in the form of natural events. Members of the Topeka, Kansas–based Westboro Baptist Church, a faith community notorious for its antigay rhetoric and religious extremism (they run a charming little website called GodHatesFags), see signs of God's homophobic wrath in just about every catastrophe known to man. To them, the natural world is constantly chattering and abuzz with antigay slogans. In a seemingly bizarre twist of logic, the group frequently pickets the funerals of (heterosexual) fallen American soldiers who have died in Iraq, convinced that the war, like every other tragedy, is a God-hewn disaster caused by the nation's relaxing moral attitudes toward gays and lesbians. One such picketing event was at the memorial service of twenty-year-old Army Specialist Brushaun Anderson from Columbus, Georgia, who had died of non-combat-related injuries in Baghdad on the first day of 2010. "These soldiers are dying for the homosexual and other sins of America," read a Westboro Baptist flyer announcing their "peaceful" protest at Anderson's funeral. "God is now America's enemy, and God Himself is fighting against America." Church members proudly held up signs reading "Thank God for Dead Soldiers" and "Fags Doom Nations" only yards away from the young man's casket. In their minds, God is kindly sending us not-so-subtle messages, warning us through natural disasters to stop supporting the gay rights movement, or else it's going to get much, much worse. God hurts because He loves.[26]

Most of us, of course, believe that Westboro Baptist Church members have lost something in translation. Yet, recent findings by University of Chicago psychologist Nicholas Epley and his colleagues reveal that, wherever our attitudes happen to lie on certain hot-button issues, most of us are overwhelmingly certain that God also shares our opinion. This means that, whether we fall left or right in a political sense, we believe that God is on our side on everything from gay marriage to embryonic stem cell research to prayer in public schools to North Korea's nuclear weapons program. And when we genuinely change our minds about these things after hearing persuasive counterarguments, we're convinced that God—but not other people—has changed His mind as well (or at least we become convinced that our own revised stances on these touchy subjects reflected His *real* attitudes all along). Epley and his group didn't explore people's opinions about the devil's personal beliefs, but perhaps it's his job to lead us astray, coaxing us into making bad decisions with misleading signs in the guise of natural events.

In any event, the important take-home point is that natural events *outside the head* are filtered through our evolved theory of mind and interpreted subjectively *inside the head*. And our reasoning about anything outside of our own skulls does not necessarily reflect any intrinsic reality about what we perceive.

As an analogy, consider how we make sense of odor, a perceived cue that's much more mundane than meaning. You may be surprised to learn, but it's worth pointing out, that there really is no such thing as an intrinsically "bad smell." Rather, there are only olfactory stimuli; and how we perceive them is largely an artifact of our particularly human evolutionary heritage. To say that rotting flesh is disgusting is similar to saying that the sunset is beautiful: There's no "beautiful-ness" quality intrinsic to the sunset, just as there's no "disgusting-ness" intrinsic to rotting flesh. Rather, rotting flesh and sunsets are only perceived this way by the human mind; as phenomenological qualities, adjectives such as "beautiful" and "disgusting" and "wonderful" merely describe how we subjectively experience the natural world. I can assure you that whatever particular scents you find repulsive, my dog, Gulliver, would likely perceive as irresistibly appealing. And I mean rotting flesh and just about anything else you can think of, with the exception perhaps of skunk odor and his own feces, for which I can only hope you'd share a mutual disdain. Neither you nor Gulliver is "correctly perceiving" these smells; you're both simply sensing and translating them through perception according to your species' evolved dispositions.

Likewise, just because we humans see, feel, and experience meaning doesn't make meaning inherently so.

———◆———

When I moved to my current house in a small village in Northern Ireland in late 2007, there was still quite a bit of work to be done, including laying flooring in an intolerably small, outdated bathroom in the garage. So for about ten seconds each day, over a period of about a year, whenever I stood in my bare feet on that cold concrete floor doing what it is that human males do at a toilet, my eyes would inevitably zero in on an area of flooring just at the crook of the plumbing and the wall. Here the mysterious word "ORBY" appeared mockingly in white paint, scribbled on the cement like the singular flash of an artist signing a masterpiece in proud haste. For the longest time, in my usual groggy state first thing in the morning, this "Orby" character didn't particularly weigh on my thoughts. Rather, more often than not I would simply stumble back to bed, pondering why anyone—perhaps a contractor, a builder, a plumber, maybe the previous owner of the house—would have left this peculiar inscription on the floor behind a toilet. What blue-collar ribaldry between workers could have led to such an inscrutable act? Was it an inside joke? A coded message to someone special, someone who once stood at the very same toilet? And what kind of word or name was "Orby" anyway? Then, also more often than not, I'd drift off to sleep again and forget all about Orby, at least until my bladder would stir me awake next. That is, until one night when, snapping out of a drowsy, blinking delirium, I leaned down and studied it more closely. When I did this, it became embarrassingly obvious that "ORBY" wasn't a signature at all—just some randomly dribbled droplets of paint that looked, from a height, as if it spelled something meaningful and cryptic. "What an idiot I am!" I thought to myself.

Perhaps I shouldn't be so hard on myself. After all, several recent studies with young children have revealed that, from a very early age, humans associate the appearance of order with intentional agency. For example, in a study by Yale University psychologist George Newman and his colleagues, published in the *Proceedings of the National Academy of Sciences*, a group of four-year-olds was told a story about a little boy named Billy. Billy had been busy playing with his toys in his bedroom before deciding to go outside to play. The children were shown a picture of Billy's room when he left it, a picture focusing on several piles of toys arranged in a particular way. Next they were shown two cards, each depicting different changes to the bedroom that allegedly happened while Billy was outside. One card showed the piles of toys in the room stacked neatly together, arranged by color and size and so on. The other image showed these same objects, but in disarray. Half of the children in the study were told that a strong gust of wind had come in through an open window and changed the things in the room, whereas the other half were told that Billy's older sister, Julie, had made the changes. Then all of the children were simply asked, "Which of these piles looks most like if [Julie, the wind] changed it?" Those in the wind condition pointed strictly to the disordered objects, whereas those in the older-sister condition were just as likely to point to the disordered as they were to the ordered objects. In other words, these preschoolers believed that whereas inanimate causal forces such as wind can lead only to disorder, intentional agents (such as Billy's older sister, Julie) can cause either order *or* disorder. Amazingly, Newman and his coauthors used nonverbal measures to discover that even twelve-month-old infants display this same cognitive bias.[27]

These findings have clear implications for understanding the ineradicable plague of religious creationism discussed in the previous chapter. Newman and his colleagues write that "the tendency to use intentional agents to explain the existence of order has often been cited as the reason why people have used versions of the 'Argument from Design' to motivate intentional deities who create an ordered universe."[28] In *The Blind Watchmaker* (1986), Richard Dawkins famously criticized eighteenth-century theologian-philosopher William Paley's natural theology by showing clearly how mechanical evolutionary processes can create the appearance of creative intent without any forethought or intelligence being involved at all. But all those pre-Darwinian, "ecumaniacal," and unenlightened thinkers such as Paley weren't just swooning over some basic insinuation that God produced order simply for the sake of producing order. That in itself wasn't terribly interesting. Rather, these naturalists wanted to know why He organized things this way and not some other way.

One of the more intriguing implications of Newman's work, therefore, is its relevance to our search for meaning in nature. For the faithful, God is seen not only as a tidy homemaker who makes things nice and orderly, but as having left us clues—a sort of signature in the seams—so we'd know and understand His intentions in His use of order. If Julie went into her little brother's room and made a mess, for example, it's hard not to see this act as her also giving Billy a sneering message ("this is what you get when you tattle on me"), just as she would be sending a more positive message by thoughtfully organizing his toys ("I don't say it enough, but you're not half-bad as little brothers go"). Likewise, God is seen as embedding messages in the secret language of plants, organisms, genes, and all the poetic contingencies threading these things continuously together. At least, that's been the view of many famous naturalists throughout history who've strained to use their empiricism to solve the riddle of God, especially, of course, those employing their craft before the mainstreaming of Darwin's theory of natural selection.

On his deathbed in 1829, for example, an eccentric British aristocrat named Francis Egerton (also known as the 8th Earl of Bridgewater)—eccentric, among other things, because he was known to throw dinner parties for his dogs while dressing them up in the day's trendiest couture—left the Royal Society a portion of his financially swollen estate. The money was to be used to commission a group of prominent naturalists to write a major apologist creed "on the Power, Wisdom and Goodness of God, as manifested in the Creation."[29] (In other words, let's have a look at the natural world to see what's going on in God's mind.) Eventually, eight authors were selected as contributors, each paid a thousand pounds sterling, a handsome sum at the time. The individual books that were published as part of the project—what became known as *The Bridgewater Treatises*—trickled out over a period of seven long years (1833–1840). One of these, a hefty two-volume work by noted entomologist William Kirby,[30] sought to reconcile popular theological teachings with the extraordinary and subtle biological diversity in the animal kingdom that was so apparent to him. Kirby, an original member of the Linnean Society who had made a name for himself studying English bees on the grounds of a rural parsonage in Suffolk, seems to have seen himself more as detective than naturalist:

Since God created nothing in vain, we may rest assured that this system of representation was established with a particular view. The most common mode of instruction is placing certain signs or symbols before the eye of the learner, which represent sounds

*or ideas; and so the great Instructor of man placed this world
before him as an open though mystical book, in which the different
objects were the letters and words of a language, from the study
of which he might gain wisdom of various kinds.*[31]

Even in their day, *The Bridgewater Treatises* were so larded with
Christian propaganda that they were dismissed by most members
of the scientific community. The anatomist Robert Knox, a known
critic of natural theology (but better known as the anatomy professor involved in the infamous Burke and Hare body-snatching case,
in which Knox paid a pair of murderers to supply him with fresh
corpses for his dissection lectures at the University of Edinburgh),
apparently had a good sense of humor too, referring to them as "The
Bilgewater Treatises."[32] But despite the dubious quality of the work,
one can see from the Kirby passage highlighted above just how central theory of mind was, at the time, to the burgeoning field of natural theology.

In fact, it continues to be central to this day, and it is part of the
reason that many contemporary natural scientists see no inherent
conflict between their faith and their work. In self-proclaimed "evolutionary evangelist" Michael Dowd's *Thank God for Evolution* (2009),
the same old theme emerges anew. Dowd, who brandishes the unusual
self-identity as both Darwinian and Christian apologist, writes that
"facts are God's native tongue!":

*The discovery of facts through science is one very powerful way
to encounter God directly. It is through the now-global community of scientists, working together, challenging one another's
findings, and assisted by the miracles of technology, that "God's
Word" is still being revealed. It is through this ever-expectant,
yet ever-ready-to-be-humbled, stance of universal inquiry that*

God's Word is discerned as more wondrous and more this-world relevant than could have possibly been comprehended in any time past.[33]

You may be surprised to learn that natural theology still has its supporters among some rather prominent philosophers and scientists. In 2008, for example, the John Templeton Foundation sponsored a major international conference on the subject at Oxford's Museum of Natural History. The primary aim of this gathering—fittingly called "Beyond Paley: Renewing the Vision of Natural Theology"—was "to review every aspect of the question of whether the divine can be known through nature."[34] Just like William Kirby, modern-day advocates of natural theology tend to view God as a sort of enigmatic foreigner speaking a foreign tongue, the intricate and beautiful language of nature. And their primary scientific task is to translate this strange, almost unintelligible language into a form that reveals His benevolent, creative intentions for humanity. (Or at least one that satisfies their own personal view of what His intentions should be.) Guest speakers at the Oxford event were well-known figures in the Christian community, such as Simon Conway Morris (a Cambridge evolutionary paleobiologist whose Gifford Lecture the previous year had been titled "Darwin's Compass: How Evolution Discovers the Song of Creation"), Justin Barrett (a psychologist who believes that the human mind evolved in the way that God intended it to evolve, for us to perceive Him more accurately), and Alister McGrath (controversial author of *The Dawkins Delusion,* and one of the principal advocates of a modern-day "scientific theology").

What is ironic is that these contemporary scholars are, in all probability, using their mindlessly evolved theory of mind to make meaning of the meaningless. Either that, or we must concur with them that meaning is in fact "out there" and that the evolution of the human brain was indeed guided by God, a God that slowly, methodically, over billions of years, placed our ancestors into the perfect selective conditions in which they were able to develop the one adaptive trait—theory of mind—that, in addition to serving its own huge, independent, adaptive functions for interacting with other human beings, also enabled this one species to finally ponder His highly cryptic ways and to begin guessing about what's on His mind.

The theory of natural selection, of course, has more than enough explanatory oomph to get us from the primordial soup of Day 1 of life on earth to the head-spinning, space-traveling, finger-pointing, technologically ripe conurbations we see today. Even if an intentional God were needed for Existence with a capital "E" (which is by no means obvious), He certainly wasn't needed for our particular human existence. Neither was He needed for the evolution of the cognitive system—theory of mind—that has allowed us to develop theories about unobservable mental states, including His. And He definitely wasn't needed to account for what we've evolved to perceive as "good" and "evil"; that, too, is the clear handiwork of natural selection operating on our brains and behaviors.

There's no more reason to believe that God frets about the social, sexual, or moral behaviors of human beings—just one of hundreds of presently living species of primates—than there is to believe that He's deeply concerned about what Mediterranean geckos have for lunch or that He loses sleep over whether red-billed oxpeckers decide to pick bloated parasites off the backs of cows or rhinoceroses in the Sudan. We are just one of billions of species occupying this carbon-infused planet spinning in this solar system, and every single one of these species, along with every single detail of their bodies, behaviors, and brains (even if they lack bodies, behaviors, and brains) can be accounted for by natural evolutionary processes. As the legendary biologist J. B. S. Haldane replied cheekily after being asked what he had learned about God from his work in studying evolution, "The Creator, if He exists, has an inordinate fondness for beetles."[35]

Isn't it astounding how all the convoluted, endless paths of thought, all the divine wild goose chases ever known or to be known, begin and end with the same cognitive capacity—this theory of mind?

4 | CURIOUSLY IMMORTAL

IN HIS NOVEL *The Counterfeiters* (1925), the French author André Gide introduces us to a disheartened, world-weary old man named Monsieur de La Pérouse. With his wife gone and his beloved grandchild painfully indifferent to his affections, La Pérouse decides to end his lonely life once and for all. For years, he has kept a pistol at his bedside for precisely this sad occasion. But oddly enough, when he finally decides to go through with his suicide, the old man finds himself in a rather unexpected psychological predicament:

I stayed a long time with the pistol to my temple. My finger was on the trigger. I pressed it a little; but not hard enough. I said to myself: "In another moment I shall press harder and it will go off." I felt the cold of the metal and I said to myself: "In another moment I shall not feel anything. But before that I shall hear a terrible noise" ... Just think! So near to one's ear! That's the chief thing that prevented me—the fear of the noise ... It's absurd, for as soon as one's dead ... Yes, but I hope for death as a sleep; and a detonation doesn't send one to sleep—it wakes one up.[1]

La Pérouse's dilemma is a good example of how our evolved theory of mind has come to play an interesting trick on us in our ability to reason clearly about death. It's not just God's or other people's minds that we're so busy thinking about, but also our own minds. And reasoning about our future selves, particularly what we'll be experiencing given an imagined set of hypothetical variables such as those believed to be present in the afterlife, is much like reasoning about what it's like to be another person. Both rest on our ability to temporarily suspend—in Rutgers University psychologist Alan Leslie's terms, "de-couple"[2]—the actual here and now of our present mental experiences and to put ourselves in the shoes of a different character faced with an entirely different set of realities. After all, who or *what* are the dead (even our own future dead selves) but bodiless minds?

For *The Counterfeiters'* old La Pérouse, who desires nothing but the peaceful obliteration of all his obsessive, depressing thoughts, who hopes to enter into the endless void of dreamless sleep, his trigger finger is paralyzed by this theory-of-mind block. As a materialist, he realizes it's silly, yet he can't help but fear the jolting boom—a sound that, in his imminently destroyed brain, wouldn't linger long enough for him to flinch.

⸺•⸺

From the perspective of a psychological scientist, the central question is not whether there is or is not an afterlife, but instead why this question arises at all. And it's not just religion where we find it flaring up. The question of what happens to us after we die is a staple of popular culture. And the assumption, in nearly every case, is that we are more than just our physical bodies—that our bodies contain an "essence," or a "soul," that unhinges itself at death. As consumers in the world of secular entertainment, we are inundated with products featuring the ghost genre. There's a virtual glut of dead souls gumming up our television channels (such as the CBS series *Ghost Whisperer*, James Van Praagh's *The Other Side,* and a spate of British paranormal "reality" shows such as *Most Haunted*); our movie theaters (everything from *The Sixth Sense* [1999] to children's films such as *Coraline* [2009] feature the translucent spirits of the dead); our bookstores (recent titles include Van Praagh's *Unfinished Business: What the Dead Can Teach Us about Life* and Sylvia Browne's *All Pets Go to Heaven*)—even our radio stations. You'd be forgiven, for example, if ever you found yourself on a quiet drive nodding your head along in agreement with the twangy, sweetly discordant lyrics of folk singer Iris Dement's "Let the Mystery Be" (1993), a humble paean about the hereafter in which Dement assures us that "no one knows for certain" what happens when we die and so we shouldn't fool ourselves into thinking otherwise.

In fact, the only real mystery is why we're so convinced that when it comes to where we're going "when the whole thing's done," we're dealing with a mystery at all. After all, the brain is like any other organ: a part of our physical body. And the mind is what the brain does—it's more a verb than it is a noun. Why do we wonder where our mind goes when the body is dead? Shouldn't it be obvious that the mind is dead too?

Yet, people in every culture believe in an afterlife of some kind or, at the very least, are unsure about what happens to the mind at death. My own psychological research in this area has led me to believe that these illogical beliefs, rather than resulting from religion or serving only to protect us from the terror of inexistence, are also an inevitable by-product of our theory of mind. In thinking about the "what's next" after death, our everyday theory of mind is inadequate; in fact, it falls flat on its face. Because we have never consciously experienced a lack of consciousness, we cannot imagine what it will feel like to be dead. In fact, it won't feel like anything—and therein lies the problem.

The common view of death as a great mystery usually is brushed aside by science-minded individuals as an emotionally fueled desire to believe that death isn't the end of the road. And indeed, a prominent school of research in social psychology called "terror management theory" contends that afterlife beliefs, as well as less obvious beliefs, behaviors, and attitudes, exist to assuage what would otherwise be crippling anxiety about the ego's inexistence.

According to terror management theorists, you possess a secret arsenal of psychological defenses designed to keep your death anxiety at bay (and to keep you from ending up in the fetal position while listening to Nick Drake on your iPod). My writing this book, for example, would be interpreted as an exercise in "symbolic immortality"; terror management theorists would likely tell you that I wrote it for posterity, to enable a concrete set of my ephemeral ideas to outlive me, the biological organism. (I would tell you that I'd be happy enough if a year from now the book still had a faint pulse.) But one sign of trouble for terror management theory is that other researchers have consistently failed to find any correlation between fear of death and belief in the afterlife. In other words, just because someone has a lot of death anxiety doesn't mean she's particularly likely to believe in life after death; there's simply no connection.

A few researchers, including me, argue increasingly that the evolution of theory of mind has posed a different kind of problem altogether when it comes to our ability to comprehend death. This position holds that, owing to their inherent inability to project themselves sufficiently into an afterlife devoid of all sensation and mental experience, our ancestors suffered the unshakable illusion that their minds were immortal. It's this cognitive hiccup of gross irrationality that we have unmistakably inherited from them. Individual human beings, by virtue of the evolved human cognitive architecture, and specifically the always-on human theory of mind, had trouble conceptualizing their own psychological inexistence from the start.

The problem applies even to those who claim not to believe in an afterlife. As philosopher and Center for Naturalism founder Thomas W. Clark wrote in a 1994 article for *The Humanist*,

> *Here . . . is the view at issue: When we die, what's next is nothing; death is an abyss, a black hole, the end of experience; it is eternal nothingness, the permanent extinction of being. And here, in a nutshell, is the error contained in that view: It is to reify noth-ingness—make it a positive condition or quality (for example, of "blackness")—and then to place the individual in it after death, so that we somehow fall into nothingness, to remain there eternally.*[3]

Consider the rather startling fact that you will never know you have died. You may feel yourself slipping away, but it isn't as though there will be a "you" around who is capable of ascertaining that, once all is said and done, it has actually happened. Just to remind you, you need a working cerebral cortex to harbor propositional knowledge of any sort, including the fact that you've died—and once you've died, your brain is about as phenomenally generative as a head of lettuce. In a 2007 article published in the journal *Synthese*, University of Arizona philosopher Shaun Nichols puts it this way: "When I try to imagine my own non-existence I have to imagine that I perceive or know about my non-existence. No wonder there's an obstacle!"[4]

This observation may not sound like a major revelation, but I bet you've never considered what it actually means, which is that your own mortality is unfalsifiable from the first-person perspective. This obstacle is why the nineteenth-century German writer Johann Wolfgang von Goethe allegedly remarked that "everyone carries the proof of his own immortality within himself."[5] And although

Sigmund Freud ultimately abandoned this line of thought in favor of the disappointingly more lackluster "wish fulfillment" theory of belief in the afterlife (essentially, the catchall skeptic's view that we believe because we want it to be true), even the father of psychoanalysis once started digging in this direction. In his essay, *Thoughts for the Times on War and Death* (1913), Freud pondered why young soldiers were so eager to join the ranks during the First World War, and he concluded that this strange glitch of the human mind probably had something to do with it. "Our own death is indeed quite unimaginable," he wrote, "and whenever we make the attempt to imagine it we can perceive that we really survive as spectators . . . in the unconscious every one of us is convinced of his own immortality."[6]

Camus wrote of an atheistic and materialist doctor in *The Plague* (1947) who once mused on the black fate of his plague-stricken patients: "And I, too, I'm no different. But what matter? Death means nothing to men like me. It's the event that proves them right."[7] We can see now how Camus' doctor is fundamentally mistaken; given that he won't be there to confirm his own hypothesis, he's apparently unaware that such proof remains eternally just out of his reach.

Psychological disorders often provide insight into normal cognitive processes gone awry. A rare delusional disorder called Cotard's syndrome frequently manifests as the belief that, though conscious, one doesn't exist, or that one is already dead yet psychologically immortal. Two French psychiatrists, David Cohen and Angèle Consoli, describe one such case in a commentary: "The delusion consisted of the patient's absolute conviction she was already dead and waiting to be buried, that she was immortal, that she had no teeth or hair, and that her uterus was malformed." The authors conclude that "the very existence of Cotard's syndrome supports [the] view of a cognitive system dedicated to forming illusory representations of immortality."[8]

It's not just existential philosophers, psychiatric patients, and eccentric characters in old French novels who err in this way. A study I published in the *Journal of Cognition and Culture* in 2002 reveals the illusion of immortality operating in full swing in the minds of undergraduate students who were asked a series of questions about the psychological faculties of a dead man, a schoolteacher with marital problems named Richard.[9] Richard, I told the students, had been killed instantaneously when his vehicle plowed into a utility pole. After the participants read a narrative about Richard's state of mind just before the accident (he was said to be busy ruminating about his wife's infidelity as he drove to work), I queried them as to whether the man, now that he was dead, retained the capacity to experience mental states. "Is Richard still thinking about his wife?" I asked them. "Can he still taste the breath mint he ate just before he died? Does he want to be alive?"

You can imagine the looks I got, because apparently not many people pause to consider whether souls have taste buds, become randy, or get headaches. Yet most of these test subjects gave answers indicative of "psychological-continuity reasoning," in which they envisioned Richard's mind to continue functioning despite his death. For example, they said things such as, "He isn't angry at his wife anymore because he sees the bigger picture now and has forgiven her," or "He still remembers what he studied last night in preparation for his lesson today, but that stuff doesn't matter anymore," or "He doesn't want to be alive, because it's better where he is now." In general, this finding of psychological-continuity reasoning came as no surprise, given that, on a separate scale, most respondents classified themselves as having a belief in some form of an afterlife.

What was surprising, however, was that many participants who had identified themselves as having "extinctivist" beliefs (they had ticked off the box that read, "What we think of as the 'soul,' or conscious personality of a person, ceases permanently when the body dies") occasionally gave such continuity responses too. In fact, 32 percent of the extinctivists' answers betrayed their hidden reasoning that Richard's emotions and desires survived his death; another 36 percent of their responses suggested that the extinctivists reasoned this way for Richard's "higher-order" mental states (such as remembering, believing, or knowing). For example, one particularly vehement extinctivist thought the whole line of questioning silly and seemed to regard me as a numskull for even asking. But just as well, he proceeded to point out that of course Richard knows he's dead, because there's no afterlife and Richard sees that now. This student reminded me of the English poet John Gay, who had this rather playful epitaph inscribed on his tombstone in 1732:

Life is a jest, and all things show it; I thought so once, and now I know it.[10]

In many cases, religious or spiritual participants rejected the possibility that Richard's bodily and perceptual states (such as being thirsty or being able to taste) survived his death by submitting that these types of mental states were "physical things" or "functions of the body," whereas Richard's emotional, desire, and knowledge states went on because they were "spiritual things." But, of course, cognitive neuroscientists would largely disagree with that assessment.

Being aware of the illusory nature of the problem does little to quell our fears. Even when we desperately want to believe that our minds end at death, that "nothingness" is just a reification, a trick of the mind, it is a real struggle to think practically in this way. Who, for instance, wouldn't squirm along with the character of Pablo as he finds himself uncomfortably living through the immediate aftermath of his pending execution in Sartre's short story "The Wall" (1939)? In this tale set during the Spanish civil war, Pablo is a resistance fighter imprisoned with two other inmates and led to believe that he's to be shot dead at dawn by a firing squad while standing blindfolded against a prison yard wall. "Something's the matter," his cell mate says to Pablo. "I see my corpse; that's not hard but I'm the one who sees it, with my eyes. I've got to think . . . think that I won't see anything anymore and the world will go on for the others. We aren't made to think that."[11] Ironically, nearly forty years after writing this story, a confused and elderly Sartre awoke in a hospital bed only to tug on his nurse's shirtsleeve demanding to know if he was dead.

———◆———

So why is it so hard to conceptualize inexistence anyway? Part of my own account, which I call the "simulation constraint hypothesis," is that in attempting to imagine what it's like to be dead, we appeal to our own background of conscious experiences—because that's how we approach most thought experiments. Death isn't *like* anything we've ever experienced, however. Because we have never consciously been without consciousness, even our best simulations of true nothingness just aren't good enough.

For us extinctivists, it's kind of like staring into a hallway of mirrors—but rather than confronting a visual trick, we're dealing with cognitive reverberations of subjective experience. In Spanish philosopher Miguel de Unamuno's existential screed, *The Tragic Sense of Life* (1912), one can almost see the author tearing out his hair contemplating this very fact. "Try to fill your consciousness with the representation of no-consciousness," he writes, "and you will see the impossibility of it. The effort to comprehend it causes the most tormenting dizziness."[12]

Wait, you say, isn't Unamuno forgetting something? We certainly do have experience with nothingness. Every night, in fact, when we're in dreamless sleep. But you'd be mistaken in this assumption. Thomas W. Clark puts it this way: "We may occasionally have the *impression* of having experienced or 'undergone' a period of unconsciousness, but, of course, this is impossible. The 'nothingness' of unconsciousness cannot be an experienced actuality."[13] The same, of course, goes for that exhaustively long epoch that was life before us—that vast, yawning stretch of time before our conception that we similarly never experienced. In fact, some preliminary evidence found by one of my graduate students, Natalie Emmons, suggests that young children reason about their preexistent minds just as they do for minds in the afterlife, looking back on this "state" as though they were a psychological entity awaiting life.[14]

If psychological immortality represents the intuitive, natural way of thinking about death, then we might expect young children to be particularly inclined to reason in this way. As an eight-year-old, I watched as the remains of our family's golden retriever, Sam, were buried in the woods behind our house. I knew very well that her brain, which was responsible for her thinking and behavior, was among these ashes. Still, I thought Sam had a mind, somehow separate from her physical brain, capable of knowing I loved her. That Sam's spirit lived on was not something my parents or anyone else ever explicitly pointed out to me. Although she had been reduced to no more than a few ounces of dust, which was in turn sealed in a now waterlogged box, it never even occurred to me that reasoning about my dead dog's feelings was a rather strange thing to be doing.

Yet if you were to have asked me what Sam was experiencing now that she was dead, I probably would have muttered something like the type of answer Gerald P. Koocher reported hearing in a 1973 study published in *Developmental Psychology*. Koocher, then a doctoral student at the University of Missouri–Columbia and later president of the American Psychological Association, asked six- to fifteen-year-olds what happens when people die. Consistent with the simulation constraint hypothesis, many answers relied on everyday experience to describe death, "with references to sleeping, feeling 'peaceful,' or simply 'being very dizzy.'"[15]

Koocher's study in itself doesn't tell us where such ideas come from. Fortunately, this question can be explored using scientific methods. If afterlife beliefs are a product of cultural indoctrination, with children picking up such ideas through religious teachings, through the media, or informally through family and friends, then one would reasonably predict that psychological-continuity reasoning increases with age. Aside from becoming more aware of their own mortality, after all, older kids have had a longer period of exposure to the concept of an afterlife. In fact, however, recent findings show the opposite developmental trend. In a 2004 study reported in *Developmental Psychology*, Florida Atlantic University psychologist David Bjorklund and I performed a puppet show for two hundred three- to twelve-year-olds. Every child was presented with the story of Baby Mouse, who was out strolling innocently in the woods. "Just then," we told them, "he notices something very strange. The bushes are moving! An alligator jumps out of the bushes and gobbles him all up. Baby Mouse is not alive anymore."[16]

Just like the adults from the previously mentioned study, the children were asked about the dead character's psychological functioning. "Does Baby Mouse still want to go home?" we asked them. "Does he still feel sick?" "Can he still smell the flowers?" The youngest children in the study, the three- to five-year-olds, were significantly more likely to reason in terms of psychological continuity than were children from the two older age groups. But here's the really curious part. Even the preschoolers had a solid grasp of biological cessation; they knew, for example, that dead Baby Mouse didn't need food or water anymore. They knew he wouldn't grow up to be an adult mouse. Eighty-five percent of the youngest kids even told us that his brain no longer worked. Yet, in answering our specific questions, most of these very young children still attributed thoughts and emotions to dead Baby Mouse, telling us that he was hungry or thirsty, that he felt better, or that he was still angry at his brother. One couldn't say that the preschoolers lacked a concept of death, therefore, because nearly all of the kids realized that biological imperatives no longer apply after death. Rather, they seemed to have trouble using this knowledge to theorize about related mental functions.

From an evolutionary perspective, some scholars believe that a coherent theory about psychological death is not necessarily vital. Anthropologist H. Clark Barrett of the University of California at Los Angeles, argues instead that understanding the cessation of bodily "agency" (for example, that a dead creature isn't going to suddenly leap up and bite you) is probably what saved lives (and thus genes) in the ancestral past. According to Barrett, comprehending the cessation of the mind, on the other hand, has no survival value and is, in an evolutionary sense, neither here nor there.[17]

In a 2005 study published in the journal *Cognition*, Barrett and psychologist Tanya Behne of the University of Manchester in England reported that city-dwelling four-year-olds from Berlin were just as good at distinguishing sleeping animals from dead ones as were hunter-horticulturalist children from the Shuar region of Ecuador.[18] So even today's urban children, who generally have very little exposure to dead bodies, appear tuned in to perceptual cues signaling death. A "violation of the body envelope" (in other words, a mutilated carcass) is a pretty good sign that one needn't worry about tiptoeing around.

On the one hand, then, from a very early age, children realize that dead bodies are not coming back to life. On the other hand, also from a very early age, kids endow the dead with ongoing psychological functions, using their theory of mind. This conception may be at least partially why the idea of brainless zombies seems to us so implausible and the stuff of horror movies, limited to only a handful of cultures, whereas some type of spiritual afterlife, with the mindful souls of the deceased passing on to the other side, is by contrast strikingly mundane. So just where do culture and religious teaching come into the mix, if at all?

In fact, exposure to the concept of an afterlife plays a crucial role in enriching and elaborating this natural cognitive stance; it's sort of like constructing an architectural scaffolding, except in this case culture develops and decorates the innate psychological building blocks of religious belief. The end product can be as ornate or austere as you like, from the headache-inducing reincarnation beliefs of Theravada Buddhists to the man in the street's "I believe there's *something*" brand of philosophy—but it's made of the same brick and mortar. The idea of an afterlife, whatever the specifics, is guided by our intuitions, and these intuitions are enabled only by our illusion-generating theory of mind. Again, our theory of mind allows us to think about our own brainless minds after death, as well as those of our dead loved ones. From a basic cognitive science perspective, then, the specific nature of the afterlife belief is largely irrelevant; it makes no difference whether the soul is believed to ascend, descend, transmigrate, slumber, hover, or recycle. The point is that the soul is likened to personal consciousness, or some mindful "essence" of the individual, and is seen as being curiously immortal all the same.[19]

In support of the idea that culture enhances our natural tendency to deny the death of the mind, Harvard University psychologist Paul Harris and researcher Marta Giménez of the National University of Distance Education in Spain showed that when the wording in children's interviews is tweaked to include medical or scientific terms, psychological-continuity reasoning decreases. In their 2005 study published in the *Journal of Cognition and Culture*, seven- to eleven-year-old children in Madrid who had heard a story about a priest telling a child that his grandmother was "with God" were more likely to attribute ongoing mental states to the decedent than were those who had heard the identical story but instead about a doctor saying a grandfather was "dead and buried."[20]

And in a 2005 replication of the Baby Mouse experiment published in the *British Journal of Developmental Psychology*, David Bjorklund and I teamed up with psychologist Carlos Hernández Blasi of Jaume I University in Spain to compare children in a Catholic school with those attending a public secular school in Castellón, Spain. As in the previous study, an overwhelming majority of the youngest children—five- to six-year-olds—from both educational backgrounds said that Baby Mouse's mental states survived after death. The type of curriculum, secular or religious, made no difference. With increasing age, however, culture clearly became a factor: the kids attending Catholic school were more likely to reason in terms of psychological continuity than were those at the secular school. There was even a smattering of young extinctivists in the latter camp.[21]

What we can make of this overall collection of findings on children's reasoning about the mind after death is that education matters, but perhaps not as much as is commonly thought. Rather than simply being inculcated by religious adults, the default belief in young children is that mental capacities survive death, albeit in some vague, unarticulated way. It would be somewhat misleading to interpret these findings as meaning that toddlers have "afterlife beliefs," because, as we've seen, the afterlife is a variable social concept that is enriched and given texture and specific cultural details through social transmission. Instead, young children are best envisioned as being naturally *prepared* to endorse the concept of an afterlife because it matches their own intuitions about the continuity of the mind after death. Just as our species' teleo-functional reasoning, erroneously applied to the category of human existence, biases us naturally toward creationist explanations and beliefs in destiny, so, too, does our theory of mind, erroneously applied to the stateless state of death, orient us toward belief in the afterlife.

———

The types of cognitive obstacles we've covered so far may be responsible for our innate sense of immortality. But although the simulation constraint hypothesis helps explain why so many people believe in something as fantastically illogical as an afterlife, it doesn't tell us why we so often see the soul as unbuckling itself from the body and floating off like an invisible helium balloon into the realm of eternity. After all, there's nothing to stop us from having afterlife beliefs that involve the still-active mind being entombed in the skull and deliriously happy, or perhaps hallucinating an eternity in the seconds before brain death. Yet almost nobody has such a belief. Rather, Pessoa sums up most people's gut feelings in *The Book of Disquiet* (1916):

> *Whenever I see a dead body, death seems to me a departure. The corpse looks to me like a suit that was left behind. Someone went away and didn't need to take the one and only outfit he'd worn.*[22]

Like our attribution of mental states to the brainless dead, this tendency to think of the invisible soul as flitting off into another, unseen world can also be explained by cognitive factors. Back when you were still in diapers, you learned that people don't cease to exist simply because you can't see them. Developmental psychologists even have a fancy term for this basic concept: *person permanence.* Such an off-line social awareness leads us to tacitly assume that the people we know are somewhere doing something. As I'm writing this sentence in Belfast, for example, my mind's eye conjures up my friend Ginger in New Orleans walking her poodle or playfully bickering with her husband—things that I know she does routinely.

The relevance of person permanence thinking for our tendency to imagine the afterlife as a *place,* in which the soul is thought to abound elsewhere, is something that several unfortunate Boca Raton, Florida, families know about all too well. One hot, mid-July afternoon in 1979, ten teenagers crammed into a gold-colored Dodge van and, probably along with a few cases of beer, left for a beach party in the nearby city of Hallandale. Afterward, some of the teens "got a wild idea" to go on a road trip,[23] perhaps taking Florida's Turnpike 150 miles north to Melbourne. Five dissenters refused to go along with this hasty plan and disembarked near a highway exit in Boca Raton. The other five—four boys and a girl—sped off in the van into the meridian sunset and would never be seen or heard from again, or so it seemed for a very long time.

For almost two decades, the families of these five young people could only speculate about what had become of them. Missing-person reports were filed, and rumors began floating around that the group had joined a hippy commune somewhere out West. A few years after their disappearance, someone even called in to the *Phil Donahue Show* to say that the missing girl was alive and well in California, where she and one of the missing boys had gotten married and were happily raising two children together. The sobering truth of that mysterious night, however, came to light in February 1997, when a fisherman wearing a pair of polarized sunglasses happened to spot the metallic glint of an immense gold object twenty feet below his boat, resting on the floor of a murky Boca Raton drainage canal. Inside the ancient van, caked with algae and encrusted with mud, were the skeletal remains of the five missing teenagers. But would knowing that their loved ones died that night have stopped the family members from imagining the teens as being "out there" somewhere anyway? Probably not. "I'm glad to know that [he's] been with God the last seventeen years," said one of the dead boy's sisters on learning of the discovery.[24] The afterlife, too, is a place.

Human cognition is not equipped to update the list of players in our complex social rosters by accommodating a particular person's sudden inexistence. We can't simply switch off our person permanence thinking just because someone has died. This cognitive inability becomes especially relevant, of course, for those whom we were closest to and whom we frequently imagined to be actively engaging in various activities when out of our sight. The central character of John Fowles's cult classic *The Magus* (1966) finds himself trying to get his head around precisely this problem of person permanence when his lover unexpectedly dies:

> *I forced myself to stop thinking of her as someone still somewhere, if only in memory, still obscurely alive, breathing, doing, moving, but as a shovelful of ashes; as a broken link, a biological dead end, an eternal withdrawal from reality.*[25]

For those who believe in the afterlife, person permanence thinking also relates to how the dead are mentally represented, or envisioned in our minds, in real time. In some sense, cleaving apart bodies and souls in the dualistic manner we've just discussed doesn't seem to match our everyday pondering of particular dead people in the afterlife—namely, our loved ones. According to Queen's University Belfast philosopher Mitch Hodge, if you were to conduct a poll on the street asking people to define the soul, most would likely say that it's something that survives bodily death, shedding our miserable corpses and so on. But the truth is, Hodge argues, it's impossible for us to imagine all those souls clamoring about in the afterlife without also picturing them as being embodied in some form.[26]

Dualism is very much a this-worldly concept, then, failing to extend itself to our representation of souls in the afterlife. For example, when you think of your dead grandmother in heaven (or hell, as the case may be), she must look like something of substance, even if it's just a wispy spirit or a nebulous shadow. She probably looks to you much like you remember her in life. What's more, she's probably not naked—at least, I hope not—but wearing clothes of some kind. Just think: if the soul were truly as ethereal as we tend to say it is, a merciless tongue of fire couldn't lap the sinner's skin, and the martyr couldn't find bliss in the fleshy bosom of his promised seventy-two virgins, nor could familiar faces of those that have gone before flash us a warm, toothy grin as we "entered the light."

In other words, the gist of Hodge's argument is that when we think of the dead, and ourselves as being dead, commonsense dualism isn't easily applied in practice; it's actually more commonsensical for us to think of the soul as a sort of physical body—just elsewhere. When Richard Stockton College psychologist David Lester and his colleagues probed undergraduate students' ideas about the afterlife for a 2002 article in the journal *Omega*, they found this same apparent contradiction between the students' explicit beliefs about heaven and their practical reasoning about the bodiless souls therein:

They [undergraduate students] believe that souls leave the body,
yet they then do not foresee a problem in recognizing other bodi-
less souls in the afterlife. If I suggest that maybe the spirits wear
name-tags, they laugh but have no better suggestion to make.[27]

How to locate your loved ones in the afterlife isn't a problem we
can solve here. But it's clear that when combined with the simulation
constraints of our theory of mind, person permanence is another cognitive hurdle that gets in the way of our effectively realizing the dead
as they truly are—infinitely in situ, inanimate carbon residue. Instead
it's much more natural to imagine them as existing in some exotic,
unobservable locale, very much living their dead lives.

———◆———

The science of soul beliefs is a fascinating affair, and it's one that cognitive scientists have only just started to investigate properly using
experimental methods and controlled procedures. The findings to
date cast considerable doubt on the everyday assumption that belief
in the afterlife can be explained away by a hand-waving "wish fulfillment" theory—one positing that we believe because we wish it
to be true. Although the fear of death is undoubtedly an important
motivator in people's clinging tenaciously to the illusion of immortality once it arises, it fails to account sufficiently for the illusion in
the first place. After all, there are many things you may wish to be
true—that on December 21, 2016, the clouds will gather and rain
chocolate gloriously down upon you; that you will live to see your
five hundredth birthday, healthy and fit as a thirty-year-old but wise
as a biblical sage; or that tomorrow at noon, and every day thereafter
for twenty minutes a day, you'll turn into a beautiful butterfly. That
these examples strike us as pleasant or desirable but still patently

absurd, while the equally bizarre idea that your mental life can exist independently of your physical brain sounds completely reasonable to most intelligent and perfectly sane people, speaks directly to the cognitively seductive power of a theory of mind misplaced.

Indeed, it's only through intellectual labor, and after countless millennia of thinking intuitively otherwise, that today we can arrive at the most obvious of all possible syllogisms: *The mind is what the brain does; the brain stops working at death; therefore, after death the mind no longer exists.* The subjective feeling that the mind survives death is a psychological illusion operating in the brains of the living. Can the answer to the question of what happens to us after death, such a profound mystery, really be this simple? To argue that the mind does survive after death would require demonstrating that at least one of the two premises in the argument is in any way false.

———

So far, we have seen how evolved human cognition—in particular, our theory of mind—is directly responsible for the illusions of purpose and destiny, for the feeling that otherworldly communicative messages are encrypted in the occurrence of natural events, and, finally, for our intuitions that our mental lives will persist in the wake of our complete neurological death. But one thing we haven't yet seen is how these three fundamental illusions come together in a single mind to ground the self in a meaningful world, particularly when it comes to our moral reasoning. In the next chapter we will explore this link between the illusions of purpose, signs, and the afterlife by revisiting the old theological question, "Why do bad things happen to good people?" And, again, theory of mind can help us understand and interpret the hidden assumptions in this timeless question in a very new light.

5 | WHEN GOD THROWS PEOPLE OFF BRIDGES

WE'LL PROBABLY NEVER know the strange confluence of thoughts that converged in the head of William Cooke, proprietor of Cooke's Circus, in the spring of 1845, compelling him to float down the River Bure as "Nelson the Clown" in a bathtub pulled by four straining geese. But news of the much-anticipated stunt certainly got the good people of Great Yarmouth—a busy seaside community in the Norfolk Broads of eastern England—talking. On the second of May, Cooke and his feathered crew were ready to set sail from the British resort town's quays; and by five o'clock that evening, hundreds of people, mostly eager, wide-eyed school-children who had seen Cooke's colorful circus handbills plastered around the district, gathered anxiously on an eighty-foot iron sus-pension bridge waiting for a glimpse of the comic scene. No one seemed to notice the confederate rowboat, which was pulling the bathtub along by a hidden cable just below the surface of the water. But wishing to maximize his exposure to the audience overhead, on approaching the town Cooke signaled to the rower to adjust course ever so slightly, thus guaranteeing a direct pass under the bridge and causing the giggling throng of onlookers above to rush en masse to its center of gravity.

The rest is, alas, an unfortunate history. "There arose a dreadful cry: a loud unearthly shriek," reported the *Norfolk Chronicle* a few days after the tragedy. "And in an instant, those who were a moment earlier full of 'lusty life,' with hearts beating in joyous excitement were launched into eternity."[1] Reports vary as to the precise number of townsfolk who lost their lives that notorious day, but about a hundred people perished, among them some sixty children. Around midnight, the boatmen pulled from the water the body of a woman with a small infant still clutched to her breast, her four-year-old daughter's hand still in her own. "She had kept hold of both even in death, and her grasp was so tight that the bodies were not easily separated." Meanwhile, says the reporter, "many children were found with their heads fast in the railing of the bridge, and were extricated with difficulty, some with broken arms and legs."[2]

Nelson the Clown survived the accident thoroughly intact. Following the official inquest, he fled the city of Great Yarmouth with his infamous geese, this time in tow, with neither appearing again in the annals of historical clownery. The jury concluded that the bridge had collapsed because of a welding defect and inferior workmanship and held one William Cory, owner of the construction company that originally built the bridge, mostly responsible.

Apart from some other rather trivial details, little else is known about the Yarmouth suspension bridge disaster of 1845, but from the solemn inquest reports we can imagine the pedestrian's view of the somber scene: sodden, limp bodies of drowned toddlers plucked from the river and rushed frantically to the candlelit terraced houses near the bridge; feverishly whispered prayers heard in the darkened cobblestone alleyways; young siblings torn suddenly and forever asunder by steel and water; and wearied boatmen casting their oars listlessly about the still water for newly risen corpses of the innocents.

Little is reported about the townspeople's desperate attempts in the days, months, and years ahead to find meaning in an event of such tragic proportions. Yet, being human, and knowing what we do about our species' theory of mind, we can be sure that such a search was taking place. Records show that more than one church sermon the following Sundays belabored the ineffability of God's intelligence and grand design, admonishing parishioners to place their trust in He who does not explain Himself. Convinced that the bridge collapse was an act of divine punishment for the townspeople's sins, one local cleric, the Reverend Henry MacKenzie, delivered an especially popular series of sermons on this topic. Reverend MacKenzie felt it was especially urgent for the community to reflect "on the necessity of repentance and humiliation, faith and amendment of life."[3] Today, if you wander through the old churchyard of the reverend's former stomping grounds at St. Nicholas Parish Church, you may well stumble over the broken headstones of those who drowned that sad day—all, according to the head-shaking MacKenzie, because of a few profligate females, drunken excesses, fistfights, gambling, gossip, and all the rest of the standard coterie of human vice.

Far from being an old-fashioned psychological anomaly of God-saturated Victorian times, such thinking strikes at the heart of human nature. Life isn't fair. But it isn't unfair either. It just is. The very asking of the question, "Why do bad things happen to good people?" presupposes an intelligent, morally concerned agent, or at least a mindful instigator, behind the scenes. It's as though we're searching for an answer on top of an answer. When something bad befalls us, we very often know perfectly well *how* it happened; yet we're still left asking *why* it happened—more specifically, why it happened *to us.* This is where causal reasoning intersects with thinking about one's unique and individual place in the natural world, one of the most important, yet under-studied, areas in modern cognitive science. And curiously, the subject of doomed bridges, along with the people unlucky enough to find themselves on them at the moment of their demise, brings this psychological phenomenon into sharp relief. The statistical probability of finding a particular person, among sometimes millions of possible others, on an otherwise sturdy bridge precisely at the moment in time it comes crashing down is so infinitesimally small that it challenges us not to feel as though the person had been singled out by an unfathomable and deliberate fate.

———◆———

The working-class people occupying the Norfolk Broads of nineteenth-century England wouldn't seem to have much in common with present-day eastern Oklahomans, but the two demographics are marred by a similar black spot in their histories. On the morning of May 26, 2002, an overly tired tugboat captain with a heart condition blacked out while maneuvering his vessel beneath an interstate bridge in Webbers Falls, causing his ship to collide with a central bridge support. Gail Shanahan and Maggie Green, who were getting an early start home after attending an equestrian show in Arkansas and had their horses with them in the hitched trailer behind their truck, died along with fourteen others—including a three-year-old girl out for the day with her grandparents—when their vehicle plunged into the river below as the bridge collapsed. A year later, Shanahan's sister gave voice to what many of those left behind were probably also asking themselves: "I've questioned why here, why was she on that bridge at that particular moment? I guess you've got to trust in God and get through it."[4]

In his classic book on children's moral development, *The Moral*

Judgment of the Child (1932), Jean Piaget tells how a colleague of his, a mysterious sounding "Mlle Rambert," administered to a large group of Swiss schoolchildren a series of stories like this one:

> *Once there were two children who were stealing apples in an orchard. Suddenly a policeman comes along and the two children run away. One of them is caught. The other one, going home by a roundabout way, crosses a river on a rotten bridge and falls into the water. Now what do you think? If he had not stolen the apples and had crossed the river on that rotten bridge all the same, would he also have fallen into the water?*[5]

Consistent with Piaget's belief that young children are artificialists (tending to see objects in the world as acting in collusion with disciplinary adults), those under eight years of age answered in the negative, saying that the bridge had collapsed only because the child had stolen the apples. Older children saw what Rambert was getting at. They answered in terms of "mechanical chance," as Piaget used the term. The worn planks would have given way, they said, no matter who was on the bridge. But, as we saw in Chapter 2 regarding his suspicions about "semi-educated" adults who happily endorsed teleo-functional statements for nature (for example, "the sun is there to give us light"), Piaget didn't entirely trust these types of rational answers. Rather, he believed that instinctual superstitious thinking is often "justified by a cloak of words" in science-savvy children and adults. One of the reasons Piaget suspected this was that some of the older children told Rambert that of course it was simply coincidence that the boy had fallen into the river after stealing the apples; they couldn't help themselves from adding, however, that all the same, it was punishment for what he had done.

Another person interested in the strange naturalness of viewing the collapse of a bridge as a sort of wrathful comeuppance was American novelist Thornton Wilder. In *The Bridge of San Luis Rey* (1927), the story opens with a centuries-old rope bridge snapping over the gorges of the Peruvian Andes, sending five people plummeting to their deaths below. Seeing the disaster as an opportunity for "theology [to] take its place among the exact sciences,"[6] the town's resident monk, Brother Juniper, investigates why God settled on those particular five people to be on the bridge at that exact moment. "Some say that we shall never know and that to the gods we are like flies that the boys kill on a summer day," he muses, "and some say, on the contrary, that the very sparrows do not lose a feather that has not been brushed away by the finger of God."[7]

A scientist at heart, Brother Juniper begins sifting through old bank ledgers, diaries, and love letters of the dead for evidence they had done something deserving of such a horrible end. Yet for all his frustrated efforts to detect the mind of a just and rational God in such carefully assembled biographical tidbits, "the thing was more difficult than he had foreseen."[8] What's more, the failed experiment causes the church fathers, who can't accept that God acts arbitrarily in matters of life and death, to label Brother Juniper an instrument of the devil. It also sees to the theologian-cum-scientist's own swift denouement at a burning stake.

In writing this story, Wilder knew that there was something about unexpected tragedies that jump-starts people's reasoning about morality. In one passage, he describes the emotional aftermath among the rattled townspeople of Lima, near where the bridge of San Luis Rey fell:

> *There was great searching of hearts in the beautiful city of Lima. Servant girls returned bracelets they had stolen from mistresses, and usurers harangued their wives angrily, in defense of usury.*[9]

Wilder was onto something quite important here. As we saw in Chapter 3, our tendency to see communicative messages in natural events rests soundly on our evolved theory of mind. But this sign-reading tendency has a distinct and clear relationship with morality. When it comes to unexpected heartache and tragedy, our appetite for unraveling the meaning of these ambiguous "messages" can become ravenous. Misfortunes appear cryptic, symbolic; they seem clearly to be *about* our behaviors. Our minds restlessly gather up bits of the past as if they were important clues to what just happened. And no stone goes unturned. Nothing is too mundane or trivial; anything to settle our peripatetic thoughts from arriving at the unthinkable truth that there is no answer because there is no riddle, that life is life and that is that. It's relatively easy to say this in some breezy general way, of course, but a different thing altogether when we're applying it convincingly to our own lives.

Wisdom and age wouldn't seem to invalidate our personal moralistic contract with God either. I've been a diabetic since I was in high school, and as a result I've found myself hospitalized on a few occasions over the years, usually because of an accidental overdose of birthday cake or some other stupid miscalculation I've made in the strange alchemy of glucose and insulin. But what I've noticed from these semiregular excursions to my local area hospitals (whether in the suburbs of Fort Lauderdale, the Ozark Mountains of Arkansas, or civil war–ravaged Belfast) is that the endocrinology wing where diabetics are tended to often shares a floor with the geriatric unit. Because diabetes is common among the elderly, this makes sense of course. But an interesting consequence of this practical arrangement is that my hospital roommates are very often octogenarians and, sadly, they're also very often alone and in a lot of pain. During those long, insipid days when the only sources of entertainment are the buzzing of dying flies caught in windowpanes, muted game show applause, and the sound of trapped air escaping from ancient anuses, one can be forgiven for eavesdropping. And I must confess that I've listened in a few times to these elderly patients as they filed some of their last grievances with God. One old man wanted to know what he and his wife, both succumbing quickly to the ravages of age, could possibly have done wrong to deserve this tragic end. More than one pleaded for mercy. An eighty-four-year-old devout Irish Catholic woman once leaned over and confided in me that God should see fit to give her her health back because, after all, she was still a virgin.

In fact, recent evidence shows that God has a special affinity for suffering. In a 2010 article in the *Personality and Social Psychology Review*, Harvard psychologists Kurt Gray and Daniel Wegner argue that human suffering and God go hand in hand because our evolved cognitive systems are inherently unsatisfied with the amoral vicissitudes of life. The gist of their argument is that, because we're such a deeply social species, when bad things happen to us we immediately launch a search for the responsible human party. In being morally vigilant this way—in seeking to identify the culpable party—we can effectively punish blameworthy, antisocial people, thus preserving our group's functional cohesion and each individual's genetic interests. That's all fine and dandy, say Gray and Wegner, when someone punches us in the face, steals from us, or sleeps with our girlfriend, but when our misfortune is more abstract (think cancer, tsunamis, earthquakes) and there's no obvious single human agent to blame, we see the hand of God.

So according to these authors, attributing moral responsibility to God is a sort of residual spillover from our everyday social psychology in dealing with other people. "Without another person to blame," write the authors, "people need to find another intentional agent to imbue the event with meaning and allow some sense of control."[10] The following little vignette may help clarify the researchers' position:

138

Imagine a young family enjoying a nice picnic somewhere in a peaceful remote valley. The birds are chirping, the sun is out, a nice breeze. It's positively idyllic. A malevolent dam worker upstream, jealous of the family's happiness, causes the water level to rise suddenly. The whole family (including the pet dog) drowns in the valley that day. Did God cause the family to drown?[11]

If you're like most of the participants who read a version of this story in Gray and Wegner's study, you'll say, "Of course not. The dam worker did it, dummy." But something interesting happened when the authors removed the human agent. Half of the participants read the same story sans the malevolent dam worker. In other words, they learned only that the water level had risen suddenly and drowned the whole family; and as you might expect, these people were much more likely to attribute the event to God than were those in the "dam worker" condition. Furthermore, participants reasoned this way only when the family drowned. By contrast, when there was no "moral harm" (the lunch got ruined, but the family was fine), God wasn't to blame.

In another clever study, Gray and Wegner created a U.S. state-by-state "suffering index" and found a positive correlation between a state's relative misery (compared to the rest of the country) and its population's belief in God. To create an objective measure of such relative misery, the investigators used data from the 2008 United Health Foundation's comprehensive State Health Index. Among other manifestations of suffering, this regularly compiled index includes rates of infant mortality, cancer deaths, infectious disease, violent crime, and environmental pathogens. What Gray and Wegner discovered was that suffering and belief in God were highly correlated, *even after controlling for income and education*. In other words, belief in God is especially high in places such as Mississippi, Alabama, and South

Carolina—and so is misery, at least as it was defined in this particular study. And that, say the authors, is no coincidence. Wherever there is a trail of woe, God is curiously afoot.

Gray and Wegner are very much aware of the logical counterargument that God is also invoked for explanations of positive events and joyous occasions. The authors don't deny this fact, but nevertheless they argue that God is especially likely to arise in people's heads in response to life's unpleasantries. "God may serve as the emissary of suffering," they write, "but He can also be an emotional crutch . . . That God may be both the cause and cure of hardship suggests why harm leads us to God more strongly than help—with help people may thank Him, but with harm people both curse and embrace Him."[12] These findings shed light on why the devastating earthquake that struck Haiti in early 2010 served only to galvanize the faithful. Yes, God killed many people, acknowledged believers. But, "praise Jesus," He spared a lot of lives too—namely, theirs.

———◆———

Another piece of the puzzle may lie in the way that our neural architecture articulates with our emotions. University of California at Berkeley psychologist Alison Gopnik suggests that humans have an "innate explanatory drive" that strongly motivates us to search for causal explanations. About a decade ago, Gopnik wrote a book chapter, provocatively titled "Explanation as Orgasm and the Drive for Causal Understanding," in which she claimed that we seek answers for the same reason we're driven to achieve sexual climax—that is to say, for the sheer thrill and phenomenological bliss of it.[13] It's only an analogy; but it's a useful one. Just as those few seconds in bed or on top of the washing machine feel naturally grand and put a smile on your face, so, too, does that fleeting eureka moment in solving a mind-tickling problem leave you glowing. (So maybe doing crosswords or Sudoku isn't going to have you exactly biting your bottom lip in ecstasy, but you get the basic idea.) In short, knowing why feels good. Not knowing why leaves us aching for explanatory release.

Physiologically speaking, says Gopnik, your brain is rigged up to chase these short-lived moments of pleasure: orgasm in the one instance because sex is nature's feel-good ruse to get your genes out there, and explanation in the other because knowing why things work the way they do enables you to learn and therefore to make more adaptive responses in the future. This drive for causal knowledge is especially apparent during early childhood, a developmental period in which it's essential for individuals to gather up as many facts about the way the world works as possible. If you've ever seen a toddler use the cat's litter box as his own personal archaeological excavation site, evaded a curious five-year-old's brutal inquisition about nipples, or wrangled a barbecue lighter away from a *Blue's Clues* pajama–clad pyromaniac, then you already know how gluttonous children are for exploratory-based knowledge. These urges of curiosity settle down over time—much like our sex drive a lot later in life. But, also like the force of people's sex drive, the longevity of our raging curiosity varies from person to person. In fact, Gopnik believes that scientists who are intrinsically motivated to solve their complicated research problems are a lot like children. Both are perpetually chasing after explanatory highs.

The thing is, Gopnik points out, your explanation doesn't actually need to be correct to give you that satisfying bolus of orgasmic pleasure driving your search for answers. Again, it's similar to sex. Gopnik writes, "The function of sex is still to reproduce even if reproduction doesn't occur in the vast majority of cases."[14] Sex leads to orgasm, and that feels good as an end in itself, even if it's ultimately a fruitless cardio exercise. Likewise, when it comes to the innate explanatory drive, you've just got to believe you've solved the problem to derive the pleasure:

This may help resolve the otherwise puzzling question of whether having a bad explanation or a pseudo-explanation is the same as having no explanation at all ... Genuine explanation might take place, and yet the outcome might be [incorrect] much of the time. This is perfectly consistent with the view that the system evolved because, in general, and over the course of the long run, and especially in childhood, it gives us veridical information about the causal structure of the world.[15]

In other words, although our explanations are scattershot, questionable, and often flat-out wrong, they're also occasionally right—especially when we're working from within a scientific framework. And getting it right some of the time is a lot better than never attempting to solve problems to begin with. According to Gopnik, because the occasional truthful causal explanation gave our ancestors a competitive edge over those without the inner desire to seek such answers at all, the overall system, albeit buggy and prone to generating supernatural logic, would have been targeted by natural selection.

So, for the sort of question we're interested in here—"Why do bad things happen to good people?"—we might borrow from Gopnik's analogy and think of God as wearing the cognitive chastity belt of a brainteaser: He has His reasons for being so prudish with us in our demands for answers, but given our innate explanatory drive, we still can't keep ourselves from trying to get into His drawers. And simply concluding that "it's not for us to know" isn't without its own explanatory appeal. Using our theory of mind, many people reckon that God has His own moralistic logic but He holds the cards close to His chest and it's not for us mere mortals to comprehend. Perhaps, as one can say about the biblical character of Job, who was something of a mouse at God's paws, God sometimes completely blindsides us as a way of bringing us closer to Him. After all, we seldom give God more thought than when we're personally in the crosshairs of calamity or impending ruin.

Many nonbelievers favor the view that humans resort to such superstitious explanations without sound, scientific causal knowledge. As we increasingly understand how the natural world operates, say defenders of this view, our need for God increasingly shrivels and it can be expected to disappear altogether—eventually. In theological parlance, this view is referred to as the "God of the gaps": because we need to feel in control over the fickle doings of nature, God is plugged in by default as the responsible party wherever there are gaps in our knowledge. A good example of this commonsensical view is found in a quote by the American physicist Richard Feynman, who remarked that

> God was always invented to explain mystery. God is always invented to explain those things that you do not understand. Now when you finally discover how something works, you get some laws which you're taking away from God; you don't need Him anymore. But you need Him for the other mysteries. So therefore you leave Him to create the universe because we haven't figured that out yet; you need Him for understanding those things which you don't believe the laws will explain, such as consciousness, or why you only live to a certain length of time—life and death— stuff like that. God is always associated with those things that you do not understand.[16]

In principle, plugging God into the gaps works well because our theory of mind enables us to attribute causes to an agent who presumably knows something that we don't know. Science is hard work. Even if we're in the dark, we can rest assured that there's a reason and just leave it at that.

But there's a major problem with this everyday view that science simply replaces God in having greater explanatory power and predictive value. Even when the true causes are known, acknowledged, and embraced, many people still appeal to God for an explanation. Knowing *how* doesn't stop us from asking *why*. Consider the suspension bridge disaster in Victorian England described at the opening of this chapter. The greatest mystery of all is not why a seemingly reasonable and just God would so cruelly visit such a fate upon the hapless children and families of Great Yarmouth on that spring day back in 1845, but why the survivors, and we looking back on them, would find this question of meaning so natural to ask to begin with.

There was no ostensible need, after all, to "make sense of" the bridge's collapse, because the cause was perfectly obvious and accepted by the townspeople: just another fatal concoction of a circus proprietor's grandiose schemes, children's universal taste for the theatrically absurd, and a lazy welder whose foreman was probably too busy to notice his slacking off on the job. It wasn't a question of accountability either. The construction company owner made it perfectly clear that he, rather than God, was responsible for the catastrophe when he personally footed the bill for dozens of the victims' burials. So why does the question of meaning so instinctively arise in the wake of a rather intelligible misfortune? Why can't we turn off our theory of mind in such cases?

———◆———

In every human society ever studied by anthropologists, uncontrollable tragedies have been seen as caused intentionally by a mindful, supernatural agent. For most of us, this "agent" is God. For others, it's one god among many, or perhaps a disgruntled ancestor or a tetchy witch. And often, misfortunes are thought to be about something we've done wrong—and sometimes simply what we're thinking about doing wrong.[17] But the important point is that reasoning in such a superstitious manner and having scientific knowledge are not mutually exclusive. As the anthropologist E. E. Evans-Pritchard uncovered in his famous study on witchcraft beliefs among the Azande of Southern Sudan, although people may have no formal education, this doesn't mean they're naive, and it certainly doesn't mean they're oblivious to logical, scientific, natural causes. Rather, misfortunes are simply the means whereby witches conduct their trade.

One of the most famous passages of all anthropological ethnographies is from Evans-Pritchard's *Witchcraft, Oracles and Magic among the Azande* (1937), in which the author gives an example of the villagers' typical reaction to misfortune:

> *Sometimes an old granary collapses. There is nothing remarkable in this. Every Zande knows that termites eat the supports in [the] course of time and that even the hardest woods decay after years of service. Now a granary is the summerhouse of a Zande homestead and people sit beneath it in the heat of the day and chat or play the African hole-game or work at some craft. Consequently it may happen that there are people sitting beneath the granary when it collapses and they are injured, for it is a heavy structure made of beams and clay and may be stored with eleusine [millet] as well. Now why should these particular people have been sitting under this particular granary at the particular moment when it collapsed? That it should collapse is easily intelligible, but why should it have collapsed at the particular moment when these particular people were sitting beneath it?*[18]

Evans-Pritchard discovered that such naturally occurring questions among the villagers inevitably led them to accusations of witchcraft. More recently, University of Texas psychologist Christine

Legare, along with Susan Gelman from the University of Michigan, discovered that Sesotho-speaking South Africans are reasonably well versed in the biological causes of AIDS, but their knowledge about the disease doesn't stop them from viewing infected people as being cursed by a witch also. What this means is that in a country where a devastating 30 percent of pregnant women are HIV positive, scientific education may not be the silver bullet to the disease's eradication we presume it to be. Clever witches, for example, can interfere with one's decision making, or put an especially attractive—and infected—young woman in a young man's path on the same day he forgot to tuck a condom into his wallet.

After running several psychological studies probing children's and adults' reasoning about the spread and nature of the virus that causes AIDS, Legare and Gelman reported their findings in a 2008 issue of *Cognitive Science*: "Although biological explanations for illness were endorsed at high levels, witchcraft was also often endorsed. More important, bewitchment explanations were neither the result of ignorance nor replaced by biological explanations."[19] In fact, adults were more likely to give witchcraft explanations than were children, even though the adults also had a better understanding of the disease's biology.

Borrowing from an account by author Tracy Kidder in his *Mountain Beyond Mountains* (2003), a book about the legendary humanitarian doctor and Harvard anthropologist Paul Farmer, Legare and Gelman also provide a humorous example of this natural coexistence of super-natural and biological explanations in the individual's mind. In the example, Farmer, credited with developing a free, modern health care system among the poorest of nations, is described as having a tongue-in-cheek conversation with an elderly Haitian woman suffering from tuberculosis:

When he had first interviewed her, about a year before, she'd taken mild offense at his questions about sorcery. She'd been one of the few to deny she believed in it. She stated, "I'm not stupid. I know tuberculosis comes from people coughing germs." She'd taken all her medicines. She'd been cured. But now, a year later, when he asked her again about sorcery, she said that of course she believed in it. "I know who sent me my sickness, and I'm going to get her back," she told him. "But if you believe that," he cried, "why did you take your medicines?" "Cheri," she said. "eske-w pa ka kon-prann bagay ki pa senp?" The Creole phrase pa senp means "not simple," and implies that a thing is freighted with complexity, usually of a magical sort. So, in free translation, she said to Farmer, "Honey, are you incapable of complexity?"[20]

Many individuals expect to be punished by God even when their secret misdoings have gone unpunished by other people. And when this doesn't happen, something seems to them fundamentally off-kilter with the moralistic universe. As social psychologists have known for a very long time, most people are guided by expectations of a just world. But God lurks in these shadows. If the world is perceived as being just (even, as studies show, among many nonbelievers), then wouldn't some watchful, knowing agent be required to keep tabs on people's social behaviors, adjusting the scales of nonhuman justice? Or, for "godless" Buddhists, who exactly is it that's making sure the bad guys are being reborn as dung beetles and lab rats?

In *The Moral Judgment of the Child* (1932), Piaget provides an illustrative, though somewhat strange choice of an example of just world beliefs. These days, masturbation isn't exactly a felony, but there were different sexual mores back in Piaget's conservative Switzerland. "It cannot be denied," he writes, "that we observe in masturbators a systematic fear of the retribution residing in things— not only the fear of the result their habits may have upon their health, the fear of making themselves stupid, etc., but also a tendency to interpret all the chance misfortunes of life as punishments intended by fate."[21]

Before you go patting yourself on the back for your more rational mind, see if you can stomach your own psychological instincts when mulling over the real-life fate of Justo Antonio Padron. On November 12, 2007, Padron, a career criminal, wiped the sweat from his brow as he jimmied open yet another lock while burglarizing vehicles at a popular Miccosukee Indian resort in South Florida. When police caught him red-handed and blared their sirens, Padron tried to make a getaway by diving into the casino's retention pond, where a fussy nine-foot alligator named Poncho made an impromptu meal out of him. And it works the other way around too. Take lucky Michigan resident Fred Toupas Jr., who back in 2008, not long after being released from prison for raping a thirteen-year-old girl, hit the jackpot in his state's fifty-seven-million-dollar lotto.

If you're logically minded, chances are you would say that these things just happen; you'd shrug them off as ironic but coincidental. But I bet you'd nevertheless feel that Padron got what he deserved and that something's not quite right about Toupas's situation. In fact, Toupas's windfall prompted a cavalcade of angry Internet users to chime in after reading the story, many of whom were atheists asking believers what more evidence they could possibly need that God didn't exist than a level 3 sex offender winning the megalottery. But our evolved theory of mind provides God with a lot of loopholes. One woman, for example, used her very creative theory of mind to discern a certain cleverness in this tale. She reminded these cynical atheists that God will always outfox humans when it comes to unraveling His unknowable motives:

> *There is a God and He certainly does know the things we all have done. Let's wait and see where this man ends up after a year of extravagant spending and whatever else he may be up to. We will all see just what money can do to the wrong kind of people.*

In certain rare cases, though, even the wildest stretch of the imagination wouldn't seem to grow a loophole large enough to accommodate God's elusive logic. According to Holocaust survivor Elie Wiesel, in Nazi Germany some people reportedly thought that God had gone insane. But an even darker prospect emerged. A few Jews began to revise their theological views and surmised that God had become morally corrupt. In his semiautobiographical chronicle, *Gates of the Forest* (1966), Wiesel describes a particularly telling scene:

> *In a concentration camp, one evening after work, a rabbi called together three of his colleagues and convoked a special court. Standing with his head held high before them, he spoke as follows: "I intend to convict God of murder, for He is destroying His people and the law He gave to them . . . I have irrefutable proof in my hands. Judge without fear or sorrow or prejudice. Whatever you have to lose has long since been taken away." The trial proceeded in due legal form, with witnesses for both sides with pleas and deliberations. The unanimous verdict: "Guilty" . . . [But] after all, [God] had the last word. On the day of the trial, He turned the sentence against His judges and accusers. They, too, were taken off to the slaughter. And I tell you this: if their death has no meaning, then it's an insult, and if it does have a meaning, it's even more so.*[22]

———

Cosmic punishment is often in the eye of the beholder. For Janet Landman, a psychologist at Babson College, the dramatic story of Katherine Anne Power is a case in point. In an edited volume called *Turns in the Road: Narrative Studies of Lives in Transition* (2001), Landman describes some of her discussions with Power while the latter was incarcerated in federal prison for a crime that had shattered the lives of many people, including Power's own. "Narrative psychologists," such as Landman, believe that dramatic life stories allow us to glimpse universal aspects of human psychology not easily captured by laboratory methods.[23]

Power's tale is the prototype of karmic anticipations. One late summer day in 1970 in Brighton, Massachusetts, the articulate, starry-eyed sociology major from nearby Brandeis University, and also a fervent Vietnam War protester, sat behind the wheel of an idling getaway car as her heavily armed partners in crime liberated a bank of its "warmongering" funds. (To properly overthrow the government, the group believed, one must first pilfer and then cleanse its dirty loot by reinvesting in antiwar causes.) Unbeknownst to Power, one of her peace-loving compatriots shot a police officer in the back as he fled, which was the making of a widow and nine fatherless children. Reportedly shocked by this robbery gone bad, Power assumed the identity of an infant who had died a year before she was born and reinvented herself as "Alice Louise Metzinger." The others were eventually caught. But Power went underground in the small northwest Oregon town of Lebanon, where, reminiscent of Jean Valjean in Victor Hugo's *Les Misérables* (1862), she dedicated herself to a life of contrition. Power became a doting mother to a young son and a loving wife to the local meat cutter; she bought into a popular restaurant, became an active volunteer, taught a class at the community college, and even gave her car to a neighbor in need.

Yet this former high school valedictorian, Catholic Girl Scout, and onetime winner of the Betty Crocker Cooking award was on the FBI's Ten Most Wanted list for fourteen of her twenty-three years on the run. Haunted by feelings of shame, guilt, and paranoia, Power often tried tempting a vengeful fate. In her earlier years on the run, she even returned to her natural hair color so that she'd more closely resemble her own image in the "Wanted" posters hanging in her favorite bar. But nobody ever recognized her; the few people she confided in with her dark secret (her husband and a few close friends) were understanding and loyal, and there was only continued good kismet in her new life. By 1984, the few leads that had once trickled in had all dried up, and the FBI removed her from their Most Wanted list. For Power, it began to feel as though her punishment was the excruciating sense of undeserved normalcy and "happiness" she had achieved. It was so insufferable, in fact, that in 1993, honoring, as she called it, her "contract with God," she turned herself in to puzzled Boston authorities and served six years of an eight-year sentence.

Like Power, many of us also can't help but mentally replay past events that continually nip at our emotional heels, and we have experienced life-changing episodes that—at least in our heads—represent a sort of sharp dividing line between everything that was before and everything that came after. According to some social psychologists, the sort of subjective spin that we put on these nightmarish events, and particularly how we see them as having shaped our current and future selves, says much about our personalities.

As director of the Foley Center for the Study of Lives at Northwestern University, Dan McAdams has spearheaded a new brand of social science research in the study of personality called the "narrative study of lives." In an article published in a 2001 issue of the *Review of General Psychology*, McAdams points out that autobiographical memory is intriguingly creative:

> *Life stories are based on biographical facts, but they go considerably beyond the facts as people selectively appropriate aspects of their experience and imaginatively construe both past and future to construct stories that make sense to them and to their audiences, that vivify and integrate life and make it more or less meaningful.*[24]

Using quasi-structured interview methods in which older individuals are asked about the major turning points in their lives and how these events affected them, McAdams sorts through the responses using an elaborately detailed coding system, one designed to detect subtle, underlying themes in the way people frame these important events in their own minds.

McAdams has found that there are two types of people in this world. First, there are those who view life-altering experiences during young adulthood (such as death, crime, addiction, abuse, relationship woes, loss, failure, and other abysmal yet often unavoidable plights of the human saga) as "contaminative episodes" in their life stories. Retrospectively, everything before the event is seen through rose-tinted glasses, with the event viewed as a type of toxic incident that corrodes into the present and ruins the rest of the life course. In a contamination sequence, a good life suddenly goes bad. The key personal misfortune is treated as a sort of foreign body rather than integrated into the narrative. For those prone to such reasoning, it's as though a happy fairy tale had been rudely interrupted: something—or someone—vandalized God's plans for them.[25]

And then there are those who view such dramatic events as

"redemptive episodes" in their self-narratives. Like Katherine Ann Power, these people eventually transform or redeem bad scenes into good outcomes by becoming better people and benefiting society. As one might expect, those older folks who look back on their lives and see their various crises as redemptive episodes that taught them valuable life lessons and changed them for the better (rather than ruining everything) are also the ones who tend to score high on scales of "generativity," which is a measure of their positive, or prosocial, contributions to others, particularly to younger generations. Yes, these events were painful, but "everything happens for a reason." This is the case for Power, anyway; she's now working at an AIDS nonprofit organization in Boston.

So McAdams believes that investigating how people cobble together their life stories is revealing in more ways than one. "Some people construct life stories that are modeled on classical tragedy," says McAdams, "whereas others convey their identities as television sitcoms."[26] The irony is that real life is seldom portrayed in our heads as the dramaturgical genre that it actually is: the existential narrative where things just happen. In this genre, there is no tidy narrative arc, but just a rather messy, conductorless train of interconnected events hitched together in an impersonal and deterministic fashion, the links between them invisible to the naked eye and beyond the ken of everyday human intelligence. Rather, in most people's minds, their own lives appear to be moving in a linear progression, one mostly of their own making, and toward a satisfying climax. Dartmouth College psychologist Todd Heatherton, for example, has found that most people tend to unreasonably denigrate their own past, casting their distant, flawed selves as naive, hapless third-person characters.[27] So in comparison, our current selves appear more advanced, or developed, in the full autobiographical plot.

This ubiquitous expectation that life progresses toward a pinnacle moment of revelation—a moment where wisdom will be attained in the full understanding of why those jarring roadblocks were placed where they were along the highways of our lives—can be especially frustrating when we're caught in the grips of serious suffering. An especially vivid (and painful) glimpse of such a case is portrayed in John Gunther's poignant memoir, *Death Be Not Proud* (1949). In this book, Gunther, an acclaimed journalist and author, chronicles his seventeen-year-old son Johnny's struggle with a malignant, furiously growing brain tumor. The boy was apparently something of a prodigy. He was Harvard bound, with aspirations of being both a mathematician and a poet; by sixteen he had developed a correspondence with Albert Einstein about a revision to the theory of relativity. In a diary entry written shortly before his death, Johnny wrote these simple but profound lines: "[My new] philosophy: Get yourself off your hands. Happiness is in love. Accept disappointments. Relieve oneself by confession of sins. I am growing up at last."[28] For a boy with such extraordinary insight, sensitivity, intelligence, and creative ambition, it seemed uncannily cruel to his father that the cancer should be eating away at the very core of all these singular gifts: his brain. Gunther reflects,

> *Why was Johnny being subjected to this merciless experience? I tried to explain that suffering is an inevitable part of most lives, that none of this ordeal was without some purpose, that pain is a constituent of all the processes of growth, that perhaps the entire harrowing episode would make his brain even finer, subtler, and more sensitive than it was. He did not appear to be convinced. Then there was a question I asked myself incessantly. Why—of all things—should Johnny be afflicted in that part of him which was his best, the brain? What philosophical explanation could one find for that? Was all this a dismal accident, purely barren*

and fortuitous? Beethoven was struck deaf and Milton blind and I met a singer once who got cancer of the vocal cords. But if the connection of circumstances was not fortuitous, not accidental, where was justice?[29]

———◆———

As the rather depressing song by Kansas goes, we really are "dust in the wind." And it's a breathless wind, at that. But it doesn't matter. With the possible exception of a few especially lucid occasions, such as the one we're engaged in now, nobody really sees their lives this way. We can squint our mind's eye so that the glare of our subjective biases is reduced, but in general we've evolved a powerful set of cognitive illusions preventing us from sustained moments of clarity. Even when one feels robbed of meaning (as in the case of those who view their misfortunes as contaminative sequences) there's still the presumption that meaning *should* be there, that it all *should* work out in the end, and that everything *should* one day make sense and be revealed to us. When it doesn't happen this way, we feel cheated, our emotional limbs flailing about wildly, grasping for answers. As William James said in *The Varieties of Religious Experience* (1902), "The world now looks remote, strange, sinister, uncanny. Its color is gone, its breath is cold, there is no speculation in the eyes it glares with."[30]

You'd be hard-pressed to find anybody who understands this better than David Chase, the Emmy Award–winning producer and creator of the HBO television drama *The Sopranos*—a dark but humorous offering centering on the everyday tribulations of Tony Soprano (played by James Gandolfini), the head mafioso of a New Jersey organized crime syndicate. When Chase wrapped up production in 2007 on his immensely popular six-season run of the show, he ended the story line in an unprecedented and, as it turns out, controversial way.

The final scene of *The Sopranos* takes place at a local diner. It's a consciously everyday scene: silverware clinking in the background, a group of Boy Scouts at a nearby booth, a young couple in love out on a date, and other urban banalities. Tony is shown waiting impatiently for the rest of his family to arrive, flipping idly through song choices on the tabletop jukebox—eventually selecting Journey's "Don't Stop Believin'" (1981), which plays for the remainder of the scene. His wife, Carmela Soprano (played by Edie Falco) arrives, and the two look disinterestedly over the menu and roll their eyes over their college-age daughter's appointment with her gynecologist. Soon their teenage son A.J. (played by Robert Iler) sits down at the table and bickers with his father while daughter Meadow (Jamie-Lynn Sigler) is shown having trouble parallel parking outside. Throughout all this, the camera periodically steals away ominously to a man at the counter who seems to be looking over at Tony—presumably a hit man. The man gets up and goes to the restroom, a waitress delivers a plate of onion rings, Meadow finally manages to park her car and presumably comes into the restaurant, Tony looks up, and—cut to black. The End.

Many fans were outraged. Some cursed their unreliable television sets or thought that their cable had gone out. It just seemed so . . . *unsatisfying*. But, defended Chase, so is life—and that's the point. Human lives aren't the equivalent of complete, grammatically correct sentences; the period can come anywhere and anytime, even in the middle of a mouthful of onion rings as presumably happened to Tony Soprano. And as we saw in Chapter 4 on the oxymoronic fallacy of "being dead," death in real life doesn't even offer the comparative luxury of a cut-to-black scene. Four months after the finale aired, with the audience still fuming, Chase decided to finally address his critics in an interview published in *The Sopranos: The Complete Book*

(2007). When asked why people seemed so intent on getting closure on the story line and whether the abrupt ending was really just a big prank, Chase answered,

> I remember I would tell my kid and her cousins bedtime stories. Sometimes I would want to get back to the grown-ups and have a drink, so I would say something like, "And they were driving down the road and that's it. Story over." They would always scream, "Wait a minute! That's no ending!" Apparently that need for finality exists in human beings. But we're not children anymore. Especially watching a show like The Sopranos that's got sex and violence.[31]
>
> I saw some items in the press that said, "This was a huge 'f—-you' to the audience." That we were s—-ting in the audience's face. Why would we want to do that? Why would we entertain people for eight years only to give them the finger? We don't have contempt for the audience. In fact, I think The Sopranos is the only show that actually gave the audience credit for having some intelligence and attention span.[32]
>
> But I must say that even people who liked it misinterpreted it, to a certain extent. This wasn't really about "leaving the door open." There are no esoteric clues in there. No Da Vinci Code. Everything that pertains to that episode was in that episode. And it was in the episode before that and the one before that and seasons before this one and so on.[33]

Chase, like other television producers, finds himself in the very godlike role of Master Narrator. And the audience's frustrations with his ending reveal their strong need for an edifying climax, something that wraps everything up in a revelatory way. Even if the camera had shown Tony Soprano being shot in the head, or having a massive stroke, or even a nuclear bomb obliterating New Jersey—anything but this incomplete sentence used to end the Sopranos' story—viewers would have had more closure than what they got. Many people flocked to the show because of its gritty, lifelike dimensions. But, in the end, the story was perhaps a little too lifelike for them.

Narrative psychologists believe that we secretly portray ourselves as living out a sort of preauthored screenplay—much like the fictional stories we read or see on television and in the movies—one with the promise of an intelligent narrative climax that will eventually tie all the loose ends together in some meaningful, coherent way. These hidden expectations may not come to the surface until someone we love drops dead on the kitchen floor of a brain aneurism, is hit head-on in a fatal car collision on the way to pick up the kids from soccer practice, or even falls off a bridge. "Yes, man is mortal," wrote Mikhail Bulgakov in *The Master and Margarita* (1967), "but that's only half the trouble! The problem is that he's unexpectedly mortal, there's the trick!"[34] Then, suddenly, we become ravenous for meaning, disoriented by the blazing clarity of disorder. No matter how much we profess to know differently, such events strike us in the gut as a fundamental violation of how life works.

That we privately see ourselves as characters in our own life stories raises, of course, the more intriguing question of just who we think is writing the script. Many life-changing events are thrown at us by chance circumstances beyond our control rather than caused directly or even indirectly by us. For religious people, the identity of this enigmatic author isn't implicit at all; it's obviously God. But even atheists occasionally lapse blatantly and unknowingly into this overt pattern of thinking. For many believers, God is a passive god, an entity that lets things happen to us rather than one that deliberately punishes or rewards us—but this still means ascribing to Him the intention not to act. Still others believe that God is incapable of causing misfortune, but rather He can only observe; so when children die, sweet old ladies are raped, and earthquakes hit, He gets just as sad and angry as we do.

This was the theme of Rabbi Harold S. Kushner's best-selling book, *When Bad Things Happen to Good People* (1981). Kushner, who wrestled with his own religious beliefs when his young son was diagnosed with the rapid-aging disease progeria, tells us that God sowed the seeds for all Creation, including those that led ultimately to the evolution of human nature, but (as we're told in the book of Genesis) then He "rested," which in Kushner's opinion means that God could no longer intervene, because nature took on a life of its own, with laws that couldn't be circumvented. What's more, God might not have even completed the job. "The world is mostly an orderly, predictable place, showing ample evidence of God's thoroughness and handiwork, but pockets of chaos remain."[35]

Whatever your particular theological view, all such theories invoke, in different doses, your theory of mind, and all inevitably have something to say about the relation between these two natural bedfellows: morality and this-worldly pain. In any event, it's very hard to shake that mysterious sense that someone or something is keeping watch over us. Something that is emotionally invested in our moral behaviors, our feelings, and, ultimately, our ability to understand our own stories. Something that, well, *cares*.

———◆———

As a nonbeliever, Cindy Chupack, one of the lead writers and producers of another acclaimed HBO television series, *Sex and the City*, is reluctant to say that God has had anything to do with her success. Yet in a 2009 interview with *Psychology Today* magazine about how she's managed to cope with her own failures and disappointments in life, Chupack betrays a cognitive processing style that shares much in common with the believer's worldview. And the common denominator is a generous helping of theory of mind in interpreting these illusory "trials":

> *I play fast and loose with religion. I don't really believe. I'm Jewish, but I like to believe we're in control of things. But I do believe—I don't attribute it to God, but I do believe there's something—how would I say this? I believe for many people there's something you're meant to do, whether or not you believe that's something God meant for you to do, or something because of your talents you're meant to do, or because of your experience with love or what's missing that you're meant to experience. And sometimes I think those are even hardships that you're sort of meant to go through to be tested.*[36]

Chupack has had her own share of hardships. When her husband came out of the closet after two years of marriage in her midtwenties, Chupack was devastated. The ensuing years were rocky ones and included, as she puts it, awkward bouts of "kamikaze dating," an endless series of embarrassing conversations with relatives, and a renewed appreciation of her friendships with other single women. All of this, of course, was perfect fodder for her later hit television show:

> *What I'm most proud of in my life was* Sex and the City, *and it never would have happened had I stayed married, and had he not been gay, and had that not been my backstory.*[37]

Chupack isn't the only nonbeliever who, perhaps without even realizing it, sees inherent purpose in a life that she otherwise believes is inherently purposeless. In a series of studies published in the late 1990s in the *European Journal of Social Psychology*, psychologists Albert Pepitone and Luisa Saffioti reported that a significant proportion of young adults culled from the relatively nonreligious Netherlands, as well as a communist organization in Italy, while rebuffing a belief in God, nevertheless deferred to fate when interpreting stories that contained a "salient life experience" over which the central character had no control, such as running into a long-lost relative in some obscure, faraway place. There's still a Master Narrator seen in such "meaningful coincidences." Fate is really just God stripped of His identity but retaining His storytelling abilities.

In her unpublished doctoral dissertation, one of my PhD students, Bethany Heywood, found similar evidence of atheists' covert believing tendencies when they were asked to think about the major turning points in their own lives. Throughout 2009, Heywood conducted a series of online interviews using Instant Messenger with thirty-four atheists and thirty-four believers, including American and British samples. To prevent them from answering dishonestly (because many atheists bristle at even the insinuation that they're irrationally minded and superstitious), the participants were given the impression that the study was about their memory of personal life events, otherwise known as "autobiographical memory." In fact, Heywood wasn't so much interested in the respondents' memory skills as in their subjective interpretations of why these particular things had happened to them. In her careful analysis of their responses to her questions—such as, "Did you learn any lessons from this experience?" "How has this event changed your life?" "Looking back, are you better able to understand why this event happened to you than you were at the time?"—Heywood found that about two-thirds of the atheists had made at least one response betraying their implicit view that "everything happens for a reason." As expected, more believers gave such responses—often noting the suspicion that their most trying times were actually God's creative handiwork. But the overall difference in ascribing some inherent reason or purpose to momentous, life-altering events was, curiously, statistically negligible between the two groups.[38]

A typical example of the atheist's reasoning in this manner is shown in a response given by a British undergraduate student who considered herself to be an unflinching nonbeliever, the type that might keep surplus "Darwin fish" bumper stickers in her knapsack. One of the major turning points in her life, this student said, was failing an important university course and losing her prestigious scholarship. It changed everything. But when she was asked why this had happened to her—an ambiguous question that appealed to her poor study habits, challenges at home, or ineptitude as much as anything else—she answered, "So that I could see that even if I failed a course, my life wouldn't actually end."[39] Other atheists confessed that they often caught themselves thinking in such a fashion too, but then immediately corrected this subjective, psychological bias in line with their explicitly logical beliefs. One was a middle-aged man who had recently botched a job interview for a position that he very much wanted, failing to get an offer from his prospective employer: "And I found myself thinking: maybe this is meant to happen so I can find a better job or move to a different country to work—something like that. But in reality I don't believe in fate, so it's strange to find oneself thinking like that."[40] Bethany Heywood's group of religious high-functioning autistics that we met in Chapter 3, by contrast, failed to even comprehend the teleo-functional pretext underlying these types of questions. For example, here is an exchange between Heywood (BH) and a man (JD) with Asperger's syndrome, a type of high-functioning autism:

BH: "Do you ever think you see meaning in events that are seemingly coincidental?"

JD: "Yes, sometimes. I'm sorry I'm not sure I understand the question fully."

BH: "I'm just wondering if you ever think there's more to coincidences than it seems like?"

JD: " Yes, to a certain degree, like someone says something to me and then later on someone else says something that is virtually the same, kind of like déjà-vu."

And another Asperger's respondent (TM):

BH: "Do you ever think there's more to coincidences than it seems like? Or do you just think coincidences are coincidences?"

TM: "If they're coincidences, by definition they are unrelated. But sometimes people mistake things for coincidence that actually are a pattern. Like people taking an unexpected dislike to me."

BH: "Do you ever see a pattern in coincidences?"

TM: "No. By definition coincidences have no pattern."

Some of the more introspective, and presumably non-autistic, novelists in modern literature have also puzzled over this bizarre cognitive push to tease apart the imaginary strands of such a shadowy web of purpose. In Milan Kundera's first novel, *The Joke* (1967), the atheistic protagonist finds himself, duly surprised, ensnared in the fiber of this very web:

*For all my skepticism, some trace of irrational superstition did sur-
vive in me, the strange conviction, for example, that everything
in life that happens to me also has a sense, that it means something, that life speaks to us about itself through its story, and that
it gradually reveals a secret, which takes the form of a rebus whose*

message must be deciphered, that the stories we live comprise the mythology of our lives and in that mythology lies the key to truth and mystery. Is it an illusion? Possibly, even probably, but I can't rid myself of the need continually to decipher my own life.[41]

This pattern of thinking strongly implies that atheism is more a verbal muzzling of God—a conscious, executively made decision to reject one's own intuitions about a faceless übermind involved in our personal affairs—than it is a true cognitive exorcism. The thought might be smothered so quickly that we don't even realize it has happened, but the despondent atheist's appeal to some reasonable, just mind seems a psychological reflex to tragedy nonetheless.

This doesn't make us weak, ridiculous, or even foolish. It just makes us human. And, as we're about to see, it may make us particularly well-adapted human beings—at least, in the evolutionary sense of the term.

6 | GOD AS ADAPTIVE ILLUSION

For millions of years before the evolution of theory of mind, our human ancestors were just like other social primates—namely, impulsive, hedonistic, and uninhibited. This isn't a character judgment against them; it's just what worked for them in maximizing their reproductive success, just as it does for most modern-day social species. It would also be rather hypocritical of us to hold such things against them. As Freud pointed out long ago with his concept of the primitive "id" component of the human personality, such limbically driven, paleomammalian tendencies are still cozily ensconced in our own human brains.

In fact, before exploring how the evolution of theory of mind shook up our social behaviors, let's have a look at what would have been the typical social behavioral profile for our ancestors *before* the evolution of a theory of mind. Presumably, it would have resembled chimpanzees' behaviors today—not exactly, of course, because chimps have also evolved since the time of the parent species. But most experts still believe that chimpanzees are a "conservative" species, meaning that they probably haven't changed all that much since the time we last shared a common ancestor with them about six million years ago.

If you've ever been to the ape exhibit at your local zoo, two things have probably struck you. First, chimpanzees are eerily similar to us, in both their behaviors and their appearance. And second, they have no shame. After all, complex social emotions such as shame and pride hinge on the presence of a theory of mind, because they involve taking the perspective of others in judging the self as having desirable or undesirable attributes. So it's not that chimps and other primates "don't care" what others think of them; it's that, without a theory of mind (or at least one as all-consuming as ours), they lack the *capacity* to care. Perhaps it's not too surprising, therefore, the sights you see at the resident primate house. All in plain view of each other, not to mention in plain view of your slack-jawed children, chimps will comfortably pass gas after copulating; cavalierly impose themselves onto screaming, hysterical partners; nonchalantly defecate into cupped hands; casually probe each others' orifices with all manner of objects, organs, and appendages; and unhesitatingly avail themselves of their own manual pleasures. They will rob their elderly of covetous treats, happily ignore the plaintive cries of their sickly group members, and, when the situation calls for it, aggress against one another with a ravenous, loud, and unbridled rage.

With typical human jurisprudence, we recoil at the mere thought of these things, cover our children's eyes, and laughingly dismiss these animals as "monkeys"—erroneously, I should add, because they are in fact great apes. What more should we ask of monkeys, we say, than for them to act as fools and clowns, as caricatures of humans, a fumbled half step toward the pinnacle of Creation? But of course that's nonsense of papal proportions. Without a theory of mind, there's simply not much reason to refrain from much of anything, except the physical presence of a dominant animal that would strike you if you did it wrong, or perhaps one that, through past exchanges, you've learned will alarm others at your provocation, thereby summoning an imposing figure to harm you on its behalf. Chimpanzees certainly have unspoken social norms, many of them quite complex. But without a theory of mind, one thing chimpanzees don't have is the often crippling, inhibiting psychological sense of others watching, observing, and critically evaluating them.

Humans, unfortunately, are not so lucky. Owing to our evolved theory of mind, other people's thoughts about us weigh especially heavy on our minds. You might claim that you don't care what others think of you, and perhaps that's truer for you than it is for many, but most people suffer immensely when perceived negative aspects of their identity—moral offenses, questionable intentions, embarrassing foibles, physical defects—are made known to others or are on the verge of exposure. In fact, we may well be the only species for which negative social-evaluative appraisals can lead to shame-induced suicide. You'd also be hard-pressed to find another animal that diets, wears toupees, injects botulism in its face, gets calf implants and boob jobs, or brandishes Gucci handbags, bleached teeth, and pierced navels, because all such vanity acts are meant to influence others' perceptions of us. And, again, all require a theory of mind.

In no other work has the sheer potency of other minds been captured more vividly than in Sartre's famous "Hell is other people" play, *No Exit* (1946). At the opening of the play, we are introduced to the three main characters, who find themselves each in the unenviable position of having just been cast into hell. There is Garcin, an assassinated left-wing journalist and draft dodger who believes he's in hell because he mistreated his wife; Inez, a sadistic postal worker with a penchant for seducing other women; and Estelle, a pretty, pampered debutante who killed her baby and drove the penniless father to suicide. Strangers to one another, these three people find themselves locked together in an average drawing room with Second Empire furniture. By all appearances, they are each intelligent, sane, and able to think rationally about the situation. For some time after their deaths, they can even continue to observe their friends and loved ones on earth. So how is this hell?

Sartre proceeds to paint a scene so disturbing that it would make even the most rapacious sinner repent, if only to escape the unbearable fate of an eternity spent with others. Sartre's allegory forces us to examine the subtle ways by which other people, by their sheer *mindful* presence, can affect us so strongly. For example, there are no mirrors or windows in the drawing room, sleep is not permitted, and the light is always on. The characters' eyelids are paralyzed, disallowing them even the luxury of blinking. Garcin reacts with muted horror to the prospect of being constantly observed by Inez and Estelle, despite the professed goodwill of both. Tensions begin to mount, especially between Garcin and Inez:

> GARCIN: Will night never come?
> INEZ: Never.
> GARCIN: You will always see me?
> INEZ: Always.[1]

To avoid unwittingly serving as one another's torturers in hell, Garcin suggests that each person stare at the carpet and try to forget that the others are there. But Inez quips,

> *How utterly absurd! I feel you there, in every pore. Your silence clamors in my ears. You can nail up your mouth, cut your tongue out—but you can't prevent your being there. Can you stop your thoughts? I hear them ticking away like a clock, tick-tock, tick-tock, and I'm certain you hear mine. [You're] everywhere, and every sound comes to me soiled, because you've intercepted it on its way.[2]*

Later in the play, when Garcin goes to strangle Inez after she merci-
lessly teases him about his military desertion, she uses his awareness
of her own judgment to drive the stake in ever further, instructing
him to feel her eyes "boring into"[3] him:

> *You're a coward, Garcin, because I wish it, I wish it—do you*
> *hear?—I wish it. And yet, just look at me, see how weak I am, a*
> *mere breath on the air, a gaze observing you, a formless thought*
> *that thinks you. Ah, they're open now, those big hands, those*
> *coarse, man's hands! But what do you hope to do? You can't*
> *throttle thoughts with hands.*[4]

As Sartre so keenly observes in this play, when we really feel
watched, our emotions and behaviors are strongly influenced. Nature
has made us exquisitely—and sometimes painfully—aware of others'
eyes on us. Although these other minds may well be "mere breath on
the air," they still are a potentially deadly miasma.

———◆———

Our acute sensitivity to being in the judgmental presence of others shouldn't come as any surprise. Sartre's theatrical drawing room
simulating hell aside, it's largely the reason why so many people stand
primping for an hour or more before the mirror every morning, why
we're more vigilant about bagging our dogs' bowel movements when
they've done their business in front of an audience, why public speaking is many people's worst nightmare, why stores invest so much
money in cameras and security guards, and why we don't publicly
excavate our belly buttons for lint.

In fact, in a wide range of recent laboratory experiments, participants have been found to act more prosocially (and less antisocially)
when cues in the environment suggest they're being observed—even

when these cues are just crude stimuli such as eyespots on a computer screen, or a toy placed on a bookshelf with big, prominent, humanlike eyes. We even leave better tips when there's a picture of a pair of eyes posted above the tip jar.

Does this mean we're well behaved only because we're concerned about our reputations? Not entirely—not in the sense of being consciously aware of this motivation anyway. But because of our peculiar evolution, one that involved theory of mind, human minds are a buzzing hive of antagonistic forces and compulsions. We harbor a beast within. It's not the devil, of course, but nature itself. Owing to the scaffolding of our psychological evolution, in which being impulsive, hedonistic, and uninhibited tended to pay off for our ancestors for millions of years, we've each got a bit of a rotten core, that·id-like carnal base that makes us lust after those we shouldn't, fantasize about things we oughtn't, and dream about doing things we mustn't. If, for example, a particularly invasive government, in attempting to better understand human nature from a scientific perspective, issued a decree for all men to wear a penile plethysmograph (a device measuring blood flow to the penis, which some people therefore believe serves as an objective measure of sexual arousal) throughout the day, we'd discover a lot of conscientious objectors. Ostensibly, men would refuse to go along with the mandate on principle: how dare the authorities even suggest such a thing, they'd say; this is a case of a government going too far. But the refusal would also be for fear of what such a study would reveal about our hidden natures, because sexual arousal is one of the few things not easily tamed by moral willpower.

If you recall from your basic biology tutorials, there's one thing that Darwinian evolution can't do, which is to start over from scratch using a blank genetic canvas. As a general rule, we humans don't like to conceive of ourselves as animals. The trouble, however, is that that is precisely what we are. Nature has left many remembrances of our primal past embedded in our inherited genotypes. These include a truncated, undeveloped tail at the base of our spines and, in women, two milk-filled udders that swell up over pregnancy with teats perfect for suckling. Although they've become blunted over the past few million years, perhaps nothing reminds us of our animal natures more than the intimate touch of our own clumsy tongues palpating against the enameled tips of our canines, those carnivorous tools designed so clearly for defleshing the bones of our prey, and occasionally for organic weaponry.

The human brain, like any other evolved physical trait or organ, is similarly built upon precursory parts from our deep mammalian past. This is because natural selection works by taking a common structure and modifying it over time. It can build on features that are already there (such as what happened with the primate visual cortex as our eyesight became more and more important for life in the trees), shrink them for the sake of neural ergonomics (such as the concomitant decrease in the primate olfactory system as our sense of smell became less and less important), or tinker with articulating structures so that they work together more efficiently. As a result, and because there's no foresight in evolution, human beings are in many ways suboptimally designed: nature could only work with the building blocks that came before. To accommodate our impressive brainpower, for example, our skulls became so large, so quickly, that compared with those of other mammalian species, women's pelvic regions are generally too narrow for giving birth. So maternal and infant mortality rates in humans are unprecedented among the rest of the primates. Yet, in terms of net genetic success, the adaptive pay-offs of our heightened cognitive abilities as allowed by these large, big brain-swaddling craniums apparently outweighed such increased risks during childbirth.

We often find just this sort of give-and-take in evolution. Nature endows a species with an improved design, but not without some cost. In the case we're most interested in here—theory of mind—our species evolved the comparatively novel capacity to reason about the unobservable mental states of others. Theory of mind had enormous survival value because it allowed our ancestors to be empathic and intensely cooperative, not to mention more Machiavellian and strategic by deliberately deceiving competitors. But the more ancient, "pre–theory of mind" brain never went away, nor did the impulsive, hedonistic, and uninhibited drives that came along with it. So, like the old primate pelvic bones forced to accommodate our new supersized human heads, there is a dangerous friction between these "old" (pre–theory of mind) and "new" (post–theory of mind) elements of our social brains, a psychological friction that continues to jeopardize our reproduction and survival to this day.

On the one hand, our "old" brains urge us to let it all hang out, as they say—genitals, passions, warts, and all. Again, apart from the threat of looming physical violence, there's no reason to hide one's peccadilloes if one does not have pride or shame. Without a theory of mind, I might as well do things in front of you that I'd do in front of any inanimate object; if I can't conceptualize your mind, you're basically just a piece of furniture, and I can hardly worry about what you're thinking about me. Frankly, says the old part of my brain, why do I care about whether the kitchen sink or the chair in the corner can see what I'm up to, much less you? But, on the other hand, our "new" brains are constantly shouting out to us, "Whoa! Not so fast! Think about the implications!" With a theory of mind, then, I realize that once you see me do X, Y, or Z (use your imagination—the more sordid the better), you *know* this about me. So, yeah, you better believe I'm going to think twice before satisfying my own immediate self-interests.

But there's still an unanswered question here. Exactly why is it that the feeling of being observed sways our social behaviors so dramatically, leading us to do things that appear altruistic, or at least keeping us from doing things we otherwise might want to do? Simply knowing that you know I'm, say, an adult bed wetter, have a particularly nasty case of gonorrhea, or enjoy watching reruns of the 1980s television series *Knight Rider* every Friday night while wearing children's racing-car pajamas might be a little embarrassing, but that in itself isn't really enough for me to bother trying to hide these things from you. After all, my dog might *see* and therefore *know* these things about me, but that wouldn't be too disconcerting. That you know these awkward (and, I hasten to add, fictitious) facts about me would probably make me a tad uncomfortable, but there's one crucial additional thing that makes your knowing very different from my dog's knowing, and that would keep me from sharing this undesirable social information about myself with you: *I realize that once you know, you're going to tell other people.*

———•———

Language. That's the problem with being human. Without a theory of mind enabling us to think about what others know and don't know, and without a means of communication to symbolically encode others' mental states, events, and concepts, there's no threat of information dissemination. Here, then, is the real crux of the matter: for every other species that currently exists or has ever existed on this earth, the specific details about what one animal knows about another is limited to what it sees firsthand. Not so, individual human beings, whose reputations precede them.

The combustive coevolution of theory of mind and language meant a game-changing development for human beings. It doesn't matter if a particular incident happened two minutes ago or two decades ago. Once you've got a single witness to your actions, or someone who has otherwise come to have specific details about you, you've got a "carrier" of strategic information about you. And a carrier can often mean trouble, especially if it involves information about your failure to heed the warnings of the new part of your social brain. As an old Chinese proverb says, "What is told in the ear of a man is often heard a hundred miles away."

With brains powered by a theory of mind, carriers realize that others don't know what they know, so they can intentionally share these juicy facts with interested, absent third parties—third parties who can punish you through anything from ostracism to execution. And, if you'll follow this reasoning through, as this communal punishment becomes publicly revealed, your public reputation deteriorates, and so also, by deductive logic, does your reproductive success. University of Edinburgh political scientist Dominic Johnson has also written on the enormity of this distinctively human evolutionary problem: "Information about person A could propagate via person B to person C, D, E and so on . . . even if person B and C do not care, it may not be until person Z hears the news, or until *enough* people hear the news, or until some authority hears the news, perhaps weeks later, that punishment will come."[5]

Through language, strategic social information (which is any information that, once exposed, could influence one's reproductive success) could be relayed to absent third parties by witnesses' reports, hearsay, allusion, rumor, or gossip, making the careful, thoughtful management of such details vitally important for our ancestors. Patience, restraint, modesty, humility—these are all desirable, biblically endorsable features of humanity not because they are heavenly virtues, but because they're pragmatic. For other apes, inhibition is often illogical, especially when witnesses are only impotent, subordinate onlookers rather than dominant or physically aggressive. For us, inhibition is very often the key to our survival. Again, this is because whenever another member of our own species—anybody with a wagging tongue really—sees us doing something, anything, this person can then go and tell someone else who wasn't there, who can tell someone else, and so on, as in the proverbial game of telephone or that figure of speech "through the grapevine." To give but one of countless examples, Temple University psychologist Ralph Rosnow describes how unsuspecting children in western Newfoundland were once used by their parents to loiter about the Roman Catholic parish, ferrying out news to teetotaling adults about the drinking patterns of the town's inhabitants.[6]

The explosive consequences of carriers are highlighted in a scene from the movie *Doubt* (2008), starring Philip Seymour Hoffman and Meryl Streep. In the film, Hoffman plays an uncomfortably avuncular priest in a small Catholic diocese in the Bronx, New York. Streep's character, a nun, is the cynical and austere principal of the attached school who comes to suspect the priest of sexually abusing a young African American boy in the church rectory. Wary of his own vulnerability to malicious rumors about the alleged molestation, the accused clergyman—whose intentions toward the boy are never confirmed (hence the title of the story)—offers the following illustrative parable in a sermon to his congregation:

> *A woman was gossiping with her friend about a man whom they hardly knew—I know none of you have ever done this. That night, she had a dream: a great hand appeared over her and pointed down on her. She was immediately seized with an overwhelming sense of guilt. The next day she went to confession. She got the old parish priest, Father O'Rourke, and she told him the whole thing. "Is gossiping a sin?" she asked the old man. "Was that God Almighty's hand pointing down at me? Should I ask for your absolution? Father, have I done something wrong?" "Yes," Father*

O'Rourke answered her. "Yes, you ignorant, badly-brought-up female. You have blamed false witness on your neighbor. You played fast and loose with his reputation, and you should be heartily ashamed." So, the woman said she was sorry, and asked for forgiveness. "Not so fast," says O'Rourke. "I want you to go home, take a pillow up on your roof, cut it open with a knife, and return here to me." So, the woman went home: took a pillow off her bed, a knife from the drawer, went up the fire escape to her roof, and stabbed the pillow. Then she went back to the old parish priest as instructed. "Did you cut the pillow with a knife?" he says. "Yes, Father." "And what were the results?" "Feathers," she said. "Feathers?" he repeated. "Feathers everywhere, Father." "Now I want you to go back and gather up every last feather that flew out onto the wind." "Well," she said, "it can't be done. I don't know where they went. The wind took them all over." "And that," said Father O'Rourke, "is gossip!"[7]

Not everything is gossip worthy, of course. In fact, most behaviors aren't. Assume that you and I are acquaintances on a cordial first-name basis. Seeing me bending over to tie my shoelaces isn't exactly something to write home about, nor is seeing me drinking a strawberry milkshake or tripping over a slab of uneven sidewalk. But if I groped you while tying my shoelaces, dumped my milkshake on your head, or removed my belt and started disciplining that misbehaving pavement, my guess is you'd be eager to share these interesting facts about me with someone else. And if word gets out about these things, or gets out to the wrong people anyway, my social life is probably going to take a hit. Now just imagine if you had seen me doing something *really* unlawful or egregious—again, you're limited only by your imagination.

Our compulsion to let others know whenever someone else has

done something wrong or unusual appears to have an innate basis. As University of Oxford psychologist Gordon Ingram and I report in a 2010 issue of *Child Development*, almost as soon as children begin speaking, tattling to adult authority figures is rampant and almost impossible to eradicate.[8] By contrast, "tootling" (letting adults know when another child has done something positive) is virtually unheard of. To get kids talking positively about other kids usually requires explicit instruction from caregivers and teachers or some special incentive.

And let's face it—even for adults, keeping a secret is hard work. You may personally be very good at keeping secrets, but consider that, in one study, 60 percent of people confessed to sharing even their best friends' secrets with a third party. Another study found that a quarter of people shared "confidential" social information entrusted to them with at least three other people. In fact, there's even some data to suggest that simply prefacing your secret sharing with a request for confidentiality (such as "Please keep this close to your chest" or "Just between you and me") can actually make your confidante *more* likely to betray your trust, because you're essentially flagging the coming information as being strategic and gossip worthy, as high-value social knowledge. Even professional therapists aren't altogether immune to the urge to share their clients' secrets among themselves, as several studies have revealed.[9]

———

As a result of our fundamental dependence on other people, humans are extraordinarily sensitive to being ostracized. Because we have vested genetic interests, we even have to worry about other people judging us on the basis of what our friends and family are up to. The sociologist Erving Goffman noted that, not very long ago, once you were seen in the company of a questionable character you were referred

to as "having smallpox," because this person contaminated your reputation by sheer association.[10] This is, of course, the Republican ploy
used against Barack Obama in the 2008 U.S. presidential election, in
which Senator John McCain's running mate, Governor Sarah Palin
of Alaska, insinuated repeatedly that Obama was "palling around"
with William Ayers. Ayers, a poisonous figure in conservative circles,
had been involved in a radical leftist organization in the 1970s, and
Obama had served on a single education reform committee with him.
It's the whole birds-of-a-feather, peas-in-a-pod thing. In the light of
this, it's not too surprising that psychologists have discovered that
we're more likely to favor punishment of transgressors—and more
severe punishment at that—when we know that there's an audience
listening to our opinions on the matter.

Things become even more complicated when the transgressor is
a biological relative. Consider the case of David Dahmer, younger
brother of the late Milwaukee serial killer Jeffrey Dahmer. How does
David cope with the stigma of having such a scandalous figure on the
twig next to his on the family tree? We'd have a hard time asking him
personally: he changed his last name, his whereabouts are unknown,
and he does his best to get by living in complete anonymity. And no
wonder. Having the last name Dahmer wouldn't exactly endear you
to the ladies (well, at least not any ladies you'd probably want raising
your children), among other things. The truth is that David indeed
carries around half of his brother's genetic material, and although
most women couldn't tell you just why they're turned off by the
prospect of touting about in their wombs or suckling at their breasts
the nephew of a necrophile who had cultivated a keen taste for the
flesh of young men (aside from the fact that it creeps them out), this
psychological aversion is nature's way of telling them that Dahmer
DNA is the equivalent of genetic plutonium. David's children would
likely be ostracized as well if people knew who their uncle was, so

their mother's own genetic success would be placed in peril because her offspring, and therefore carriers of her own genes, would be outcasts with an insufferable social handicap.

Is such automatic judgment being unfair to the Dahmer heirs? From a societal perspective, it's entirely unfair. But from the amoral perspective of natural selection, whatever genetic factors played a role in their uncle becoming a headlines-grabbing psychopath may also be incubating in their own genetic material, so this social bias probably reflects a reasonable adaptive strategy.

Similarly, studies suggest that the adult children of rapists, child molesters, and alcoholics are often extraordinarily wary of confiding these dark family secrets to romantic partners, even after marriage. Of course, just because their parents did these things doesn't mean that they themselves will inevitably end up doing the same. Quite the opposite, in most cases. But all else being equal, in the ancestral past, those who stigmatized others on the basis of their moral bloodlines would have had a leg up over those who didn't, because doing so minimized the chances of passing on to their offspring maladaptive, heritable traits such as impulsive tendencies and various social disorders.

———•———

Previously, evolutionary psychologists tended to focus on the advantages of having language. Indeed, there were certainly many advantages to sharing our mental lives with others through symbolic communication, and today there are just as many evolutionary theories to account for them. The most relevant theory for our analysis, however, was one developed by University of Oxford anthropologist Robin Dunbar. Dunbar has argued that language allowed our ancestors to abandon the type of parasite-picking, hand-in-fur grooming that eats up much of the daily routine of other social primates, because chitchat does the same thing, only better (well, minus the parasite removal, but we subsequently lost a lot of our body hair too). Gossip replaced grooming, since we could now tend to our relationships, forge alliances, and ease our social anxieties through word of mouth rather than through hand in fur. What's more, we could learn about what happened behind the scenes, collect strategic information about others that permitted us to make adaptive decisions around them, and sew facts and lies into others' heads that would spread and serve our own selfish interests.[11]

The next time you're catching up with old friends, listen carefully to how they speak about themselves. They're not too transparently pretentious, I'd bet, as that would backfire (just think how much we despise braggarts and name-droppers, given the obviousness of their manipulative intentions)—yet they're probably not too humble either. If you tune your ear just right, you'll notice just how inventive people can be at sliding into the conversation details that place themselves in a positive light. If you've ever itched to tell someone how you mastered tae kwon do in the sixth grade, sacrificed your own happiness to care for your dying uncle, scored 143 on the Stanford-Binet intelligence test, or have a brilliant daughter who was just accepted into Wellesley College, rest assured you're not alone.

If they're believable, lies can go a long way, at least in terms of serving our reproductive interests. What is especially remarkable is that human beings are the only species for which the individual's actual possession of evolutionarily relevant traits (such as intelligence, talents, selfishness, sexual proclivities, diseases, and so on) has become overshadowed in selective importance by the ability to *intentionally* manipulate others' beliefs about these traits. In today's world, for example, it doesn't matter if you've got a skin disease, a mental disorder, or one leg that's shorter than the other—all that really matters to your reproductive interests is whether you can lead others to believe that you don't have these problems, by using your theory of mind to plant false beliefs in their head (perhaps, in these cases, with the help of makeup, psychotropic medication, or a prosthetic device). This is what keeps PR companies so busy today.

But while not all information is reliable and we constantly run the risk of being deceived by others, in general the more information we have about other people, the better placed we are to make adaptive decisions around them. Gossip allows us to avoid much of the costly trial-and-error learning that other primates face. This is why we're social vultures hovering over the sensational aspects of each other's lives, and why, as our evolved psychology manifests itself today, star-driven tabloids are such a lucrative business and campaign seasons have us busily collecting dirt on politicians. It's important to know if those in a position of leadership, who are poised to have considerable say about our future welfare, have a history of corruption or dubious dealings. And because, evolutionarily speaking, there's an obvious imbalance between the costs of disbelieving and the costs of believing strategic social information, even false accusations can be especially damaging to one's reputation. All else being equal, a woman who shrugged off her fiancé's ex-wife's claims that the man, years earlier, had physically abused their infant daughter would be at a disadvantage over one who dumped this fiancé for another man. This is why the "where there's smoke, there's fire" line of reasoning is so intuitive to most people, whereas the "innocent until proven guilty" counterpoint comes only with organized judicial effort.

In one clever archival study in a 2003 issue of *Evolution and Human Behavior*, University of Guelph psychologists Hank Davis and Lyndsay McLeod sampled a random selection of news stories from eight different cultures over the past three hundred years. What they discovered was that the "essence" of sensational news—what made something particularly alluring to a human readership—was its relevance to reproductive success in the ancestral past.[12] Most of these high-profile stories dealt with things such as altruism, reputation, cheaters, violence, sex, and the treatment of offspring. In other words, what whets our appetites in the social domain today are probably the same general topics of conversation that the first humans were gabbing about 150,000 years ago in sub-Saharan Africa.[13]

Again, with all due caveats, you wouldn't knowingly marry someone who had a history of abusing children or philandering up a storm, just as you wouldn't hire someone who stole from his previous employer or who was supposedly a slacker. In today's high-tech world, you certainly wouldn't buy something from an eBay seller who had generated negative feedback.

What separates you from other animals is that you don't have to be the victim yourself. Other people have already done that for you. Ultimately, the human tendency to plant, track, and manipulate social information by way of language enabled group sizes to become larger and larger, bettering the chances of survival for individual members (and hence their genes). "At some point in our [preverbal] evolutionary history," writes Robin Dunbar, "prehuman groups began to push against the ceiling on group size. The only way they could have broken through this ceiling so as to live in groups larger than about 80 individuals was to find an alternative mechanism for bonding [other than manual grooming] in which the available social time was used more efficiently."[14]

Among other benefits, a larger group offered its members increased protection against external threats—whether other humans or tooth-and-claw predators. So when there was a bad apple in the bunch, or someone who weakened the group's defenses in some way by compromising its cohesion, strength, and size, this person invited intolerance. And language rooted out these problem figures marvelously. In groups as diverse as British undergraduate students and Zinacantán Indians in Mexico, content analyses of "free-range" conversations (essentially, data gathered by the researchers' eavesdropping) show that about 80 percent of all naturally occurring linguistic discourse involves social topics.[15] The particular rules may differ from society to society, of course, fluctuating with the prevailing social and environmental pressures. But in general, morality is a matter of putting the group's needs ahead of one's own selfish interests. So when we hear about someone who has done the opposite, especially when it comes at another person's obvious expense, this individual becomes marred by our social judgment and grist for the gossip mills. As Florida State University psychologist Roy Baumeister says, "Gossip serves as a policing device that cultures employ as a low-cost method of regulating members' behaviors, especially those that reflect pursuits of selfish interests that come at a cost to the broader community."[16]

Consider, for example, a scene in Robert Louis Stevenson's *The Strange Case of Dr. Jekyll and Mr. Hyde* (1886), in which the narrator watches in horror as, in a fit of rage, the heinous Mr. Hyde tramples a young girl whose path has accidentally collided with his own at a street corner:

> *Killing [Hyde] being out of the question, we did the next best. We told the man we could and would make such a scandal out of this, as should make his name stink from one end of London to the other. If he had any friends or any credit, we undertook that he should lose them.*[17]

Clever readers realize that Mr. Hyde is just as much a part of our own double human nature as is the kindhearted Dr. Jekyll. And Stevenson certainly wasn't alone in holding this opinion of the constant tension between the intrinsic good and evil in each of us.[18] In fact, the age-old question of our double human nature is a recurring theme in literature. In Swedish author Pär Lagerkvist's somewhat lesser-known novel *The Dwarf* (1944), a story written from the psychological vantage point of a man standing only twenty-six inches high in Renaissance Italy, the protagonist shrewdly observes,

> *I have noticed that sometimes I frighten people; what they really fear is themselves. They think it is I who scare them, but it is the dwarf within them, the ape-faced man-like being who sticks its head from the depths of their souls. They are afraid because they do not know that they have another being inside. And they are deformed though it does not show on the outside.*[19]

Here, then, in the acknowledgment of our animalistic "dark sides," is the rub. Language was indeed adaptive, just as Dunbar and other evolutionary psychologists say it was. But it was a double-edged sword; every bit as much as it solved some problems, it introduced a serious adaptive predicament for our ancestors. Not only were we talking about other people; other people were talking about us. And, given those ever-present, feel-good, ancient drives we inherited as part of our old social brains, that was a *major* problem. Even a single, impulsive, uninhibited selfish misstep would have led directly to social problems once word got out; and given our extreme dependence on others, these social problems would have translated into real, calculable genetic losses. "Words are wolves," said the French writer Jean Genet.[20]

That language posed a special adaptive problem for early humans is reflected by evolutionary changes to other areas of the brain, particularly the regions responsible for executive functioning and inhibitory control. In a chatty human society, behavioral self-regulation would have been especially important. Florida Atlantic University psychologists Kayla Causey and David Bjorklund point out that

*as social complexity and brain size increased, greater require-
ments to cooperate and compete with [other humans] . . . required
greater voluntary inhibitory control of sexual and aggressive
behaviors, which contributed to increased social harmony and
delay of gratification. Neural circuits initially involved in the
control of emotional and appetitive behaviors could then be co-
opted for other purposes, playing a critical role in the evolution of
the cognitive architecture of modern humans. Over time, inhibitory mechanisms became increasingly under cortical (and thus
intentional) control.* [21]

The inhibition of our selfish, or explosive, streaks is no less critical today than it was in the past. If you're known as a cheat, a child
abuser, a thief, or even a slacker, some of the better-case scenarios
are that you'll end up alone, poor, or in a federal penitentiary where,
despite even the best efforts with your same-sex cell mate, the forecast
for your further genetic replication is grim. In some places still, your
community might simply decide that you're not worth all the hul-
labaloo anyway and simply do away with you in some creative way,
cheaply ridding itself of a potential liability to the group.

But although the adaptive problems posed by this chronic tension
between the old and new components of our social brains are clearly
apparent still today, just imagine how powerful they would have been
for our ancestors. Only ten thousand years ago, we were still living
in close-knit societies about the size of a large lecture hall in a state
university. What today might be seen as an embarrassing faux pas
back then could have been the end of the line for you. At least, it could
have been the end of the line for your reproductive success, because
an irreversibly spoiled reputation in such a small group could have
meant a surefire death for your genes.

Imagine the very worst thing you've ever done—the most vile, scandalous, and vulgar. Now imagine all the details of this incident tattooed on your forehead. This scenario is much like what our ancestors would have encountered if their impulsive, hedonistic, and self-centered drives weren't kept in check by their more recently evolved prudent inhibitions. And this was especially the case, of course, in risky situations—that is, while being watched by potential carriers. Eyes meant carriers, and carriers, of course, meant gossip. If their previously adaptive, ancient drives overpowered them, our ancestors couldn't simply move to a brand-new town where nobody knew them. Rather, in their case it was "wherever you go, there you are." Because early humans were completely dependent on those with whom they shared a few hundred square kilometers, cutting off all connections wasn't a viable option. And effectively hiding one's identity behind a mantle of anonymity wasn't very doable either, because one couldn't exactly be just a nameless face. There was no such thing as the Internet then; the closest our ancestors had to anonymity was the cover of night.[22] So in the ancestral past, being good, being moral, by short-circuiting our evolved selfish desires, was even more a matter of life and death than it is today. Like Nathaniel Hawthorne's character Hester Prynne trapped in cloistered, seventeenth-century Puritan Boston, early humans found themselves living in a scarlet-letter savanna.[23]

———◆———

Fortunately, today most of us are skilled at behaviorally smothering our ancient drives and subscribing to moral rules, which are nothing but the logistical details by which group members can coexist without tearing each other to bits. After all, we're the direct genetic descendants of those who effectively heeded the advice of their new social brains. And, to be clear, it's not *always* the end of the world if we're seen doing something frowned on by society or if others somehow learn of our bad deeds. In fact, depending on the circumstances and the severity of one's immoral lapse, any given screwup could have a negligible effect on one's genetic fitness, even if it succumbs to loose lips. There are also preemptive damage control tactics to keep the information from being received by the wrong pair of ears or serving to ward off or lessen punishment, such as apologies, confession, restitution, crying, or blackmail.[24]

In extreme cases, murdering a carrier could also be effective, adaptively speaking. In Dostoyevsky's *The Brothers Karamazov* (1880), the priest character, Father Zossima, tells of a middle-aged man attempting to clear his conscience of murdering a young woman after she had refused his marriage offer. The woman's innocent serf had been falsely arrested for her murder, subsequently fell sick in prison, and died shortly thereafter. Plagued by guilt, the real murderer, who "was in a prominent position, respected by all, rich and had a reputation for benevolence,"[25] confesses to the priest but soon comes to regret this and considers killing Father Zossima. "The thought was unendurable that you were alive knowing everything," says the man to the monk, who had now become a dangerous carrier. "Let me tell you, you were never nearer death."[26]

We see the same basic dynamic operating in police witness protection programs today. In fact, many unexplained homicides, whose real motives may never be known, might well be the result of the victim's knowing a little too much about the murderer. I once even read a sad news story about a thief who burglarized a pet store and killed the owner's talking parrot for fear it would be able to identify him. It may have indeed done so if his partner had inadvertently said his name aloud during the heist.

In general, though, it was best for our ancestors not to find themselves in a position where such costly damage control tactics were necessary, or to become vulnerable in any way to carriers. The most adaptive strategy was usually simply to be well behaved—or restrained—in the first place. "Conscience," said the American satirist H. L. Mencken, "is the inner voice that warns us somebody may be looking."[27] So when you dig deep enough into what are apparently selfless, pure-hearted motives, cynics can still rejoice in knowing that being good is ultimately, as evolutionary biologists point out, a self-ish genetic enterprise. There really is no being good for goodness' sake—at least, not at the unconscious level of genetic replication.[28]

———•———

Lest we forget about that selfish monstrosity still rummaging about in our heads, moaning for release from the prison of such evolved incon-veniences, there are occasions still when being selfish can reap its own rewards. This is especially the case when carriers don't seem to pose a genuine threat, such as when there are no witnesses to our actions, or when we're acting in collusion with others who are gambling with their own genetic stakes. There are also occasions when, owing to any number of relational vicissitudes with others, releasing the devil inside can earn us considerable profit by causing us to be impulsive and self-centered.

But acting in such a manner is pretty much always a high-risk strategy, no matter how certain we are that we can get away with it. This is because human beings operate with an "optimism bias," a way of looking at the future that causes us to downplay the likelihood of negative personal outcomes. Among other things, this bias leads us to assume that we'll be successful at tasks in which we feel we're even remotely competent, including, sometimes, antisocial acts. As a result, we have a tendency to underestimate the presence of genuine threats—in the ancestral past, perhaps someone was in fact spying on us when we thought we were alone or perhaps our partner in crime would be discovered and subsequently rat us out. These threat miscalculations are especially dangerous to our genetic welfare today. Contemporary forensic science methods have filled our prisons with people who had very different plans for themselves. And of course the world has its generous share of regretful divorced men and women who traded in their loving spouses for a single, seemingly discreet pleasure that came to be exposed.

As we learned earlier in this chapter, however, we also possess an especially effective, adaptive safeguard to protect our genes against our evolved impulses and our vulnerably overconfident judgment: the inhibiting sense of being observed. Again, ancestrally speaking, eyes meant carriers, and carriers meant gossip. What further derails our selfish streak is the conscious awareness that an observer can identify us as an individual: a specific person with a name and a face. The more obvious—or traceable—our individual identity, the less likely we are to engage in intemperate, high-risk behaviors that, though they may well reap immediate payoffs, can also hobble our overall reproductive success, owing to the adaptive problem of gossip. Only a rather dim-witted bank robber, for example, would enter his targeted establishment without a disguise. If one is convinced of being absolutely unidentifiable, the fear of punishment—or retribution— vanishes. The famous social psychologist Leon Festinger referred to this general phenomenon as the process of "deindividuation," which occurs whenever "individuals are not seen or paid attention to as individuals."[29] Deindividuation is quite clearly a potentially dangerous scenario for the social group as a whole; if the individual actor cannot be identified, then the threat of gossip loses that personal punch, one that otherwise helps keep the actor's egoistic needs in check.

Deindividuation is, of course, at the core of a mob mentality. It can also lead to acts of brutal violence against out-group members, because a "deindividuated" person is absorbed into an anonymous group identity and no longer fears the consequences of toting around an insolvably tarnished reputation. When faced with a frenzied mass of angry, anonymous people, relatives and friends of the out-group victim wouldn't know where to begin looking for revenge against a specific perpetrator. In anthropological circles, it is well known that warriors who hide their identities before going into battle are more likely to kill, mutilate, or torture than are those who do not bother to disguise themselves. And here in Northern Ireland, where I currently live, one analysis found that of all incidents of sectarian violence reported in the region over a two-year period (1994–96), paramilitary members who wore masks during their offenses attacked more people, inflicted more serious injuries, committed more acts of vandalism, and were more likely to threaten their victims after attacking them than were paramilitary members who left their faces exposed.[30]

The coevolution of language and theory of mind came with its good side, its bad, and its downright ugly in giving our species its unique signature in the animal kingdom. So where does God—and other supernatural agents like Him—come into the evolutionary picture? As we've seen, God was born of theory of mind. But it seems Mother Nature gave birth for selfish reasons.

In an influential cross-cultural analysis on "the attributes of God" performed by the Italian scholar Raffaele Pettazzoni in the 1950s, one especially prominent and recurring feature began to emerge in the samples of all the religious groups studied. Pettazzoni discovered that, regardless of the particular religion one subscribed to, the central gods were envisioned as possessing a deep *knowing* of people as unique individuals—of their "hearts and souls."[31] Indeed, one of the inevitable consequences of thinking about God is a heightened, almost invasive sense of individuation. In one recent study, participants who were asked to think about God exhibited a huge increase in self-awareness compared to those asked to think about other people.

Many people believe that while you may be anonymous to your fellow man, rest assured that some "Other" is always surveying your actions. In the early 1980s, for example, a team of anthropologists in Borneo studying a group of people known as the Iban jotted down a prominent belief there: "Anyone who successfully cheats another, or escapes punishment for his crimes, even though he may appear to profit temporarily, ultimately suffers supernatural retribution."[32]

For many, God represents that ineradicable sense of being watched that so often flares up in moments of temptation—He who knows what's in our hearts, that private audience that wants us to act in certain ways at critical decision-making points and that will be disappointed in us otherwise. The "right decisions" are favorably inclined toward those logistical details we've just discussed, what we'd call morals and social norms, and are seen to be as right as the grass is green. Even if this sense of God's watching didn't always persuade our ancestors to act morally under such conditions, if it did so just once, it could have been the one time they'd have been caught by other people—which is, of course, the only penalty for misbehavior they'd have really ever faced. In other words, the illusion of a punitive God assisted their genetic well-being whenever they underestimated the risk of *actual* social detection by other people. This fact alone, this emotional short-circuiting of ancient drives in which immediate interests were traded for long-term genetic gains, would have rendered God and His ilk a strong target of natural selection in human evolution.

The intoxicating pull of destiny beliefs, seeing "signs" in a limitless array of unexpected natural events, the unshakable illusion of psychological immortality, and the implicit assumption that misfortunes are related to some divine plan or long-forgotten moral breach—all of these things have meaningfully coalesced in the human brain to form a set of functional psychological processes. They are functional because they breed explicit beliefs and behaviors (usually but not always of a religious nature) that were adaptive in the ancestral past. That is to say, together they fostered a cognitive imperative—a deeply ineradicable system of thought—leading our ancestors to feel and behave as though their actions were being observed, tallied, judged by a supernatural audience, and responded to in the form of natural events by a powerful Other that held an attitude toward them. By helping to thwart genetically costly but still-powerful ancestral drives, these cognitive illusions pried open new and vital arteries for reproductive success, promoting inhibitory decisions that would have been highly adaptive under the biologically novel, language-based rules of natural selection. The illusion of God, engendered by our theory of mind, was one very important solution to the adaptive problem of human gossip.

Such thinking may not lead people to reason logically about the nature of existence. But that's irrelevant. As evolutionarily minded scholars, all we really need to determine is whether or not these cognitive predispositions somehow increased our ancestors' odds of passing on their genes. And indeed, evidence that supernatural reasoning curbs our selfish and impulsive behavior is limited, but consistent, and comes from a variety of studies.

For example, one logical conclusion that follows from the theoretical model we've just sketched out is that the larger the society, the more opportunities there are for cheating others, but also the more likely it is that one would underestimate the threat of potential carriers, given the sheer number of eyes present. The inhibiting effect of feeling watched and known about by a punitive, supernatural Other would be especially vital to saving one's "genetic hide," so to speak, under such large-group conditions. And indeed, in an important cross-cultural analysis reported in a 2003 issue of *Evolution and Human Behavior*, evolutionary biologists Frans Roes and Michel Raymond found that, across cultures, large societies are associated with moralizing high gods: the larger the population, the greater the chance that the culture includes the concept of supernatural watchers concerned with human morality.[33] Note also that as long as group members genuinely believe that another's misfortune is caused by that person's sins, this erroneous causal attribution is sufficiently scary to keep the rest of the group members in line.

In another study, University of British Columbia psychologists Ara Norenzayan and Azim Shariff primed some of their research participants with "God concepts" by exposing them to words such as "spirit," "divine," and "prophet." The effect of this exposure was that, compared with those who saw only neutral words, these people donated more money to a stranger on a seemingly unrelated task. Although the authors acknowledge that these findings aren't without alternative interpretations, their particular argument favors the one being made here:

> *Activation of God concepts, even outside of reflective awareness . . . triggers this hyperactive tendency to infer the presence of an intentional watcher. This sense of being watched then activates reputational concerns, undermines the anonymity of the situation, and, as a result, curbs selfish behavior.*[34]

In addition, in a 2005 issue of *Human Nature*, Todd Shackelford, Katrina McLeod, and I reported the results of a study in which, as part of a slick cover story, we told a group of participants that the ghost of a dead graduate student had recently been seen in the lab. Compared to those who didn't hear any mention of the alleged ghost, students who received this information beforehand were much less likely to cheat on a separate game in which they were competing for fifty dollars when left alone in the room and given the opportunity to do so.[35]

More recently, University of Kent psychologist Jared Piazza and I resurrected the spirit of Princess Alice (discussed in Chapter 3) to determine whether young children left alone in the room with this friendly invisible being would also be inhibited from cheating. Five- and six-year-olds were just as likely to refrain from cheating on a game when they thought Princess Alice was sitting in a chair watching them as they were when a real human being—an unengaged stranger with a neutral facial expression—actually was in that very same chair observing them. As expected, cheating rates were highest among a control group of children who were left alone in the room with neither the stranger nor Princess Alice. In general, this pattern of findings was the case for slightly older kids as well, yet a few of the seven- to nine-year-olds in the study did in fact cheat in front of Princess Alice, shrugging her off as a fabrication devised by the experimenters. Curiously, though, even these young skeptics did so only after reaching out and waving their hands over the empty chair to make sure she wasn't there. Furthermore, those who said they believed in Princess Alice were much less likely to cheat than those who said they didn't.[36]

In sum, both logic and current evidence point to the following unavoidable conclusion: By curtailing bad behaviors, the sense of being observed by a morally invested, reactive Other (whether God, Princess Alice, the ghost of a dead graduate student, or some other supernatural agent of your choosing), especially one that created us and for whom we're eternally indebted in return, meant fewer self-destructive scraps for those ravenous wolves of gossip to feed on.

———⊙———

Is religion an adaptation? The question itself is flawed. In his important book *Religion Explained* (2002), Washington University anthropologist Pascal Boyer writes, "People have religious notions and beliefs because they acquired them from other people. On the whole, people get their religion from other members of their social group."[37] But it is not at the level of religion per se where we are likely to find a true genetic adaptation.[38] Natural selection is nondenominational. In fact, you may have noticed how seldom religion has entered our discussion over the course of this book. Instead, if an adaptation indeed exists, it's at the level of brain-based psychological processes that we have been exploring throughout—those incredibly potent cognitive factors that lead us to think that we've been created for a special purpose, or that natural events contain important messages from another realm, or that our endless psychological existence is mysteriously linked with some hazy moral pact with the universe.

These building-block illusions had to be psychologically convincing enough before more elaborate, fill-in-the-blank, culturally diverse religious ideas could emerge. By all accounts, the basic illusion of God (or some other supernatural agent) "willfully" creating us as individuals, "wanting" us to behave in particular ways, "observing" and "knowing" about our otherwise private actions, "communicating" His desires to us in code through natural events, and "intending" to meet us after we die is pretty convincing for most people. These things transcend religion and cut across almost every single human society on this planet. By contrast, religion involves culturally acquired concepts that are flexible enough to meet the particular socioecological conditions at hand—it comprises the specific content of belief, not what drives belief itself.

Does all this disprove the existence of God? Of course not. Science speaks only to the improbable, not the impossible. If philosophy rules the day, God can never be ruled out entirely, because one could argue that human cognitive evolution was directly and intentionally inspired by God, so we alone, of all species, can perceive Him (and reality in general) using our naturally evolved theory of mind. But if scientific parsimony prevails, and I think it should, such philosophical positioning becomes embarrassingly like grasping at straws.[39]

The facts of the evolutionary case imply strongly that God's existence is rather improbable. As Yale University psychologist Paul Bloom writes,

> *The driving force behind natural selection is survival and reproduction, not truth. All other things being equal, it is better for an animal to believe true things than false things; accurate perception is better than hallucination. But sometimes all other things are not equal.*[40]

Owing to the distorting lens of our evolved theory of mind—distortions that warp our perception of reality in systematic, predictable ways because they served our ancestors' genetic interests—we know now that what *feels* real (even when these thoughts are shared with other sane, healthy, completely normal people) is not always a good measure of what *is* real. The cognitive illusion of an ever-present and keenly observant God worked for our genes, and that's reason enough for nature to have kept the illusion vividly alive in human brains.

In fact, the illusion can be so convincing that you may very well refuse to acknowledge it's an illusion at all. But that may simply mean that the adaptation works particularly well in your case.

7 | AND THEN YOU DIE

BASING THEIR CONCLUSIONS on hearsay and a rather dubious narrative provenance, creationists have long held that Darwin "recanted" his theory of evolution on his deathbed and died a repentant Christian believer. As the story goes, a fervent evangelical Anglican named Lady Hope (born Elizabeth Reid Cotton, later marrying an admiral named Hope and thus adopting her noble prefix) had inveigled herself into the Darwins' close circle of friends toward the end of the great scientist's life. Lady Hope, who by all accounts was a busybody widow who had already made a name for herself in the temperance movement against drunkenness, allegedly paid her friend Charles a visit not long before his death. Her grandiloquent (and hotly contested) description of that visit was first published in a Washington, DC–based Baptist periodical called the *Watchman-Examiner* on August 19, 1915, reading partly as follows:

> *It was one of those glorious autumn afternoons, that we some-*
> *times enjoy in England, when I was asked to go in and sit with*
> *the well-known professor, Charles Darwin. He was almost bed-*
> *ridden for some months before he died. I used to feel when I saw*

him that his fine presence would make a grand picture for our Royal Academy, but never did I think so more strongly than on this particular occasion.

He was sitting up in bed, wearing a soft embroidered dressing gown, of rather a rich purple shade.

Propped up by pillows, he was gazing out on a far-stretching scene of woods and cornfields, which glowed in the light of one of those marvelous sunsets which are the beauty of Kent and Surrey. His noble forehead and fine features seemed to be lit up with pleasure as I entered the room.

He waved his hand towards the window as he pointed out the scene beyond, while in the other hand he held an open Bible, which he was always studying.

"What are you reading now?" I asked as I seated myself beside his bedside. "Hebrews!" he answered—"still Hebrews. 'The Royal Book' I call it. Isn't it grand?"

Then, placing his fingers on certain passages, he commented on them.

I made some allusions to the strong opinions expressed by many persons on the history of the Creation, its grandeur, and then their treatment of the earlier chapters of the Book of Genesis.

He seemed greatly distressed, his fingers twitched nervously, and a look of agony came over his face as he said: "I was a young man with unformed ideas. I threw out queries, suggestions, wondering all the time over everything, and to my astonishment, the ideas took like wildfire. People made a religion of them."[1]

Over the years, many Christian apologists have all but exhausted themselves in trying to confirm Lady Hope's tale of Darwin's deathbed conversion and the so-called recantation of his scientific ideas. Darwin's wife, Emma, soundly denied all such claims. Still, many years later, one scholar apparently rifled through the Darwin family's otherwise unmarked set of dusty old Bibles and found a backward pencil tick mark appearing opposite the first few verses of Hebrews 6—alleged confirmation of Lady Hope's account.[2] When skeptics questioned the flowery language attributed to Darwin by Lady Hope, others pored over Darwin's old letters and correspondence in search of previous incidents in which he had lapsed into similar purple prose. Still others pointed out that, indeed, Darwin did tend to twitch his fingers nervously on occasion, and did he not, in fact, possess a purple dressing gown?

Most evolutionists, however, fail to see the point in this creationist appeal to Darwin's religious ambivalence. So what if his never fully excised, schoolboy sinner's guilt did prick his conscience at the very end, they say. Whether Darwin died embracing the Christian Lord or slid off into death still the wary old agnostic he had been known as in life, it's quite a stretch to claim that a verbal "taking back" of the theory of evolution has any repercussions for the central tenets of evolutionary theory itself. Fortunately, the truth of natural selection doesn't depend on the firmness of any one man's convictions, even if that man is Charles Darwin. More generally, of course, we might ask whether rambling, suffering-laden thoughts on one's deathbed, a place where fear abounds and lucidity easily absconds, should trump our assessment of a person's insights and thinking during the golden times of that individual's healthy intellectual heights.

Even the staunchest of atheists, in moments of despair, can find themselves appealing to God. But this just says that atheists are human, with human brains, brains that work in predictably human ways—such as invoking God's will—in response to particular human problems. I've never understood why so many skeptics are intent on demonstrating their immunity to irrational or quasi-religious thought. Although I have little doubt that many fervent nonbelievers out there have clung tenaciously to their atheism as they faced death or impending disaster (there's even a popular website with signed testimonials from atheistic veterans proudly proclaiming their steely logical-headedness in the line of fire), foxhole atheism is still much ado about nothing, philosophically speaking. The atheist may or may not come to "God" when things appear most grim, but that doesn't mean he or she is in any way confirming God's existence. Even an atheist's coming to confess "ignorance" and acknowledging God's existence during difficult times would have zero to do with whether or not God actually exists. I, for one, don't handle suffering very well; having a low-grade fever and a sore throat is enough to have me privately asking God why He's being so unspeakably cruel to me. But I'm also pretty sure my wobbly epistemological stance during these difficult times doesn't have much bearing elsewhere in the metaphysical cosmos.

As we've seen throughout this book, our private experiences generated by thinking about our individual purpose, the meaning of life, the afterlife, why bad things happen to good people, and so on, are highly seductive, emotionally appealing, and intuitively convincing—in most cases leading directly to belief in God. It is therefore more than a little foolhardy to think that human nature can ever be "cured" of God by scientific reason. As a way of thinking, God is an inherent part of our natural cognitive systems, and ridding ourselves of Him—really, thoroughly, permanently removing Him from our heads—would require a neurosurgeon, not a science teacher. So the real issue is this: knowing what we know now, is it wise to trust our evolved, subjective, mental intuitions to be reliable gauges of the reality outside our heads, or do we instead accept the possibility that such intuitions in fact arise through cognitive biases that—perhaps for biologically adaptive reasons—lead our thinking fundamentally away from objective reality? Do we keep blindly serving our genes and continue falling for this spectacular evolutionary ruse of a caring God, or do we peek behind the curtain and say, "Aha! That's not God, that's just Nature up to her dirty little tricks!"

———◆———

Being poised to shatter the adaptive illusion of God is arguably one of the most significant turning points our species has ever faced in its relatively brief 150,000-year history. The belief instinct may never be completely deprogrammed in our animal brains, but by understanding it for what it is rather than subscribing uncritically to the intuitions it generates, we can distance ourselves from an adaptive system that was designed, ultimately, to keep us hobbled in fear. Our evolutionary ancestors required a fictitious moral watcher to tame their animalistic impulses, to keep them from miring their reputations under the real glare of human carriers. But what happens now that we know the truth about God, about our "souls," about the afterlife?

Even if it's only an intellectual liberation from these illusions and our emotions and intuitions never completely follow suit, the distracting (and often distressing) thoughts that come with seeing ourselves through the eyes of a judgmental, infallible, and unreasonable moral agent may eventually begin fading away, or at least lose their powerful influence over our decision making and behaviors. I'm not optimistic that this will happen, however, because I think nature has played too good a trick on us. Furthermore, whether shattering the adaptive illusion of God is a "good thing" or a "bad thing" isn't entirely clear. That value judgment would almost certainly differ from person to person. From our genes' perspectives, destroying this illusion may well be detrimental to our overall reproductive interests. Then again, I have a hard time believing that, upon seeing God for what He really is, people would suddenly start acting like amoral chimpanzees. With or without belief, the consequences for acting selfishly are as much a deterrent as they've always been: those who don't play by the rules will—by and large, more often than not—suffer the *human* consequences.

The philosopher Voltaire famously said, "If God did not exist, it would be necessary to invent him."[3] That was sound logic at the time. But remember, Voltaire wrote this in 1768 during the French Enlightenment. Things have changed since then, to say the least. With today's social-tracking technology (Social Security numbers, the Internet, hidden cameras, caller ID, fingerprints, voice recognition software, "lie detectors," facial expression, DNA and handwriting analysis, to name just a few particularly effective behavior-regulating devices presently in place in the modern world), Voltaire's declaration doesn't really pertain anymore—at least, not for large-scale, developed nations. Who needs Voltaire's "eye in the sky" when today we've got millions of virtual superhuman eyes trained on us from every possible angle, lodged discreetly in every pore of our lives? Human evolution hasn't quite caught up with human technology, however, and the adaptive illusion of God is likely to survive as long as theory of mind is a part of our species' cognitive blueprint.

Yet now that the illusion has started unraveling at its psychological seams, we can finally catch a glimpse of ourselves as the amazing creatures that we are. After all, compared to all the other creatures on this planet, we are strange manifestations of matter indeed, endowed with the unique capacity to think about what it's like to be others, to reflect on the very question of meaning, and to be aware of our own limited time as subjectively experiencing selves.

We are the first generation, in the history of our species, to be confronted directly by the full scientific weight of an argument that renders a personal God both unnecessary and highly unlikely. The many loopholes of a more humble agnosticism have suddenly become unreasonable places to continue burying our heads. Yet being in the full godless light of this shattered illusion is, I think, a spectacular position to find oneself in.

Where I sit writing these words, the view is of an old Irish parishioner's graveyard, and as such places go, it is a field of mildewed, pockmarked old headstones for the forgotten villagers who preceded me here in time. Certainly, many people in my village feel that these extinct individuals are more than just their ossified remains. If one has faith in an improbable Second Coming, a reanimated two-hundred-year-old corpse might one of these days crawl out of her tomb, straighten out her bodice, shout over to me that she's dying for a cold pint of Guinness, and say, "Would you be so kind, love, as to fetch me one." If that happened, and were I not already having my intestines gnawed on by some fiendish devils in hell as one of the wicked myself, I would be delighted to do so for her, from the very same pub where she preferred to drink in her own day, no less, since it's still pouring Guinness for her heirs on the main street today. I would also endeavor, once the alcohol made her comfortable enough to share such a personal experience with me, to find out from this woman all that I could about what it's like to be dead.

The seventeenth-century French philosopher Blaise Pascal may well regard me as a fool for betting on an atheistic extinctivism on the grounds of his famous, and eponymous, wager. He argued that one should always wager that there is a God and an afterlife, because the believer has everything to win and nothing to lose, whereas the nonbeliever has everything to lose and nothing to win.[4] (In fact, according to "Bering's wager," which deals in earthly currency, the believer has considerably more to lose.) My money is on this type of resurrection scenario never happening. The dead are the dead, nothing more and nothing less. Somewhere, there's an extinct butcher in that overflowing graveyard across from my window, whose callused hands once skinned fatted calves, disposed of offal in the vacant fields behind the old abattoir, and brushed tenderly against his wife's rosy cheeks. Now these hands are but yellowed phalanges layered with a delicate moss. The most beautiful woman in the village is somewhere under those dreary stones too, still wearing the same expensive silk-and-lace gown sent to her by the wealthy suitor she met while holidaying in Bath a hundred years ago. But, were we to disturb the earth and peel back the lid of her antique casket, no trace would remain of her once lovely face or her voluptuous breasts. Nor would we find any sign of the tuberculosis-riddled lungs beneath those breasts that stole her away from so many hopeful young men.

It's not these people's bodies that are buried six feet under the fertile Irish soil—they didn't "occupy" their bodies or lease them out from God for the short time they were here. They were their bodies, and now they are my very quiet neighbors across the way. But using our theory of mind, we can imagine what it was like to be them on the eve of their deaths, preparing to "meet their maker" and to reunite with their loved ones (those mindless stones in the stratified tombs beneath theirs). Perhaps, alone with their thoughts, the butcher and the belle looked deeply in the mirror, gazed piercingly into their own eyes, and pictured themselves as the prone cadavers they were soon to turn into. And maybe they wondered what it's all been for.

In fact, because we're going to flatline sooner or later too, because there's a plot of land, an urn, or even a bit of hungry sea out there patiently awaiting our own lifeless remains, we might ask ourselves the very same question. The difference between our skeletal predecessors and us, however, is that we can actually arrive at a reasonably informed answer. It's an answer that was unobtainable in their day because the psychological science wasn't yet in place to allow them to understand the question properly, and therefore to recognize it as the nonquestion that it is.

What's it all for? In the end, that's probably a false riddle. But never mind the mind of God. We can live for each other—here and now, before it's too late, sympathetically sharing snapshots from inside our still-conscious heads, all 6.7 billion heads containing just as many hypothetical universes, most of them, unfortunately, spinning feverishly with the illusions we've just shattered. But what you choose to do with your brief subjective existence is entirely up to you. If you choose to ignore this precautionary tale of a fleeting life without supernatural consequences, there will be no hell to pay. Only missed opportunities. And then you die.

And that's the truth. I swear to God.

NOTES

INTRODUCTION

1. In many courtrooms across the Western world with slightly more serious cases on the docket, my little act of rebellion would be translated as a breach of the Bible-handed oath "Do you swear to tell the truth, the whole truth, and nothing but the truth, so help you God?" And in the ancient Hebrew world, there was the similar "oath by the thigh"—where "thigh" was the polite term for one's dangling bits—since touching the sex organs before giving testimony was said to invoke one's family spirits (who had a vested interest in the seeds sprung from these particular loins) and ensured that the witness wouldn't tell any fibs. I rather like this older ritual, in fact, as it's more in keeping with evolutionary biology. But in general, swearing to God, in whatever way it's done, is usually effective in persuading others that you're telling the truth. We know from controlled studies with mock juries that if a person swears on—or better yet, kisses—the Bible before testifying, the jury's perception of that person's believability is significantly enhanced.

   Psychologically speaking, there's a lot happening when we swear to God like this—at least when we do so sincerely. At the top of that list is the assumption that, whereas you can fool your fellow man, you can't fool God. Only God *knows*. Pierre Bovet, a Swiss psychologist working in the 1920s, reasoned that the significance of God's omniscience is first grasped by children when they realize that their parents aren't as all-knowing as they once thought. That is to say, at some point in early childhood, every kid figures out that even the smartest mothers and fathers can be deceived

207

through treachery and lies. Not so, God. According to Bovet, God therefore becomes something of a brighter bulb, replacing the rather dim, or at least fallible, parental figure.

An experiment conducted by Justin Barrett and his colleagues lends some support to Bovet's assumptions. In this study, children were shown that a closed saltine cracker box actually contained a bunch of rocks. After the perfunctory "you got me" laugh, they then were asked what their mother would think was inside the box if she saw it sitting there (no shaking allowed) and also what God, or an ant, or a tree, or a bear would think. Three-year-olds were egocentric and answered "rocks" for all of these characters. They figured that if they knew something, everyone else must know it too; it doesn't matter if you sip lattes while driving your Subaru, shed your leaves in late September, have a brain smaller than a dust mite, or played Job like he was a mouse at your paws. Developmental psychologists have, in fact, long known that, prior to the age of about four or so, children have difficulty taking the perspective of another person; rather, it's as if the entire world were looking through their own eyes. Older children, in contrast, distinguished between what these characters could and couldn't know. Whereas God was privy to the rock secret, they reasoned, the others would be duped just like they had been into thinking there were crackers inside. (Well, except for the bear, which a few clever children reasoned could smell that there wasn't any food.) What's especially interesting about these findings, the authors point out, is that "for children to 'get God right' all they had to do is keep answering like a young 3-year-old," hinting that our natural egocentrism makes us "developmentally prepared" to conceptualize God's all-knowing mind. Justin L. Barrett, Rebekah A. Richert, and Amanda Driesenga, "God's Beliefs versus Mother's: The Development of Nonhuman Agent Concepts," *Child Development* 72 (2001): 50–65.

2. In one of the very few theoretical papers to explore the question of our closest living relatives' existential concerns, psychologists Jack Maser and Gordon Gallup surmised two decades ago that fear of death is the major motivational force behind God beliefs. "The organism, which is aware of itself, and bearing witness to the demise of its associates, should be able to take the next logical step and conceive of a nonself, or its death." Furthermore, "chimpanzees have minds. They may even be able to conceive of a God, but without foreknowledge that they will die, there is no great motivational reason for the notion of God to be a paramount feature in their lives." Maser and Gallup,

"Theism as a By-product of Natural Selection," *Journal of Religion* 70 (1990): 515–32.

3. Miguel de Unamuno, *Tragic Sense of Life,* trans. J. E. Crawford Flitch (Charleston, SC: BiblioBazaar, 2007), 55. Originally published in 1912.

4. Richard Dawkins, *The God Delusion* (London: Bantam, 2006), 172.

CHAPTER 1

1. Rosamond Kent Sprague, ed., *The Older Sophists: A Complete Translation by Several Hands of the Fragments in Die Fragmente der Vorsokratiker, edited by Diels-Kranz. With a New Edition of Antiphon and of Euthydemus* (Columbia: University of South Carolina Press, 1972; Indianapolis, IN: Hackett, 2001), 32.

2. Ibid., 39.

3. Ibid., 37.

4. Nicholas Humphrey, "The Society of Selves," *Philosophical Transactions of the Royal Society of London. Series B, Biological Sciences* 362 (2007): 745–54.

5. This is certainly not to say that other social species cannot experience loneliness. A dog tethered to a tree and neglected by its owner undergoes great anguish. Domesticated canines, through generations of artificial selection, are designed to live social lives alongside human caregivers. And as the psychologist Harry Harlow's notorious 1960s research on socially deprived rhesus macaques amply demonstrated, most primates also suffer symptoms of severe psychological distress if physically removed from others for extended lengths of time. (Harry F. Harlow, Robert O. Dodsworth, and Margaret K. Harlow, "Total Social Isolation in Monkeys," *Proceedings of the National Academy of Sciences, USA* 54 [1965]: 90–97.) And humans are no exception. The effects of solitary confinement on prisoners, for example, may include memory loss, severe anxiety, hallucinations, and delusions. Yet by contrast to the type of "intersubjective" loneliness we're interested in here—in which other minds are insufferably just out of reach—in these more conventional cases of physical loneliness the socially isolated organism is maladapted to survive in a climate of complete social deprivation.

6. W. B. Yeats (1949), quoted in Christopher Ricks, *Keats and Embarrassment* (Oxford: Oxford University Press, 1976), 64.

7. Gorgias may have been the first *official* solipsist, but it's doubtful he was the first human being ever to stumble naively upon such thoughts. In his book *Kinds of Minds* (1996), the philosopher Daniel Dennett reports that roughly a

third of his undergraduate students claim they spontaneously questioned the presence of other minds—long before they ever heard of the formal concept of solipsism. For example, these students will describe, at a specific, abrupt moment in their childhood, how they cast skeptical glances at those around them, searching the eyes of others for an irrefutable glimmer of a "soul."

8. Daniel M. Wegner, Betsy Sparrow, and Lea Winerman, "Vicarious Agency: Experiencing Control over the Movements of Others," *Journal of Personality and Social Psychology* 86 (2004): 838–48.

9. Gordon G. Gallup Jr. and Steven M. Platek, "Cognitive Empathy Presupposes Self-awareness: Evidence from Phylogeny, Ontogeny, Neuropsychology, and Mental Illness," *Behavioral and Brain Sciences* 25 (2002): 36–37.

10. Fernando Pessoa, *The Book of Disquiet,* trans. Richard Zenith (New York: Penguin, 2002), 268. Originally published in 1916.

11. Paul Bloom, *Descartes' Baby: How the Science of Child Development Explains What Makes Us Human* (New York: Basic Books, 2004), 177–78.

12. Peter Koval, Joonha Park, and Nick Haslam, "Human, or Less than Human?" *In-Mind* (April 13, 2009), www.in-mind.org/issue-8/human-or-less-than-human.html.

13. Many other thinkers, of course, preceded Dennett in the question of other minds (Thomas Hobbes, John Stuart Mill, Sir William Hamilton, Friedrich Nietzsche, and Bertrand Russell, to name just a few). But it was Dennett who first began piecing together the evolutionary story behind this capacity to reason about thought, recognizing it to be as much a matter for evolutionary theorists and biologists as it was for philosophers.

14. Daniel C. Dennett, *Kinds of Minds: Toward an Understanding of Consciousness* (New York: Basic Books, 1996), 26.

15. Alison Gopnik, Andrew N. Meltzoff, and Patricia K. Kuhl, *The Scientist in the Crib: Minds, Brains, and How Children Learn* (New York: Morrow, 1999), 5.

16. Jane Goodall, "Learning from the Chimpanzees: A Message Humans Can Understand," *Science* 282 (1998): 2184–85.

17. "A Self Worth Having: An Interview with Nicholas Humphrey," *Edge: The Third Culture* (June 30, 2003), www.edge.org/3rd_culture/humphrey04/humphrey04_index.html. Ironically, this important contribution to our understanding of human cognitive evolution happened in the shade of a family tree with a very famous branch attached to it. Although he's not a direct descendent of Charles Darwin, Nicholas Humphrey comes very close

to it, being able to trace his genealogical history to the most famous scientist of all time. As he explains it, Humphrey's grandmother's brother Geoffrey Keynes married Charles Darwin's granddaughter Margaret Darwin.

18. David Premack and Guy Woodruff, "Does the Chimpanzee Have a Theory of Mind?" *Behavioral and Brain Sciences* 1 (1978): 515–26.

19. Frans B. M. de Waal, "Cultural Primatology Comes of Age," *Nature* 399 (1999): 635.

20. As quoted by C. Dreifus, "Going Ape," *Ms.* 9, no. 5 (August–September 1999): 48–54.

21. Charles Darwin, *The Descent of Man* (New York: Modern Library, 1982), 445. Originally published in 1871.

22. Roger S. Fouts, "Apes, Darwinian Continuity, and the Law," *Animal Law* 10 (2004): 99–124.

23. Ibid.

24. Derek Bickerton, "Darwin's Last Word: How Words Changed Cognition," *Behavioral and Brain Sciences,* 31 (2008): 132.

25. Frederick L. Coolidge and Thomas Wynn, *The Rise of* Homo sapiens*: The Evolution of Modern Thinking* (Malden, MA: Wiley-Blackwell, 2009), 192–93.

26. Daniel J. Povinelli, Jesse M. Bering, and Steve Giambrone, "Toward a Science of Other Minds: Escaping the Argument by Analogy," *Cognitive Science* 24 (2000): 509–41.

27. Daniel J. Povinelli and Timothy J. Eddy, "What Young Chimpanzees Know about Seeing," *Monographs of the Society for Research in Child Development* 61, no. 3 (1996).

28. Christophe Boesch, "What Makes Us Human (*Homo sapiens*)? The Challenge of Cognitive (Cross-Species) Comparison," *Journal of Comparative Psychology* 121 (2007): 227–40 (italics added).

29. Brian Hare, Josep Call, Bryan Agnetta, and Michael Tomasello, "Chimpanzees Know What Conspecifics Do and Do Not See," *Animal Behaviour* 59 (2000): 771–86.

30. Josep Call and Michael Tomasello, "Does the Chimpanzee Have a Theory of Mind? 30 Years Later," *Trends in Cognitive Sciences* 12 (2008): 187–92.

31. Derek C. Penn and Daniel J. Povinelli, "On the Lack of Evidence That Non-human Animals Possess Anything Remotely Resembling a 'Theory of Mind,'" *Philosophical Transactions of the Royal Society of London. Series B, Biological Sciences* 362 (2007): 731–44.

32. "Child Star, Now Grown Up, Re-releases 'Red Balloon'" (interview with Pascal Lamorisse), *National Public Radio* (December 14, 2007), www.npr .org/templates/story/story.php?storyId=17253102.

33. György Gergely and Gergely Csibra, "Teleological Reasoning in Infancy: The Naïve Theory of Rational Action," *Trends in Cognitive Sciences* 7 (2003), 287–92.

34. Fritz Heider and Marianne Simmel, "An Experimental Study of Apparent Behavior," *American Journal of Psychology* 57 (1944), 243–59. To see if you can avoid attributing these humanlike characteristics to the images on the screen, check out Heider and Simmel's original animation online. At the time of this writing, the clip is readily available on YouTube.

CHAPTER 2

1. Charles Darwin, *The Autobiography of Charles Darwin 1809–1882*, ed. Nora Barlow (London: Collins, 1958), 92–93.

2. Jean-Paul Sartre, *Words*, trans. Irene Clephane (London: Penguin, 1964), 65.

3. Unfortunately, we know very little at this stage about what makes one individual liable to become an atheist and another a believer—even when the two are raised together, share the same general upbringing, and are exposed to the same parental beliefs. It's certainly not just a matter of genes, of course, because even heritable traits are influenced profoundly by the environment. But learned values, ideologies, and belief systems can take on considerable strength when they nuzzle into the head of an especially receptive genetic host. Evidence suggests, for example, that the personality variable of *religiosity* (basically, how much passion someone tends to feel about religious topics, wherever she falls on the belief scale) is largely determined by genes. Your identical twin brother may be an evangelical preacher while you're a screaming atheist, but these genetics data help explain why you're both so hot and bothered by God.

4. Jean-Paul Sartre, *Existentialism and Human Emotions* (New York: Philosophical Library, 1957), 14.

5. In other work, such as *The Flies* (1946), Sartre targets the quandary of morality in the absence of a human nature designed by God. In doing so, he foreshadows the many earnest attempts of recent evolutionary theorists who argue that good and evil, the soul, the afterlife, and God are phantoms of the evolved human mind rather than ontological realities. Unlike Sartre, however, many of these recent writers struggle to articulate a nondeterministic morality that allows any room for free will. This is because, when followed to

its full, logical conclusion, evolutionary psychology can lead only to a deterministic moral philosophy. This is not to say that evolutionary processes themselves are deterministic; rather, they are "epigenetic" (bidirectionally driven by genetic and environmental factors). But when it comes to the discrete social behaviors of individual human beings, and the psychological forces that are responsible for such behaviors, the subjective self is impotent to affect the person's biological destiny. If, for example, a middle-aged man hires a prostitute, it is because the decision is in accordance with his present physiology, which has arisen as a consequence of his unique developmental experiences, which occurred within a particular cultural environment in interaction with a particular inherited genotype, which he inherited from his particular parents, who inherited genetic variants of similar traits from their own particular parents, ad infinitum. What's more, this man's brain acted without first consulting his self-consciousness; rather, his neurocognitive system enacted evolved behavioral algorithms that responded, either normally or in error, in ways that had favored genetic success in the ancestral past. This man's self merely plays the role of spectator in his body's sexual affairs; so there is no one here to hold personally accountable for his behavior, even though he may be exposing his wife to a sexually transmitted disease or exploiting a young drug addict for his own pleasure. There is only the embodiment of a man who is helpless to act in any way that is contrary to his particular nature, which is a derivative of a more general nature.

In this sense, evolutionary psychology is antithetical to Sartre's humanistic thesis; here, the self is only a deluded creature that thinks it is participating in a moral game when in fact it is just an emotionally invested audience member. So just as he did with any religious portrayal of a human nature purposefully crafted by God, Sartre similarly derided any biological portrayal of a universal human nature. In his view—which was rightly held, if one appreciates the full philosophical implications of the complex interplay of biology, genetics, and psychology—a biological explanation would excuse the individual from accountability in the moral domain. If there is, in reality, no such thing as free will, then how can the individual have responded any other way to the stimuli he or she was confronted with? Attributing responsibility to others becomes merely a social convention that reflects only a naive psychology of the causes of their behaviors.

6. Rick Warren, *The Purpose Driven Life: What on Earth Am I Here For?* (Grand Rapids, MI: Zondervan, 2002), 18.

7. Steve Paulson, "The Flying Spaghetti Monster" (interview with Richard

Dawkins), *Salon* (October 13, 2006), www.salon.com/books/int/2006/10/13/dawkins.

8. There are certainly many scholars today who, while being well informed of very complex matters concerning evolutionary biology, remain subtle (or not-so-subtle) advocates of some type of "natural theology"—a quasi-scientific branch of religious study that, in modern manifestations, seeks to understand God's creative intentions in "guiding" evolution. The fallacies of natural theology are discussed in detail elsewhere in the book (Chapter 3). But in general, there are of course many people for whom evolutionary logic and religious belief are not obviously incommensurable and who suffer no apparent conflict or tension by simultaneously endorsing the former without abandoning the latter.

9. Simon de Beauvoir, *Adieux: A Farewell to Sartre,* trans. Patrick O'Brien (New York: Pantheon, 1984), 438 (italics added).

10. Albert Camus, *The Fall,* trans. Justin O'Brien (New York: Vintage, 1991), 27. Originally published in 1956.

11. David Albert Jones, *The Soul of the Embryo: An Enquiry into the Status of the Human Embryo in the Christian Tradition* (London: Continuum, 2004), 11.

12. Job 10:10–11 (New International Version).

13. William James, "Thought before Language: A Deaf-Mute's Recollections," *Philosophical Review* 1 (1892): 613–24.

14. Ibid.

15. Ibid.

16. In fact, D'Estrella strongly influenced the impressionist painter Granville Redmond when the latter's parents admitted their hearing-impaired son to the school. As an adult, Redmond in turn befriended the silent film star Charlie Chaplin, who admired his paintings, and eventually the two became so close that Chaplin incorporated some of his deaf companion's exaggerated gestures—copied from D'Estrella, no less—into his famous cinematic pantomime acts.

17. James, "Thought before Language."

18. Jean Piaget, *The Moral Judgment of the Child,* trans. Marjorie Gabain (New York: Free Press, 1997), 257. Originally published in 1932.

19. Deborah Kelemen, "Are Children 'Intuitive Theists'?: Reasoning about Purpose and Design in Nature," *Psychological Science* 15 (2004): 295–301.

20. Krista Casler and Deborah Kelemen, "Developmental Continuity in the Teleo-Functional Explanation: Reasoning about Nature among Romanian Romani Adults," *Journal of Cognition and Development* 9 (2008): 340–62.

21. Tania Lombrozo, Deborah Kelemen, and Deborah Zaitchik, "Inferring Design: Evidence of a Preference for Teleological Explanations in Patients with Alzheimer's Disease," *Psychological Science* 18 (2007): 999–1006.

22. Deborah Kelemen, Maureen A. Callanan, Krista Casler, and Deanne R. Pérez-Granados, "Why Things Happen: Teleological Explanation in Parent-Child Conversations," *Developmental Psychology* 41 (2005): 251–64.

23. E. Margaret Evans, "Beyond Scopes: Why Creationism Is Here to Stay," in *Imagining the Impossible: Magical, Scientific and Religious Thinking in Children,* ed. Karl S. Rosengren, Carl N. Johnson, and Paul L. Harris (Cambridge: Cambridge University Press, 2000), 305.

24. Kayoko Inagaki and Giyoo Hatano, "Young Children's Conception of the Biological World," *Current Directions in Psychological Science* 15, no. 4 (August 2006): 177–81.

25. Albert Camus, *The Myth of Sisyphus, and Other Essays,* trans. Justin O'Brien (New York: Vintage, 1991), 94. Originally published in 1943.

26. Jeanette Walls, "Gossip," MSNBC (November 27, 2006), www.msnbc.msn .com/id/15516583.

27. Bill O'Reilly, *A Bold Fresh Piece of Humanity* (New York: Broadway Books, 2008), 242.

28. Ibid., 254.

29. Letter to Asa Gray, February 8 or 9, 1860. In Frederick Burkhardt and Sydney Smith, eds., *The Correspondence of Charles Darwin,* vol. 8, *1860* (Cambridge: Cambridge University Press, 1993), 275.

30. "CNN March 1997 Interview with Osama bin Laden," FindLaw, http:// news.findlaw.com/hdocs/docs/binladen/binladenintvw-cnn.pdf (accessed November 7, 2004).

31. Paula Hancocks, "Kids TV Praises Gaza Mom's Suicide Bombing," CNN (July 16, 2009), http://edition.cnn.com/2009/WORLD/meast/07/15/tv.show/ index.html?iref=allsearch.

32. "Obama's Religious Beliefs: An Interview with Barack Obama on His Religious Views," WantToKnow.info (March 27, 2004), www.wanttoknow .info/008/obama_religious_beliefs_views.

33. Tim P. German and H. Clark Barrett, "Functional Fixedness in a Technologically Sparse Culture," *Psychological Science* 16 (2005): 1–5.

34. Jean-Paul Sartre, *Saint Genet: Actor and Martyr,* trans. Bernard Frechtman (New York: Braziller, 1963).

35. "Miss California Sparks Furor with Gay Marriage Comments on Miss USA Telecast," FOXNews.com (April 20, 2009), www.foxnews.com/entertainment

/2009/04/20/miss-california-sparks-furor-gay-marriage-comments-miss-usa-telecast.

36. Ibid.

37. Richard Dawkins, *The God Delusion* (London: Bantam, 2006), 289.

38. Fyodor Dostoyevsky, *The Diary of a Writer*, 2 vols., trans. Boris Brasol (New York: Scribner, 1949), 96.

CHAPTER 3

1. Brett Martel, "Storms Payback from God, Nagin Says," *Washington Post* (January 17, 2006), www.washingtonpost.com/wp-dyn/content/article/2006/01/16/AR2006011600925.html.

2. Banesh Hoffman, *Albert Einstein: Creator and Rebel* (New York: Plume, 1972), 146.

3. This was one of the central points in William James's *The Varieties of Religious Experience* (1902): that religion is quintessentially an individual, personal affair. James tightened his fists in thoughtful revolt at the overly simplistic, common scientific shorthand prevalent in his day (and ours) that tended to reduce God to a force that doesn't concern itself with particular human problems: "The God whom science recognizes must be a God of universal laws exclusively, a God who does a wholesale, not a retail business. He cannot accommodate his processes to the convenience of individuals." *The Varieties of Religious Experience: A Study in Human Nature* (New York: Megalodon Entertainment, 2008), 417. Originally published in 1902.

4. Simon Baron-Cohen, *Mindblindness: An Essay on Autism and Theory of Mind* (Cambridge, MA: MIT Press, 1997).

5. Simon Baron-Cohen, "The Cognitive Neuroscience of Autism: Implications for the Evolution of the Male Brain" (2000), http://autismresearchcentre.com/docs/papers/2000_BC_cognitive.pdf (accessed November 26, 2008).

6. Digby Tantum, "Adolescence and Adulthood of Individuals with Asperger Syndrome," in *Asperger Syndrome*, ed. Ami Klin, Fred R. Volkmar, and Sara S. Sparrow (New York: Guilford, 2000), 382.

7. Temple Grandin, *Thinking in Pictures: And Other Reports from My Life with Austim* (New York: Doubleday, 1995), 189.

8. Ibid., 191.

9. Ibid., 200.

10. Edgar Schneider, *Discovering My Autism: Apologia Pro Vita Sua (with Apologies to Cardinal Newman)* (London: Kingsley, 1999), 54.

11. Ibid., 72.

12. Ibid., 73.

13. Harvey Whitehouse, *Modes of Religiosity: A Cognitive Theory of Religious Transmission* (Lanham, MD: AltaMira, 2004).

14. Jonathan Kenneth Burns, "An Evolutionary Theory of Schizophrenia: Cortical Connectivity, Metarepresentation, and the Social Brain," *Behavioral and Brain Sciences* 27 (2004): 840.

15. Albert Camus, *The First Man,* trans. David Hapgood (New York: Knopf, 1995), 314.

16. Tamar Szabó Gendler, "Alief and Belief," *Journal of Philosophy* 105 (2008): 634–63.

17. Ryan T. McKay and Daniel C. Dennett, "The Evolution of Misbelief," *Behavioral and Brain Sciences* 32 (2009): 493–561.

18. Chimpanzees display some rather enigmatic behaviors around other dead chimps, and cognitive theorists have yet to contribute seriously to the debate over just what exactly is occurring with these death responses. The primate ethologist Frans de Waal, however, made this provocative statement: "Seeing the termination of a familiar individual's life, chimpanzees may respond emotionally as if realizing, however vaguely, what death means." (*Peacemaking among Primates* [Cambridge, MA: Harvard University Press, 1996], 55.) Surely the death of another with whom an animal is emotionally attached can lead to outward displays of intense grief, even bereavement. What causes these emotions, however, is not necessarily an awareness of what death *means*—but is perhaps an anxiety-laden response to the sudden and unexpected severing of the attachment relationship. The mother-infant bond is so strong in nonhuman primates, for instance, that the aesthetic horrors of decomposition are seemingly overridden by emotional attachment; mothers will often carry the carcasses of their deceased infants until the small body has undergone substantial decay. Yet De Waal's statement refers more to the responses of chimps to fallen group members than to dead offspring or mothers. He writes of one group's response to the death of a former alpha-male chimpanzee severely maimed by rivals: "They were completely silent during the time that Luit's body was lying in his cage. The following morning, even at feeding time, hardly any sounds were heard. Vocal activity resumed only after the corpse had been carried out of the building." (Ibid., 66.)

Another primatologist, Geza Teleki, details how a group of chimpanzees at Gombe reacted to the accidental falling death of one of its own: at first there was raucous displaying and contagious fear response, followed by a period of intense quietude, careful visual inspection and overall attention directed toward the body, and finally, after several hours of corpse-centered activity, the reluctant moving off of the remaining group members. ("Group Responses to the Accidental Death of a Chimpanzee in Gombe National Park, Tanzania," *Folia Primatologica* 20 [1973]: 81–94.)

Before we can credit chimpanzees with a conscious death concept, however, we must be careful not to fall prey to our own anthropomorphizing theory of mind. What are we to make of the "ceremonial" gathering of black-billed magpies in response to the sudden death of another bird? Are we willing to say that they, too, have a vague notion of what death "means"? Given what we are learning of the ostensible mind blindness of other animals, it is perhaps more prudent at this stage to say that neither chimpanzees nor black-billed magpies have the cognitive hard wiring needed to represent death as the end of personal existence. Rather, both species are probably engaging in a response that reflects their basic understanding of perceptual cues of animacy (self-propelled movement, respiration, and so on) in combination with the unexpected termination of a social relationship. But in any event, experiencing the dead as giving communicative signs to the living in the form of natural events seems an unlikely psychological attribute in other species.

19. Justin L. Barrett, *Why Would Anyone Believe in God?* (Lanham, MD: AltaMira, 2004); Stewart Guthrie, *Faces in the Clouds: A New Theory of Religion* (New York: Oxford University Press, 1993).

20. "International Angel Day with Doreen Virtue and Charles Virtue," Hay House, www.hayhouse.com/event_details.php?event_id=695.

21. Doreen Virtue and Charles Virtue, *Signs from Above: Your Angels' Messages about Your Life Purpose, Relationships, Health, and More* (New York: Hay House, 1999), 45.

22. Jesse M. Bering and Becky D. Parker, "Children's Attributions of Intentions to an Invisible Agent," *Developmental Psychology* 42 (2006): 253–62.

23. In fact, a recent set of unpublished data by University of Oxford psychologists Florian Kiessling and Yvan Russell reveals that preschoolers' understanding of "invisible" probably translates to something more like "not present" than it does "transparent" ("Theory of Mind and Religion" [paper presented at the Second "Explaining Religion" (EXREL) Conference, Centre for Anthropology and Mind, University of Oxford, 2009]), so their failure to see Princess Alice as causing the picture to fall and the light to flash makes sense. If she's not actually in the room, how could she act on objects inside of it?

24. All children were, of course, "debriefed" following their participation in the

study—the experimenter made it clear to each child that Princess Alice was only pretend, and showed the child how the picture was made to fall by the magnet's being lifted on the other side of the door and how the light was made to flash on and off by a pocket-sized remote control. Nevertheless, some parents claimed that upon similar, unexpected events happening in the child's home (such as a lightbulb flickering or fuse blowing) children from the experimental condition would spontaneously invoke Princess Alice as the cause. It's unclear, however, whether they were serious or only joking. Yet it is remarkably easy to create novel, difficult-to-extinguish supernatural agents. University of Texas at Austin psychologist Jacqueline Woolley and her colleagues, for example, invented a Halloween character named "The Candy Witch" for their study and discovered that, for many children, belief remained high a year after the study was completed, especially for those children who had received a "visit" from the Candy Witch as part of the initial experiment. Jacqueline D. Woolley, Elizabeth A. Boerger, and Arthur B. Markman, "A Visit from the Candy Witch: Factors Influencing Young Children's Belief in a Novel Fantastical Being," *Developmental Science* 7 (2004): 456–68.

25. Josef Perner and Deborrah Howes, "'He Thinks He Knows': And More Developmental Evidence against the Simulation (Role-Taking) Theory," *Mind & Language* 7 (1992): 72–86.

26. God Hates Fags website, www.godhatesfags.com.

27. G. E. Newman, F. C. Keil, V. Kuhlmeier, and K. Wynn, "Sensitivity to Design: Early Understandings of the Link between Agents and Order," *Proceedings of the National Academy of Sciences, USA* (forthcoming).

28. Ibid.

29. William Kirby, *On the Power, Wisdom, and Goodness of God as Manifested in the Creation of Animals and in Their History, Habits, and Instincts*, 2 vols. (London: Pickering, 1835), 1:vii.

30. Ibid.

31. Ibid., 2:384–85.

32. Quoted in Philip F. Rehbock, *Philosophical Naturalists: Themes in Early Nineteenth-Century British Biology* (Madison: University of Wisconsin Press, 1983), 56.

33. Michael Dowd, *Thank God for Evolution: How the Marriage of Science and Religion Will Transform Your Life and Our World* (New York: Plume, 2009), 80.

34. "International Conference on Natural Theology: Beyond Paley: Renewing

the Vision for Natural Theology, 23–25 June 2008, Museum of Natural History, Oxford University," Thomist Tacos for the Soul, www.thomist tacos.com/?p=124 (accessed March 15, 2010).

35. Mark Williamson, "Haldane's Special Preference," *Linnean* 8 (1992): 14.

CHAPTER 4

1. André Gide, *The Counterfeiters: A Novel* (New York: Vintage, 1973), 249. Originally published in 1927.

2. Alan M. Leslie, "Pretense and Representation: The Origins of 'Theory of Mind,'" *Psychological Review* 94 (1987): 412–26.

3. Thomas W. Clark, "Death, Nothingness, and Subjectivity," in *The Experience of Philosophy,* ed. Daniel Kolak and Raymond Martin, 3rd ed. (New York: Wadsworth, 1996), 480–90. Originally published in *The Humanist* 54, no. 6 (1994): 15–20, www.naturalism.org/death.htm.

4. Shaun Nichols, "Imagination and Immortality: Thinking of Me," *Synthese* 159 (2007), 215–33.

5. Cited as "Attributed to Goethe (Johann Peter Eckermann, *Conversations with Goethe,* 1852)" in Shaun Nichols, "Imagination and Immortality: Thinking of Me," *Synthese* 159 (2007): 215–33.

6. Sigmund Freud, "Thoughts for the Times on War and Death," in *Collected Works of C. G. Jung,* ed. Herbert Read, Michael Fordham, and Gerhard Adler, vol. 4, *Freud and Psychoanalysis* (London: Hogarth, 1953), 304–5. Originally published in 1913.

7. Albert Camus, *The Plague,* trans. Stuart Gilbert (New York: Vintage, 1991), 119. Originally published in 1947.

8. David Cohen and Angèle Consoli, "Production of Supernatural Beliefs during Cotard's Syndrome, a Rare Psychotic Depression," *Behavioral and Brain Sciences* 29 (2006): 468–69.

9. Jesse M. Bering, "Intuitive Conceptions of Dead Agents' Minds: The Natural Foundations of Afterlife Beliefs as Phenomenological Boundary," *Journal of Cognition and Culture* 2 (2002): 263–308.

10. John Gay, "My Own Epitaph," inscribed on Gay's monument in Westminster Abbey; also quoted as "I thought so once; but now I know it."

11. Jean-Paul Sartre, *The Wall,* trans. Lloyd Alexander (New York: New Directions Paperback, 1969), 8. Originally published in 1939.

12. Miguel de Unamuno, *Tragic Sense of Life,* trans. J. E. Crawford Flitch (Charleston, SC: BiblioBazaar, 2007), 71. Originally published in 1912.

13. Clark, "Death, Nothingness, and Subjectivity" (italics added).

14. N. Emmons, "Children's Beliefs about Themselves as Babies, In Utero and Before They Were Conceived" (unpublished manuscript).

15. Gerald P. Koocher, "Childhood, Death, and Cognitive Development," *Developmental Psychology* 9 (1973): 369–75.

16. Jesse M. Bering and David F. Bjorklund, "The Natural Emergence of Reasoning about the Afterlife as a Developmental Regularity," *Developmental Psychology* 40 (2004): 217–33. Research on children's understanding and reasoning about the subject of death is, for obvious reasons, methodologically challenging, given the serious ethical considerations. For example, parents are especially wary of experimenters "teaching" their children ideas about what happens after death, so interview scripts must be worded in such a manner that the child makes no insinuations about what is a "correct" or "incorrect" answer. Many parents are concerned that questioning their children about death will prove disturbing or prematurely expose the children to these dark matters of the human condition. The present study—the puppet show with the mouse and alligator—was conducted on the heels of September 11, 2001, so parents were unusually sensitive about having their children encountering the topic of death. But in fact, we found that the children in our studies were overwhelmingly curious about the subject of death and enthusiastically welcomed the opportunity to discuss their views on the issue with attentive adults. Certainly, no children were disturbed by our questioning about the workings of a dead mouse's mind. Nevertheless, with the exception of fairly innocuous stories, quizzing children about actual dead human beings remains largely off-limits in psychological science, and therefore our full understanding of children's death concepts remains in a state of methodological limbo.

17. H. Clark Barrett and Tanya Behne, "Children's Understanding of Death as the Cessation of Agency: A Test Using Sleep versus Death," *Cognition* 96 (2005): 93–108.

18. Ibid.

19. The difference between minds and souls is a very subtle one, and most people struggle with teasing the two apart. According to University of California at Irvine psychologist Rebekah Richert and Harvard University psychologist Paul Harris, however, people differentiate minds and souls on several shady grounds. First, most people find the mind to be a more believable entity than the soul. In a 2008 study reported in the *Journal of Cognition and Culture*, Richert and Harris found that, out of 161 undergraduate students surveyed, 151 (93.8 percent) claimed that the mind exists, whereas only 107

(66.5 percent) felt the same about the soul. Second, people tend to conceptualize the soul as coming into existence earlier than the mind. Whereas only 8.1 percent of study participants believed the mind begins "prior to conception," 26.1 percent stated that the soul predated the union of egg and sperm. An equal number of students thought that minds and souls appeared simultaneously at the moment of conception, but more people thought that the mind begins at some point "during pregnancy" (35.4 percent) than thought the same of the soul (12.4 percent). Third, more people conceptualize the mind as changing over the life span (86.3 percent) than they do the soul (51.6 percent). Whereas only 4.4 percent of the study respondents claimed that the mind remains unchanged over the life span, 28.0 percent were certain that this was the case for the soul. In addition, for most people (83.9 percent) the soul is envisioned as continuing "in some way" after death, whereas the mind is more likely to be seen as ceasing to exist at death (70.8 percent). When Richert and Harris asked their participants whether they thought a human clone would have a mind, 67.1 percent said "yes," 21.1 percent were unsure, and 11.8 percent said "no." By contrast, only 32.3 percent thought a human clone would have a soul, 34.4 percent were unsure, and 33.5 percent were convinced it would be soulless. Furthermore, the more "spiritual" the participants considered the soul to be (in terms of performing special spiritual functions such as journeying to the afterlife and connecting to a higher power), and the more they distinguished between mind and soul, the less likely they were to support using embryos for stem cell research, disconnecting people from life support, and cloning humans. Interestingly, Richert and Harris discovered that, "people's concepts of the soul predicted their ethical decision making [on these issues] independently of religious affiliation." Rebekah A. Richert and Paul L. Harris, "The Ghost in My Body: Children's Developing Concept of the Soul," *Journal of Cognition and Culture* 6 (2006): 409–27.

20. Paul L. Harris and Marta Giménez, "Children's Acceptance of Conflicting Testimony: The Case of Death," *Journal of Cognition and Culture* 5 (2005): 143–64.

21. Jesse M. Bering, Carlos Hernández Blasi, David F. Bjorklund, "The Development of 'Afterlife' Beliefs in Religiously and Secularly Schooled Children," *British Journal of Developmental Psychology* 23 (2005): 587–607.

22. Fernando Pessoa, *The Book of Disquiet,* trans. Richard Zenith (New York: Penguin, 2002), 41. Originally published in 1916.

23. "Mystery of Missing Teens Believed Solved: Discovery Brings Grief, Relief," *Palm Beach Post* (March 3, 1997), http://nl.newsbank.com.

24. Penny Owen, "Soldier Leaves Behind Wife, 4 Children," *The Oklahoman,* May 30, 2002.

25. John Fowles, *The Magus* (New York: Back Bay Books, 2001), 427. Originally published in 1966.

26. K. Mitch Hodge, "Descartes' Mistake: How Afterlife Beliefs Challenge the Assumption That Humans Are Intuitive Cartesian Substance Dualists," *Journal of Cognition and Culture* 8 (2008): 387–415.

27. David Lester, Megan Aldridge, Christine Aspenberg, Kathleen Boyle, Pam Radsniak, and Chris Waldron, "What Is the Afterlife Like?" *Omega* 44 (2001–02): 113–26.

CHAPTER 5

1. "A Dreadful Accident," *Norfolk Chronicle* and *Norwich Gazette* (May 10, 1845), www.gotts.org.uk/Yarmouth%20bridge.htm.

2. Ibid.

3. Henry MacKenzie, *Sermon, Preached on Whitsunday, 1845: Being One of a Series Delivered after the Fall of the Bridge, at Great Yarmouth* (London: Smith, Elder, and Co., 1845).

4. Kurt Kelly, "Hundreds Gather to Mourn Victims of Bridge Collapse," *NewsOK* (May 27, 2003), http://newsok.com/hundreds-gather-to-mourn-victims-of-bridge-collapse/article/1030595. One of the other victims to perish was Andrew Clements, a young army captain and father of four from California en route to his new home in Alexandria, Virginia, where his family had flown in a few days earlier and was waiting anxiously for him to arrive. Clements's commanding officer "pondered the odds of making a 2,929-mile drive and landing on a 500-foot stretch of bridge that, in the most bizarre of accidents, had plummeted precisely as he crossed it. 'If [he] just stopped at a rest stop or stopped to get gas . . . There's just so many variables—and the timing.'" Ibid.

5. Jean Piaget, *The Moral Judgment of the Child,* trans. Marjorie Gabain (New York: Free Press, 1997), 252. Originally published in 1932.

6. Thornton Wilder, *The Bridge of San Luis Rey* (New York: Washington Square Press, 1955), 7. Originally published in 1927.

7. Ibid., 10.

8. Ibid., 163.

9. Ibid., 4.

10. Kurt Gray and Daniel M. Wegner, "Blaming God for Our Pain: Human Suffering and the Divine Mind," *Personality and Social Psychology Review* 14 (2010): 7–16.

11. Ibid.

12. Ibid.

13. Alison Gopnik, "Explanation as Orgasm and the Drive for Causal Understanding: The Evolution, Function, and Phenomenology of the Theory-Formation System," in *Cognition and Explanation*, ed. F. Keil and R. Wilson (Cambridge, MA: MIT Press, 2000), 299–323.

14. Ibid.

15. Ibid.

16. Quoted in P. C. W. Davies and Julian Brown, eds., *Superstrings: A Theory of Everything?* (Cambridge: Cambridge University Press, 1992), 208–9.

17. For example, consider this passage from the Bible: "Whosoever looketh on a woman to lust after her hath committed adultery with her already in his heart." Matt. 5:28 (New International Version).

18. E. E. Evans-Pritchard, *Witchcraft, Oracles, and Magic among the Azande* (New York: Oxford University Press, 1976), 22. Originally published in 1937.

19. Cristine H. Legare and Susan A. Gelman, "Bewitchment, Biology, or Both: The Co-existence of Natural and Supernatural Explanatory Frameworks across Development," *Cognitive Science* 32 (2008): 607–42.

20. Ibid.

21. Piaget, *Moral Judgment of the Child*, 259.

22. Elie Wiesel, *The Gates of the Forest*, trans. Frances Frenaye (New York: Holt, Rinehart, Winston, 1966), 197.

23. Janet Landman, "The Crime, Punishment, and Ethical Transformation of Two Radicals: Or How Katherine Power Improves on Dostoevsky," in *Turns in the Road: Narrative Studies of Lives in Transition*, ed. Dan P. McAdams, Ruthellen Josselson, and Amia Lieblich (Washington, DC: American Psychological Association, 2001), 35–66.

24. Dan P. McAdams, "The Psychology of Life Stories," *Review of General Psychology* 5 (2001): 100–122.

25. Ibid.

26. Ibid.

27. Todd F. Heatherton and Patricia A. Nichols, "Personal Accounts of Successful versus Failed Attempts at Life Change," *Personality and Social Psychology Bulletin* 20 (1994): 664–75.

28. John Gunther, *Death Be Not Proud: A Memoir* (Cutchogue, NY: Buccaneer, 1997). 206–7. Originally published in 1949.

29. Ibid., 63.

30. William James, *The Varieties of Religious Experience: A Study in Human Nature* (New York: Megalodon Entertainment, 2008), 128. Originally published in 1902.

31. "David Chase Takes On Angry Sopranos Fans," *The Chicago Syndicate* (October 19, 2007), www.thechicagosyndicate.com/2007/10/david-chase -takes-on-angry-sopranos.html.

32. Ibid.

33. Ibid.

34. Mikhail Bulgakov, *The Master and Margarita* (CreateSpace [www.cre atespace.com], 2009), 11. Originally published in 1967.

35. Harold S. Kushner, *When Bad Things Happen to Good People* (New York: Avon, 1983), 52.

36. Jay Dixit, "Cindy Chupack on Failure," *Brainstorm* blog (*Psychology Today*), May 18, 2009, www.psychologytoday.com/blog/brainstorm/200905/cin dy-chupack-failure.

37. Ibid.

38. Jesse M. Bering and Bethany T. Heywood, "Do Atheists Reason Implicitly in Theistic Terms? Evidence of Teleo-functional Biases in the Autobiographical Narratives of Nonbelievers" (paper presented at the Annual Meeting of the Society for Personality and Social Psychology, Las Vegas, NV, January 2010).

39. Ibid.

40. Ibid.

41. Milan Kundera, *The Joke* (New York: Harper Perennial, 1993), 164. Originally published in 1967.

CHAPTER 6

1. Jean-Paul Sartre, *No Exit, and Three Other Plays* (New York: Vintage International, 1989), 45. Originally published in 1946.

2. Ibid., 22.

3. Ibid., 35.

4. Ibid., 44.

5. Dominic D. P. Johnson, "God's Punishment and Public Goods: A Test of the Supernatural Punishment Hypothesis in 186 World Cultures," *Human Nature* 16 (2005): 410–46.

6. Ralph L. Rosnow, "Gossip and Marketplace Psychology," *Journal of Communication* 27 (2006): 158–63.

7. "Memorable Quotes for 'Doubt' (2008/I)," Internet Movie Database, www.imdb.com/title/tt0918927/quotes (accessed March 25, 2010).

8. G. P. D. Ingram and J. M. Bering, "Children's Tattling: Early Communicative Biases in the Reporting of Other Children's Behavior," *Child Development* 81 (2010): 945–57.

9. Anita E. Kelly, "Revealing Personal Secrets," *Current Directions in Psychological Science* 8 (1999): 105–9.

10. Erving Goffman, *Stigma: Notes on the Management of a Spoiled Identity* (New York: Simon & Schuster, 1963).

11. R. I. M. Dunbar, "Coevolution of Neocortical Size, Group Size and Language in Humans," *Behavioral and Brain Sciences* 16 (1993): 681–735.

12. Hank Davis and S. Lyndsay McLeod, "Why Humans Value Sensational News: An Evolutionary Perspective," *Evolution and Human Behavior* 24 (2003): 208–16.

13. Dalhousie University anthropologist Jerome Barkow has argued persuasively that one of the reasons we become so interested in celebrities is that our evolved minds are essentially duped into thinking these people are among our close circle of friends (or at least, in-group members). Because television, cinema, newspapers, tabloids, the Internet, and so on are all evolutionary novelties—that is, they certainly weren't present in the ancestral past when human social brains evolved—today our minds largely operate as though these strangers in our living rooms and on the front pages matter in our day-to-day social lives. So, sensationalized stories from the world of entertainment (such as, say, the intriguing "love triangle" of Angelina Jolie, Brad Pitt, and Jennifer Aniston) make for especially good gossip. Jerome H. Barkow, "Beneath New Culture Is Old Psychology," in *The Adapted Mind: Evolutionary Psychology and the Generation of Culture,* ed. Jerome H. Barkow, Leda Cosmides, and John Tooby (New York: Oxford University Press, 1992), 626–37.

14. R. I. M. Dunbar, "Gossip in Evolutionary Perspective," *Review of General Psychology* 8 (2004): 100–110.

15. Ibid.

16. Roy F. Baumeister, Liqing Zhang, and Kathleen D. Vohs, "Gossip as Cultural Learning," *Review of General Psychology* 8 (2004): 111–21.

17. Robert Louis Stevenson, *The Strange Case of Dr. Jekyll and Mr. Hyde* (Clayton, DE: Prestwick House, 2005), 11. Originally published in 1886.

18. Goethe, the author of *Faust* (1808), once acknowledged of himself, "There is no crime of which I do not deem myself capable." Far be it from us to say how secretly deranged our dear Goethe was, but I suspect this was probably a stretch—there are some pretty scary criminals. You get the idea, though. We're only human, after all.

19. Pär Lagerkvist, *The Dwarf* (London: Chatto & Windus, 1953), 20. Originally published in 1944.

20. Jean-Paul Sartre, *Saint Genet: Actor and Martyr,* trans. Bernard Frechtman (New York: Braziller, 1963).

21. K. Causey and D. F. Bjorklund, "The Evolution of Cognition," in *Evolutionary Psychology: A Critical Reader,* ed. V. Swami (London: British Psychological Society, forthcoming).

22. In fact, a recent study by University of Toronto psychologist Chen-Bo Zhong and colleagues demonstrated that ambient darkness—even darkness that is artificially induced by having participants wear sunglasses—encourages antisocial behavior in the laboratory. Presumably, argue the authors, this is because darkness renders in human beings the (often incorrect) perception of increased anonymity. Chen-Bo Zhong, Vanessa K. Bohns, and Francesca Gino, "Good Lamps Are the Best Police: Darkness Increases Dishonesty and Self-Interested Behavior," *Psychological Science* 21 (2010): 311–14.

23. After a long historical period during which people may have been able to emigrate to new social groups and start over if they spoiled their reputations, the present media age, in some ways, more accurately reflects the conditions faced by our Pleistocene ancestors. With newspapers, telephones, cameras, television, and the Internet at our disposal, personal details about medical problems, spending activities, criminal and financial history, and divorce records (to name just a few tidbits potentially costly to our reputations) are not only permanently archived, but can be distributed in microseconds to, literally, millions of other people. The Internet, in particular, is an active microcosm of human sociality. From background checks to matchmaking services, to anonymous website browsing, to piracy and identity theft; from Googling ourselves and peers to flaming bad professors (e.g., www.ratemy professor.com) and stingy customers (e.g., www.bitterwaitress.com)—the Internet is ancient social psychology meeting new information technology.

24. Consider, for example, the rather curious case of confession. From an evolutionary perspective, it seems counterintuitive that a person would ever confess to a wrongdoing, even if guilty. After all, although we humans are expert at making theoretical inferences about unobservable mental states,

we are not literally mind readers. Knowing this, and knowing that confession guarantees social exposure of our transgression and usually some form of punishment, it seems the human mind would be designed to motivate absolute discretion in response to accusations of wrongdoing. Yet the urge to confess is real, and it is powerful. (I suspect just as many people have the urge to confess their sins to the dying as the dying are apt to confess to the living, since the dead, of course, tell no tales, which in the present case means that they are the terminal stumps of the gossip line.)

Florida Atlantic University psychologist Todd Shackelford and I have argued that confession is a preemptive strategy against *statistically probable* exposure of a moral offense. (Jesse M. Bering and Todd K. Shackelford, "Evolutionary Psychology and False Confession," *American Psychologist* 60 [2005]: 1037–38.) Anxiety may be the primary emotional state that precipitates confession, with confession being the only available recourse that has a positive, anxiety-relieving effect; in conditions of likely exposure, confession should be the default response and should be difficult to inhibit. When the probability of exposure is high (as when there is incontrovertible evidence or there are witnesses to the crime), confession might serve to lessen inevitable punishment. In fact, in a study conducted with inmates of Arkansas penitentiaries, all of whom pled guilty to their offenses, we found that retrospective urge-to-confess feelings were significantly and positively correlated with the number of people who the convicts believed knew they had committed the crime. In other words, if they hadn't confessed, exposure was virtually inevitable anyway, given the number of carriers.

False confessions are another mystery. Saul Kassin, a forensic psychologist at Williams College, describes several standard police interrogation tactics—including lying about evidence, witnesses, and/or informants—that may contribute to the production of false confessions. (Saul M. Kassin, "On the Psychology of Confessions: Does Innocence Put Innocents at Risk?" *American Psychologist* 60 [2005]: 215–28.) But keep in mind that punishment is the product of the group's belief in the individual's guilt rather than the actual truth of the matter. If innocents perceive the likelihood of their vindication to be outweighed by the reality of other people's false belief in their guilt, then false confession may have been an adaptive strategy under certain conditions, particularly in ancestral environments in which trial by jury, judicial appeals, or DNA exclusion could not provide exoneration.

Through confession, the individual has available multiple means of achieving payoffs in genetic fitness terms. For example, social psychologists have found that when confession is coupled with remorse signals (such as those accompanying genuine guilt), observers are more likely to reason that recidivism is unlikely or that the person has suffered enough through feeling ashamed. This combination of confession and remorse promotes forgiveness and a reduced punishment. In the ancestral past, the advantages of false confession may have therefore overridden the natural inclination to protest one's suspected guilt; denying guilt, even if one was truly innocent, may actually have had a more calamitous impact on reproductive success if such protests fell on the ears of group members who held uncompromising false beliefs.

25. Fyodor Dostoyevsky, *The Brothers Karamazov,* trans. C. Garnett (New York: Modern Library, 1950), 360. Originally published in 1880.

26. Ibid., 374.

27. H. L. Mencken, *A Mencken Chrestomathy* (New York: Vintage, 1982), 617. Originally published in 1949.

28. Human sociality displays a number of characteristics revealing that our behaviors are designed to work for the good of the group, if only for selfish genetic reasons. For present purposes, it is useful to highlight two such categories of cooperative heuristics. With direct reciprocity, or "reciprocal altruism," rational actors adopt a straightforward rule of thumb: do unto [specific] others as they have done unto you. Indirect reciprocity, or "thirdparty altruism," by contrast, is of more direct relevance to the present discussion. Here, the rule of thumb is, do unto [specific] others as you have observed them do unto others. According to Harvard University mathematical biologist Martin Nowak and evolutionary game theorist Karl Sigmund of the University of Vienna, indirect reciprocity involves "information storage and transfer as well as strategic thinking and has a pivotal role in the evolution of cooperation and communication. The possibilities for games of manipulation, coalition-building and betrayal are limitless. Indirect reciprocity may have provided the selective challenge driving the cerebral expansion in human evolution." (Martin A. Nowak and Karl Sigmund, "Evolution of Indirect Reciprocity," *Nature* 437 [2005]: 1291–98.)

Nowak and Sigmund concede, however, that, "the co-evolution of human language and cooperation by indirect reciprocity is a fascinating and as yet unexplored topic." (Ibid.) Indeed, Richard Alexander's original 1987 definition of "indirect reciprocity" described it as "occurring *in the presence of* interested audiences—groups of individuals who continually evaluate the members of their society as possible future interactants from whom they would like to gain more than they lose" (Richard D. Alexander, *The Biology of Moral Systems* [Hawthorne, NY: De Gruyter, 1987], 110 [italics added]), therefore overlooking entirely the role of language in indirect reciprocity.

29. L. Festinger, A. Pepitone, and T. Newcomb, "Some Consequences of Deindividuation in a Group," *Journal of Abnormal and Social Psychology* 47 (1952): 382–89.

30. Andrew Silke, "Deindividuation, Anonymity and Violence: Findings from Northern Ireland," *Journal of Social Psychology* 143 (2003): 493–99. On the other side of the coin, an increased sense of being identifiable and knowable by others lends itself to "good" social behaviors. As University of Kent psychologist Jared Piazza and I reported in a 2009 issue of *Evolution and Human Behavior*, people share more money with a stranger when they're under the impression that a bystander in the room might relay personally identifying information to the stranger, such as the participant's name and degree major. Jared Piazza and Jesse M. Bering, "Concerns about Reputation via Gossip Promote Generous Allocations in an Economic Game," *Evolution and Human Behavior* 29 (2008): 172–78.

31. R. Pettazzoni, "On the Attributes of God," *Numen* 2 (1955): 1–27.

32. Benedict Sandin, *Iban Adat and Augury* (Penang, Malaysia: Penerbit Universiti Sains Malaysia for School of Comparative Social Sciences, 1980), xxviii.

33. Frans L. Roes and Michel Raymond, "Belief in Moralizing Gods," *Evolution and Human Behavior* 24 (2003): 126–35.

34. Ara Norenzayan and Azim F. Shariff, "The Origin and Evolution of Religious Prosociality," *Science* 322 (2008): 58–62.

35. Jesse M. Bering, Katrina McLeod, and Todd K. Shackelford, "Reasoning about Dead Agents Reveals Possible Adaptive Trends," *Human Nature* 16 (2005): 360–81.

36. Jesse M. Bering and Jared Piazza, "Princess Alice Is Watching You: Children's Belief in an Invisible Person Promotes Rule Following" (unpublished manuscript).

37. Pascal Boyer, *Religion Explained: The Evolutionary Origins of Religious Thought* (New York: Basic Books, 2001), 40.

38. The primary paradigm within the cognitive science of religion for the past decade can be described as the "cultural epidemiological" model of religious concept transmission and acquisition. Conceptualized originally by the French anthropologist Dan Sperber, this approach has been most extensively developed by Washington University anthropologist Pascal Boyer. Boyer lays out a very elegant scientific model that shows how the evolved

human mind is especially susceptible to religious concepts because they exploit our everyday, mundane, run-of-the-mill thought processes. What makes a particular concept "religious" or supernatural, says Boyer, is its counterintuitiveness—the extent to which it violates our innate assumptions about basic aspects of the natural world. Boyer sometimes uses the term "sticky" to describe religious concepts. They're especially hard to shake, he says, because they are continually grabbing our attention by virtue of the fact that they challenge our innate understanding of the humdrum world. With Boyer's catalogue of supernatural ideas, just about any religious concept you can conjure up has this same basic formula: take a run-of-the-mill bit of the everyday, and add a flash of color in the form of a contradiction in terms. (Pascal Boyer, *Religion Explained: The Evolutionary Origins of Religious Thought* [New York: Basic Books, 2001].)

The beauty of Boyer's model is that it can account for otherwise mind-boggling cross-cultural variation in religious concepts. His counterintuitiveness formula explains why thousands of people flocked recently to a home in Bangalore city to witness what many hailed as a miracle. It seems a small marble statue of the nineteenth-century Indian saint Shirdi Sai Baba fluttered its lashes during a routine cleaning and decided to spring open its left eye to have a peak at the world. Boyer's model can also explain the Lord Ganesha phenomenon that occurred a few months prior, just a stone's throw away on the map, in Mumbai. Statues of this elephant-headed deity, who happens to be the Hindu patron of sciences among other things, started slurping milk from spoons offered by religious devotees. What possessed the very first person to raise a tablespoon of milk to a piece of stone carved into the shape of an elephant's trunk we may never know, but like the one-eyed Sai Baba, these thirsty Lord Ganesha statues really got people talking.

The reason such religious statues garner our attention, argues Boyer, is that we have an inborn concept of what makes an inanimate object inanimate. Moving on its own accord, seeing, and having biological functions just aren't on that list. So when word gets out that a lifeless artifact has breached natural law—bleeding paintings, crying figurines, blinking statues—the news spreads like wildfire, propagating myths, sparking debate, and renewing faith.

39. In 1967, for example, a well-known philosopher from the University of Notre Dame named Alvin Plantinga wrote an influential little book titled *God and Other Minds*. Over the years, Plantinga has tinkered with some of the details of his argument for the existence of God, and he appears slightly embarrassed

by the youthful brashness of his earlier writing, but his central position on the matter has not changed. "I remain unrepentant about the main epistemological conclusions of the book," he wrote in the preface to a new edition twenty-three years later. "The chief topic of *God and Other Minds* is the question of the rationality, or reasonability, or intellectual propriety of belief in God. My contention was that the strongest argument for the existence of God and the strongest argument for other minds are similar, and fail in similar ways; hence my 'tentative conclusion': 'if my belief in other minds is rational, so is my belief in God. But obviously the former is rational; so, therefore, is the latter.'" (Alvin Plantinga, *God and Other Minds: A Study of the Rational Justification of Belief in God* [Ithaca, NY: Cornell University Press, 1991], xi. Originally published in 1967.)

Were it not for the focus of the present book, it would be rather cruel of me to dawdle unnecessarily over this quote of Plantinga's, which I've admittedly cherry-picked as a shining example of the type of theological acrobatics of reason that tend to pass for logical argument. Yet, I really do think Plantinga ought to be not only repentant about this logic, but deeply so. Yes, as we saw in Chapter 1, philosophically, other human minds can never be proven to exist—hence the term "*theory* of mind." But to say that the two cases—God's mind and other human minds—are "in the same epistemological boat" (as Plantinga puts it) (ibid., xvi) is something of a stretch. More than the patent silliness of Plantinga's argument, this sort of intellectualistic obfuscation of the God question seems to me almost deliberately made to cause confusion among readers.

40. Paul Bloom, *Descartes' Baby: How Child Development Explains What Makes Us Human* (New York: Basic Books, 2004), 222–23.

CHAPTER 7

1. "Did Darwin Become a Christian on His Deathbed?" Christian Apologetics & Research Ministry, www.carm.org/secular-movements/evolution/did -darwin-become-christian-his-deathbed (accessed March 25, 2010).

2. Ibid.

3. Voltaire, *Épître à l'Auteur du Livre "Des Trois Imposteurs"* [Epistle to the Anonymous Author of the Book, "The Three Impostors"] (1768).

4. Blaise Pascal, *Pensées,* trans. A. J. Krailsheimer (New York: Penguin, 1995). Originally published in 1670.

SUGGESTED ADDITIONAL READING

CHAPTER 1

Bloom, Paul. *Descartes' Baby: How the Science of Child Development Explains What Makes Us Human.* New York: Basic Books, 2004.

Call, Josep, and Michael Tomasello. "Does the Chimpanzee Have a Theory of Mind? 30 Years Later." *Trends in Cognitive Sciences* 12 (2008): 187–92.

Herrmann, Esther, Josep Call, María Victoria Hernàndez-Lloreda, Brian Hare, and Michael Tomasello. "The Cultural Intelligence Hypothesis: Humans Evolved Specialized Skills of Social Cognition." *Science* 317 (2007): 1360–65.

Humphrey, Nicholas. "The Society of Selves." *Philosophical Transactions of the Royal Society of London. Series B, Biological Sciences* 362 (2007): 745–54.

Penn, Derek C., Keith J. Holyoak, and Daniel J. Povinelli. "Darwin's Mistake: Explaining the Discontinuity between Human and Nonhuman Minds." *Behavioral and Brain Sciences* 31 (2008): 109–78.

Povinelli, Daniel J., and Jesse M. Bering. "The Mentality of Apes Revisited." *Current Directions in Psychological Science* 11 (2002): 115–19.

Wellman, Henry M. "Developing a Theory of Mind." In *The Wiley-Blackwell Handbook of Childhood Cognitive Development* (2nd ed.), edited by Usha Goswami. Malden, MA: Wiley-Blackwell, 2010.

CHAPTER 2

Evans, E. Margaret, Cristine H. Legare, and Karl S. Rosengren. "Engaging

Multiple Epistemologies: Implications for Science Education." In *Evolution, Epistemology, and Science Education: Understanding the Evolution vs. Intelligent Design Controversy,* edited by M. Ferrari and R. Taylor. New York: Routledge, forthcoming.

German, Tim P., and H. Clark Barrett. "Functional Fixedness in a Technologically Sparse Culture." *Psychological Science* 16 (2005): 1–5.

Kelemen, Deborah. "Are Children 'Intuitive Theists'?: Reasoning about Purpose and Design in Nature." *Psychological Science* 15 (2004): 295–301.

Lombrozo, Tania, Deborah Kelemen, and Deborah Zaitchik. "Inferring Design: Evidence of a Preference for Teleological Explanations in Patients with Alzheimer's Disease." *Psychological Science* 18 (2007): 999–1006.

Rosset, Evelyn. "It's No Accident: Our Bias for Intentional Explanations." *Cognition* 108 (2008): 771–80.

CHAPTER 3

Baron-Cohen, Simon. *Autism and Asperger Syndrome.* Oxford: Oxford University Press, 2008.

Barrett, Justin L. *Why Would Anyone Believe in God?* Lanham, MD: AltaMira, 2004.

Bering, Jesse M. "The Existential Theory of Mind." *Review of General Psychology* 6 (2002): 3–24.

Bering, Jesse M., and Becky D. Parker. "Children's Attributions of Intentions to an Invisible Agent." *Developmental Psychology* 42 (2006): 253–62.

Epley, Nicholas, Benjamin A. Converse, Alexa Delbosc, George A. Monteleone, and John T. Cacioppo. "Believers' Estimates of God's Beliefs Are More Egocentric Than Estimates of Other People's Beliefs." *Proceedings of the National Academy of Sciences, USA* 106 (2009): 21533–38.

CHAPTER 4

Astuti, Rita, and Paul L. Harris. "Understanding Mortality and the Life of the Ancestors in Madagascar." *Cognitive Science* 32 (2008): 713–40.

Bering, Jesse M. "The Folk Psychology of Souls." *Behavioral and Brain Sciences* 29 (2006): 453–98.

Gottfried, Gail M., Susan A. Gelman, and Jennifer Shultz. "Children's Understanding of the Brain: From Early Essentialism to Biological Theory." *Cognitive Development* 14 (1999): 147–74.

Greenberg, Jeff, Sander L. Koole, and Tom Pyszczynski, eds. *Handbook of Experimental Existential Psychology*. New York: Guilford, 2004.

Harris, P. L. "Death in Spain, Madagascar, and Beyond." In *Children's Understanding of Death: From Biological to Supernatural Conceptions*, edited by V. Talwar, P. L. Harris, and M. Schleifer. New York: Cambridge University Press, forthcoming.

Slaughter, Virginia, and Michelle Lyons. "Learning about Life and Death in Early Childhood." *Cognitive Psychology* 46 (2003): 1–30.

CHAPTER 5

Gray, Kurt, and Daniel M. Wegner. "Blaming God for Our Pain: Human Suffering and the Divine Mind." *Personality and Social Psychology Review* 14 (2010): 7–16.

Heatherton, Todd F., and Patricia A. Nichols. "Personal Accounts of Successful versus Failed Attempts at Life Change." *Personality and Social Psychology Bulletin* 20 (1994): 664–75.

Legare, Cristine H., and Susan A. Gelman. "Bewitchment, Biology, or Both: The Co-existence of Natural and Supernatural Explanatory Frameworks across Development." *Cognitive Science* 32 (2008): 607–42.

McAdams, Dan P. *The Redemptive Self: Stories Americans Live By*. New York: Oxford University Press, 2006.

Preston, Jesse, and Nicholas Epley. "Science and God: An Automatic Opposition between Ultimate Explanations." *Journal of Experimental Social Psychology* 45 (2009): 238–41.

CHAPTER 6

Bering, Jesse M., Katrina McLeod, and Todd K. Shackelford. "Reasoning about Dead Agents Reveals Possible Adaptive Trends." *Human Nature* 16 (2005): 360–81.

Johnson, Dominic D. P. "God's Punishment and Public Goods: A Test of the Supernatural Punishment Hypothesis in 186 World Cultures." *Human Nature* 16 (2005): 410–46.

McAndrew, Francis T., Emily K. Bell, and Contitta Maria Garcia. "Who Do We Tell, and Whom Do We Tell On? Gossip as a Strategy for Status Enhancement." *Journal of Applied Social Psychology* 37 (2007): 1562–77.

Norenzayan, Ara, and Azim F. Shariff. "The Origin and Evolution of Religious Prosociality." *Science* 322 (2008): 58–62.

Piazza, Jared, and Jesse M. Bering. "Concerns about Reputation via Gossip Promote Generous Allocations in an Economic Game." *Evolution and Human Behavior* 29 (2008): 172–78.

Roes, Frans L. "Moralizing Gods and the Arms-Race Hypothesis of Human Society Growth." *Open Social Science Journal* 2 (2009): 70–73.

INDEX